EVALUATION IN STUDENT AFFAIRS

George D. Kuh, Editor

American College Personnel Association

EVALUATION IN STUDENT AFFAIRS

ACPA MEDIA PUBLICATION NUMBER 26

Editor
George D. Kuh

Copyright 1979 by the American College
Personnel Association

All Rights Reserved. No part of this
publication may be reproduced without prior
written permission of the Chairperson of
ACPA Media.

Publication Sales: ACPA Media
350 T.U.C., M.L. #159
UNIVERSITY OF CINCINNATI
CINCINNATI, OHIO 45221

Editor & Chairperson, ACPA Media and Editorial Boards
Janet D. Greenwood, University of Cincinnati

Assistant Managing Editor
Betty Asher, University of Cincinnati

Editorial Assistant
Eva Horwitz, University of Cincinnati

Editorial Board
James Aiken, California Polytechnical State University
Rosalind Andreas, Oakland University
Willard W. Blaesser, Arizona State University
Katherine Boardman, University of Georgia
John Borgard, Virginia Commonwealth University
Edward H. Hammond, University of Louisville
Robert Huss, University of Georgia
James Marine, Ball State University
Robbie L. Nayman, Colorado State University
Ed Nolan, University of Tampa
Gary Rankin, South Oklahoma City Junior College
John Schuh, Indiana University
Carolyn Smith, University of Houston
Emil R. Spees, Southern Illinois University
Bonnie Titley, Colorado State University
Bob Young, University of Connecticut
Tom Zarle, Bentley College

Media Board
David Borland, North Texas State University
Douglas H. Lamb, Illinois State University
Norma P. Simon, Private Practice, New York
Emil R. Spees, Southern Illinois University
Jay Stormer, Cleveland State University
Marvalene H. Styles, San Diego State University

ACPA President
Phyllis Mable

ACPA President-Elect
Cynthia S. Johnson

ACPA Past President
Don G. Creamer

Publication May Be Ordered From:
ACPA Media
Janet D. Greenwood
350 T.U.C., M.L. #159
University of Cincinnati
Cincinnati, Ohio 45221

PREFACE

Every day judgments are made by a variety of groups about the relative value of student affairs. In some subtle and not so subtle ways, students tell us whether they appreciate our programming efforts or are satisfied with their living environments. Administrators and decision-makers decide whether our contributions are important enough to warrant continued financial support at comparable levels. In self-appraisal, we sometimes hold up the mirror to ourselves at the end of a workweek and ask, "How well am I doing?"

The information required to determine how well we are doing is often readily available. In the past, however, student affairs staff (as well as other educational personnel) have often based evaluations of their performance and institutional contributions on hunches or, at best, incomplete data. Considering that a variety of approaches are presently available to help frame educational evaluation questions and to gather information relevant to these questions, rendering judgments based on hunches or impressions is no longer necessary or sufficient. Nevertheless, existing evaluation strategies and models have rarely been used in a systematic fashion to determine the merit or worth of student affairs programs.

The need for a compilation of suggested best practices in the evaluation of student affairs was personally underscored as I began to teach a seminar in evaluation for students in the college student personnel administration preparation program at Indiana University. A major component of this course is to design and conduct an evaluation in student affairs. While students were able to spend a considerable amount of time translating evaluation textbooks and articles into meaningful applications for student affairs, it became obvious that to expect student affairs practitioners to invest a comparable amount of time discovering and subsequently interpreting the principles of program and staff evaluation for use in their respective work settings was both unreasonable and unrealistic. As I verbally shared my need for materials which would communicate the various evaluation strategies in ways which would be beneficial to student affairs staff, I discovered there were others who also perceived the need for synthesizing best practices in evaluation of student affairs. After discussions with Robert Brown of the University of Nebraska and Oscar Lenning of NCHEMS, I drafted a proposal for Commission IX and the Media Board of the American College Personnel Association, both of which subsequently endorsed the project. Commission IX also graciously provided funds from their limited financial resources to underwrite the production costs for preparation and reproduction of various drafts of the manuscripts.

I am deeply indebted to each of the contributors who made my work enjoyable as well as edifying. Their willingness to work within a relatively tight time line was important in delivering a timely and necessary product. Jan Greenwood, chairperson of the ACPA Media Board, took responsibility for providing the technical assistance required for producing a volume of this length. I and the other contributors are also indebted to several members of the media board who anonymously offered their suggestions to improve the manuscript. As always, my colleagues at Indiana, the late Betty Greenleaf and Bob Shaffer, were supportive throughout this undertaking and always willing to share their widsom. Mary Konanz skillfully prepared the various drafts of the manuscript and B. J. Bischoff, a master's candidate in College Student Personnel Administration at Indiana University, designed the cover.

It is also important to acknowledge the many latitudes extended to me during the editing of the manuscript by my children, Kari Ann and Kristian, and particularly by my wife, Martha McCarthy, an acknowledged authority in the area of school law. Without their unselfish support and love, this volume would have remained a topic of discussion between friends.

George D. Kuh
Bloomington, Indiana
April, 1979

CONTENTS

PART ONE: EVALUATION – WHAT IS IT?

I   Evaluation: The State of the Art in Student Affairs 1
    George D. Kuh

II   Key Issues in Evaluating Student Affairs Programs 13
    Robert D. Brown

III   Evaluator Roles and Evaluation Strategies:
    A Consumer's Introduction 33
    Robert D. Brown

PART TWO: ISSUES IN EVALUATING STUDENT SERVICES

IV   Admissions 53
    L. J. Abernathy

V   Orientation 63
    Margaret J. Barr, Sharon H. Justice and Bernard D. Yancey

VI   Residence Life 77
    Barbara A. Phillips and John H. Schuh

VII   Counseling Center 87
    John G. Corazzini

VIII   Student Activities 95
    Richard N. McKaig and Sharon M. Policello

IX Career Planning and Placement 104
    Marvalene H. Styles and Sara Beth Hull

X   The Chief Student Affairs Administrator 121
    Robert H. Shaffer

PART THREE: TOWARD A COMPREHENSIVE APPLICATION
OF EVALUATION IN STUDENT AFFAIRS

XI   Evaluating Experimental Student Affairs Programs 133
     Carl L. Harshman

XII Staff Evaluation 149
     J. Roger Penn

XIII Evaluation of Student Development Programs 163
     Gary R. Hanson and Oscar T. Lenning

XIV Needs Assessment in Student Affairs 185
     Oscar T. Lenning and Andrea C. McAleenan

PART FOUR: CASE STUDIES

XV   A Student Affairs Application of the CIPP
     Evaluation Model 207
     Robert F. Rodgers

XVI Comparing Apples and Oranges: Coordinating
     Evaluation and Decision Making 225
     Jack McKillip

XVII Evaluating a Living-Learning Program 239
      Philip C. Chamberlain

PART FIVE: A FINAL WORD

XVIII Building A Wolf-Proof House: Integrating Evaluation
      in Student Affairs 253
      George D. Kuh

Subject Index 267

Name Index 271

CONTRIBUTORS

LUCKY J. ABERNATHY is Program Officer for Special Services for the College Board with responsibility for several placement and assessment programs. Prior to joining the College Board, he worked in university admissions and research and served as a secondary school guidance director and as a teacher. He received his Ph.D. from Indiana State University.

MARGARET J. BARR is Assistant Dean of Students, University of Texas at Austin. She has worked in student affairs for 14 years and has extensive experience in training programs, staff development activities, new student orientation, housing, and the college union.

ROBERT D. BROWN is Professor of Educational Psychology at the University of Nebraska-Lincoln where his teaching and research interests include student development and program evaluation. He has served as a teacher, counselor, and administrator in a variety of educational institutions.

PHILIP C. CHAMBERLAIN is Associate Professor of Higher Education at Indiana University. He has served as Director of Admissions at the University of Louisville and as Associate Director of Institutional Research at Indiana University-Bloomington where he earned his Ph.D.

JOHN G. CORAZZINI is Assistant Director of the University Counseling Center and Assistant Professor in the Department of Psychology at Colorado State University. He received his Ph.D. from the University of Notre Dame. He is currently a Directorate Body member for Commission VII of ACPA.

GARY R. HANSON is Assistant Dean of Students for Student Life Studies at the University of Texas at Austin where he evaluates student service programs and conducts environmental impact research. He has also served as a research psychologist at the American College Testing Program where he focused on the career development of college students. He received his Ph.D. from the University of Minnesota.

CARL L. HARSHMAN is Dean of Metropolitan College and Associate Professor of Higher Education at St. Louis University. He has been a faculty member, administrator and institutional researcher at Ohio Dominican College, Wright State University and The Ohio State University. He received his Ph.D. from Ohio State.

SARA BETH HULL is Director of Career Planning and Placement and of the Student Development Center at Seattle University. Previously she was associated with the Arts and Sciences Placement Office at Indiana University, and with the Career Services and

Placement Center at the University of Iowa where she earned the Ph.D.

SHARON H. JUSTICE is Assistant Dean of Students responsible for new student orientation at the University of Texas at Austin. She received her Ph.D. from Southern Illinois University, Carbondale and has eight years of experience in orientation, student activities, and housing.

GEORGE D. KUH received his Ph.D. from the University of Iowa and is presently Associate Professor of College Student Personnel and Higher Education Administration at Indiana University-Bloomington. Previously he was a faculty member and Assistant Director of the Drug Counseling Program at the University of Iowa and Assistant Director of Admissions at Luther College.

OSCAR T. LENNING is Senior Staff Associate at the National Center for Higher Education Management Systems. Formerly he was Assistant Director for Research Services at the American College Testing Program and Chairperson of Commission IX of ACPA. He received his Ph.D. from the University of Iowa.

ANDREA C. McALEENAN is Associate Dean for Academic Affairs at Azusa Pacific College and a doctoral student in Higher Education Administration at the Claremont Graduate School. She was formerly Chairperson of the Department of Student Development at Azusa Pacific and has worked in student affairs at the University of Hawaii and California State University at Northridge. She earned the masters degree in student personnel from Michigan State University.

RICHARD N. McKAIG received his M.S. in Student Personnel Administration from Ball State University and is currently an Ed.D. candidate at Indiana University. Formerly Director of Student Activities at the University of Wisconsin-Stevens Point, he serves as Director of Student Activities at Indiana University-Bloomington and as Chairperson of Commission IV of ACPA.

JACK McKILLIP is Associate Professor of Psychology at Southern Illinois University at Carbondale where he also serves as a consultant on evaluation for various student affairs units. His teaching and research interests are in the areas of needs assessment and program evaluation.

J. ROGER PENN received his Ph.D. from Oregon State University where he is Assistant to the Vice President of Student Services, Director of Special Programs, and Associate Professor in the Division of Post-Secondary Education. Formerly, he was associated with the University of Wisconsin-Center System and Colorado State University.

BARBARA A. PHILLIPS is Acting Associate Dean of Student Life at Indiana State University and is also a doctoral student at Indiana University where she earned the M.S. in College Student Personnel Administration. She has previous work experience in residence life and as a generalist in student affairs at Kutztown State College and Indiana University.

SHARON M. POLICELLO is Director of Campus Activities at Ithaca College and an Ed.D. candidate at Indiana University where she earned the M.S. in College Student Personnel Administration. She has additional work experience in student affairs at Eureka College and Indiana University-Bloomington.

ROBERT F. (BOB) RODGERS is Director of the Student Personnel Assistant Program and Assistant Professor of Education at The Ohio State University where he teaches and does research in the areas of developmental theory, group interventions, and paraprofessional counseling. He has work experience with financial aids, fraternities and residence life, and formerly was Assistant Vice President for Student Services at Ohio State where he earned his Ph.D.

ROBERT H. SHAFFER received his Ph.D. from New York University. He is currently professor of Education and Business Administration and Chairman of the Department of Student Personnel at Indiana University, Bloomington where he was formerly Dean of Students. He has held major offices in a number of student affairs associations and has served as editor or editorial board member of *The NASPA Journal, The Journal of College Student Personnel,* and *The Personnel and Guidance Journal.*

JOHN H. SCHUH is Director of the Department of Residence Life and part-time Associate Professor of Education at Indiana University-Bloomington. Previously, he was Assistant Director of Housing and Adjunct Assistant Professor of Education at Arizona State University where he earned his Ph.D. He serves on the executive committee of ACUHO and on the Directorate Body of Commission III of ACPA.

MARVALENE H. STYLES received the Ph.D. from Florida State University. She has served as a student affairs administrator, professor and counselor in institutions of higher education in Florida and California. Currently she is Director of the Center for Counseling Services and Placement at San Diego State University.

BERNARD D. YANCEY is a Computer Programmer in the Office of the Dean of Students at the University of Texas at Austin. He has four years experience in research, evaluation and student life studies within student affairs and related areas.

1
EVALUATION: THE STATE OF THE ART IN STUDENT AFFAIRS
George D. Kuh

During the 1960s, postsecondary education enjoyed a period of unprecedented yearly growth, both in the numbers of students matriculating and the numbers of dollars provided by legislatures and private donors. Following the turbulent campuses of the late 1960's, waning public confidence in higher education was reflected in more conservative appropriation levels for state colleges and universities (Flentje & Sample, 1973). Several years later, enrollment shortfalls resulted in financial exigency in some institutions occasionally culminating in the dismissal of tenured faculty and, in the most extreme cases, institutional demise. In some instances student affairs staff members were reassigned to other units or terminated as part of an institution's fiscal austerity program; e.g., Illinois State University (Boyer, 1979; Escott, 1979). Even though many of these institutions soon found it difficult to do without a full complement of persons adequately prepared to perform student affairs functions, a dangerous precedent had been established. In other instances academic program discontinuation led to tenured faculty being reassigned to student affairs. Often these reassignments necessitated additional educational coursework and experiences in college student personnel before faculty were prepared to assume their new roles. By 1978, enrollments appeared to have stabilized somewhat although a sharp decline in the numbers of potential traditional aged (18-22) college students was expected a few years later (Henderson, 1977; Hodgkinson, 1976).

How institutions will respond to the "baby bust" is not yet clear. Few colleges have publicly articulated the decision rules which will be used during the next decade of shrinking enrollments. It seems reasonably accurate to assume, however, that more accountability procedures will be mandated to satisfy the information needs of external (legislatures, trustees, students' parents, donors, taxpayers) as well as internal audiences (Vice President for Finance, Chief Student Affairs Officer, faculty, students).

In addition to demands for accountability, challenges to college student affairs staff to determine *how well* they are doing their jobs appear periodically in the literature. During the past five years, Burck and Peterson (1975), Dressel (1973), Harpel (1976), and Oetting and Hawkes (1974) have reminded student affairs staff that systematic *evaluation* of programs and personnel is necessary to insure that

1

students are provided satisfactory services. These writers represent the "humanitarian" perspective of the need for evaluation (Perloff & Perloff, 1977), "the social conscience of student affairs" which monitors the impact and effectiveness of student affairs programs.

DEFINITIONS

While the terms accountability and evaluation are often used interchangeably in the student affairs literature, in fact they describe related but somewhat different processes. In fact, accountability — "a set of procedures that collates information about accomplishments and costs to facilitate decision-making" (Krumboltz, 1974, p. 639) — can be considered a part of a comprehensive evaluation process. Evaluation, however, should be more than the audit of a program to justify its existence. It should also attempt to determine the relative merit and worth of a program or how well it does what it sets out to do.

Just as evaluation and accountability are often incorrectly assumed to be synonymous, so are the terms evaluation and research. Indeed, evaluation and research are both inquiry activities. However, several important distinctions between the two activities should be noted because "the failure to distinquish between research and evaluation often results in the failure to collect the kinds of data needed to decide about continuing or modifying a given program" (Miller & Prince, 1976, p. 135).

Kerlinger (1973) has defined research as "systematic, controlled, empirical, and critical investigation of hypothetical propositions about the presumed relations among natural phenomena" (p. 11). To qualify as research, inquiry should be consistent within a particular theoretical framework and be generalizable to some degree. It may or may not have immediate utility (Burck & Peterson, 1975; Worthen & Sanders, 1973).

Over the past several decades, evaluation has been defined in a variety of ways:
— The collection, and use of information to make decisions about an educational program (Cronbach, 1963);
— The comparison of performance against standards (Provus, 1969) or behaviorally anchored objectives (Tyler, 1942);
— The process of delineating, obtaining, and providing useful information for judging alternatives (Stufflebeam, Foley, Gephart, Guba, Hammond, Merriman & Provus. 1971).

In the following chapters, evaluation is considered to be a purposeful set of activities which has as its ultimate objective the rendering of judgments about the merit or worth of a student affairs program. In most instances, decisions concerning the program's existence will be made based on these judgments. Brown (Chapter 2) expands on this definition for student affairs evaluators and decision-makers.

The distinction between evaluation and research is somewhat easier to discern when the purposes of the forms of inquiry are considered. Research is typically stimulated by intellectual curiosity and seeks to discover the relationships between events or variables primarily to explain a particular phenomenon. On the other hand, an evaluation is not usually designed to document why a program succeeds but rather to determine a program's worth or how well it succeeds. Because an evaluation is undertaken to provide relevant information about a program or service to decision-makers, it has immediate social utility (see Oetting, 1976a, 1976b; Worthen & Sanders, 1973).

As an example, consider a residence life program designed to foster autonomy among hall residents. The researcher is interested in learning the relationship between gains on some measure of autonomy (perhaps a fall and a spring administration of the Autonomy scale of the *Onmibus Personality Inventory* or some observations of participant behavior and a particular hall program. To some extent, the evaluator is also interested in the researcher's data and conclusions. But more importantly, the evaluator must answer additional questions about program efficacy. To what extent did the program meet its goals? How much staff time and financial support was required? To what extent did the program outcomes contribute to the overall objectives of the student affairs division? To what extent does an experimental or pilot program suggest another stage in a developmental sequence of programs? Do the evaluation data indicate program changes are required if the program is to be continued?

The distinctions between research and evaluation should not be ignored. In reality, however, researchers often provide information from which administrative decisions are made about the worth of a program. For student affairs staff to debate whether these data resulted from a research project or an evaluation effort would not be a particulaly productive way to invest our time. As long as the *purposes* of these two methods of inquiry are clear, sharing both research and evaluation information with decision-makers should be encouraged.

In addition, there are other processes or activities which can be used to examine the functioning of a division of student affairs. For example, during the 1970s, Management By Objectives (MBO) became popular as an accountability system. By requiring staff to set forth personal and program objectives, administrators are able to determine whether these objectives have been accomplished. However, MBO procedures do not necessarily emphasize quality control because there is nothing inherent in the MBO process which requires data be gathered to estimate the *merit* or *worth* of the respective program or staff member's contribution. Nevertheless, MBO has served a useful purpose and, if its limitations are recognized, this process can be a useful accountability tool for the administrator.

Organizational development (OD) is a term used to encompass another set of interventions which can be employed to improve the functioning of a student affairs division. Typically, OD is used to identify and solve problems. While a successful OD intervention can result in improved performance on the part of student affairs staff, estimates of merit or worth of program or staff performance will most likely be serendipitous because the focus of the OD activity probably will be on problem solving, not evaluation.

This book emphasizes evaluation as an important, necessary activity for divisions of student affairs and only passing reference is made to related activities such as MBO and OD. In practice, however, it is not easy to distinguish between MBO, OD, and evaluation; and successful student affairs divisions are likely to use these as well as other interventions in concert. In order to determine which or what combination of these activities is appropriate, staff must become cognizant of the respective purposes and technologies associated with each and then employ the type of activity which will provide the desired result.

A CLEAR CHALLENGE

It is evident that evaluation in higher education — certainly including student affairs — is a process whose time has come. The importance of evaluation to student affairs was recently emphasized at a meeting of midwestern chief student affairs officers at Allerton, Illinois where this topic was identified as the top priority for discussion (Shaffer, 1978). That "evaluation" was the theme of the first volume of the *New Directions for Student Services* (Hanson, 1978) series further substantiates the relative importance of evaluation to contemporary student affairs. It is time for the profession to examine more thoroughly existing evaluation strategies and adapt them for use in student affairs. Dressel's (1976) assessment of the need for more evaluations in student affairs programs presents a straight-forward challenge: "Student personnel services ... requires rigorous evaluations today, but I ... have not thus far seen or been involved in an adequate evaluation in this area" (p. xiii).

PURPOSES

The purposes of this book are fourfold: (1) to illustrate the need for and purposes of evaluation as an important and necessary set of professional behaviors in student affairs; (2) to describe various ways (strategies) through which student affairs programs and staff can be evaluated; (3) to identify salient evaluation issues in a variety of functional areas; and (4) to demonstrate the efficacy of evaluation in student affairs through examples and case studies.

When should an evaluation be conducted? Who in the institution should be responsible for evaluating student affairs programs? Do evaluation issues differ from one functional area to another? How can evaluation aid decision-making about student affairs programs? What skills and behaviors will be required of student affairs staff to evaluate programs and staff? Some answers to these questions and many more can be found in the following chapters. It is hoped that the ideas and suggestions presented here will be of use to most student affairs staff and to teachers, consultants, and students involved with student affairs programs.

OVERVIEW

A variety of procedural questions must always be raised when planning an evaluation in student affairs.[1] Is this evaluation designed to modify an existing program or is it to provide information culminating in decisions about whether programs should be continued? What will be done with the information after it has been collected? Who should conduct the evaluation? These and other related concerns which must be considered when planning an evaluation are addressed in Chapter 2.

One of the major obstacles to adequate evaluation of student affairs programs and staff is that many staff members are not familiar with the evaluation strategies that are available. In Chapter 3, various evaluation strategies appropriate for use in student affairs are discussed.

Each functional area of student affairs presents some unique evaluation needs and concerns. Chapters 4 through 9 are overviews of some of the more salient but common evaluation issues from a variety of areas. In Chapter 10, the different types of problems associated with evaluating the performance of the chief student affairs officer are addressed. Chapter 11 identifies the concerns related to the evaluation of experimental programs. In Chapter 12 the issues which need to be considered by student affairs staff when planning and conducting staff evaluations are presented.

Evaluating the programming specifically designed to influence

---

[1]The term "student affairs" is used throughout the book to describe the various functions typically performed by college student personnel and/or student affairs staff members. "Student development" is used in specific reference to programs or staff activities which are, in a generic sense, designed to influence in a patterned and orderly way the growth and development of college students.

the growth and development of students is essentially an assessment procedure. Numerous value choices must be made when determining the particular student characteristics to be influenced and measured. Some of the problems inherent in the evaluation of student development programming are discussed in Chapter 13. Similarly, conducting needs assessments is an important activity but relatively few suggestions have been put forward in the literature as to how needs assessments in student affairs can be systematically mounted. In Chapter 14, the importance of needs assessment is emphasized, needs assessment is differentiated from other types of measurement efforts, and an explication of how to conduct a needs assessment in student affairs is provided.

Chapters 15 through 17 are case studies of actual evaluations conducted in student affairs. Each describes the planning and implementation complexities associated with evaluating student services. The first presents the application of an existing evaluation model (C.I.P.P., see Stufflebeam et al., 1971) to a fraternal affairs system in a university; the second uses a university's health service setting to emphasize the dilemma administrators face when decisions about a variety of programs must be made; and the third case study describes an evaluation of a living-learning residence hall program.

Accountability demands from various sources (legislature, donors, alumni, etc.) and the need to evaluate post-secondary programs are not likely to abate appreciably in the next decade. The division of student affairs can capitalize on this opportunity and provide leadership to other divisions or within the institution by responding to requests for data related to program efficacy with enthusiasm and resoluteness. The final chapter considers some of the training needs and institutional issues which must be resolved if evaluation is to become an ongoing, budgeted, and viable activity in student affairs.

THE STATE OF THE "ART" OF EVALUATION IN STUDENT AFFAIRS

Do student affairs staff reflect an understanding of and exhibit skills required for evaluation activities? The best answer seems to be, "It depends." It depends on what information is used to assess the current state of the "art" and it also depends on how evaluation is defined. To determine whether evaluation is reasonably well understood by student affairs staff, a review of the student affairs literature found two types of publications: (1) articles which encourage practitioners to evaluate their programs and services; and (2) articles in which practitioners/professors report their evaluation findings and offer guidelines for conducting evaluations. There are a number of publications which can be included in the first category and fewer in the second.

Within the first category are a series of articles about accountability which have provided student affairs staff with a rationale for conducting evaluations. For example, Levy and Schreck (1975) have suggested that for purposes of accountability, "Goal clarification is essential. Programs and services must be defined in terms of desired results ... Evaluative measures, both quantitative and qualitative, must be developed that will produce hard evidence of goal attainment" (p. 143). Bishop (1975) has outlined five basic features of a good accountability system: (1) staff input, (2) flexibility, (3) availability of specific data, (4) realistic time demands, and (5) ease of compilation and simplicity of reporting.

In general, these contributions reflect some interest and knowledge about evaluation as an important responsibility of student affairs administrators. However, the accountability model tends to emphasize monitoring or activity measures of program personnel and/or clients (usually students). Oetting (1976a) has warned that evaluation should be more than program monitoring. Yet, these behaviors are often equated with evaluation (e.g., Harpel, 1976).

In other instances, writers misinterpret the purposes of evaluation. As a result, they confuse rather than clarify the uses of evaluation as an important tool for student personnel workers. For example, Miller and Prince (1976) stipulate that evaluation be an integral component of the student development programming process to *test theory*, implementation plans, effectiveness of staff, and goal-outcome discrepancy. Evaluations usually will not be used to examine theory, however, because theory testing is more appropriately the function of research.

In the second category, a few articles were found which reported evaluation results. For example, a unique evaluation approach was used by the Student Life Division of the University of Houston (Freeman, Nudd B. O'Donnell, 1972) to obtain information about effectiveness of services. Also, Sims and Kozall (1974) described a management by objectives system instituted in 1968 at the University of Georgia. The process requires all departments and persons to set objectives annually and to evaluate performance on the basis of objectives met. Casse, Gillis and Mullen (1974) described a management information system which was used at the University of Iowa to determine and analyze process criteria for counseling activities in terms of effort, cost, and function.

Articles which provide pedagogical assistance to practitioners in their evaluation efforts have not appeared with any regularity in the student affairs literature. In one of the few articles of this kind, Harshman and Harshman (1974) provided a detailed description of the process they used to design the Resident Counselor Evaluation Scale for Ohio Dominican College. This process can be replicated by other professionals when attempting to evaluate programs and services. Although Fisher and Howell (1972) do not report results of the evaluation of the staff at the University of South Florida, they do describe the methodology used with sufficient specificity that it can have utility for other administrators.

OBSTACLES

For the most part, evaluation has been treated somewhat superficially in the student affairs literature. Staff have been encouraged to state goals, assess needs, design appropriate programs and note outcomes (e.g., Burck & Peterson, 1975) but few writers have offered specific concrete suggestions for applying existing strategies to student affairs evaluation problems (e.g., Brown, 1978) or for designing new, comprehensive evaluation strategies specifically for use in student affairs. While Miller and Prince (1976) emphasize that evaluation should be a component in student development programming, well developed methods of conducting evaluations in many areas of student affairs are not readily available.

It is possible that the blurred distinction between research and evaluation has created some confusion. Even when the purposes of these forms of inquiry become clearer to staff, the fact remains that most student affairs professionals have had some coursework in research methodology, but few have had specific training or experience in evaluation theories and techniques. In addition, some student affairs divisions or functional areas may lack the financial and/or staffing resources to effectively conduct an internal evaluation. Further complicating the situation is the fact that the goals and objectives articulated by divisions of student affairs sometimes lack the clarity required to conduct a satisfactory evaluation.

Ideally, evaluations should be conducted to determine the value of a particular contribution and to provide information which will facilitate program or service improvement (Stufflebeam et al., 1971). While evaluations can be used to improve services for students, it is also possible that the findings will identify some individuals or programs which are inadequate (Perloff & Perloff, 1977). Therein lies perhaps the greatest obstacle to encouraging and conducting evaluations in student affairs.

As a group, student affairs staff tend to be more person-oriented, rather than thing or product oriented. Of necessity perhaps, the profession is predominately "field-dependent" (see Cross, 1976), and is comprised of "people who need love and affection ... (and) to be appreciated" (Stamatakos, 1978, p. 328). As a result, the student affairs staff member's concern for others may often mitigate against rigorous evaluation of colleagues' performance. The tendency for an organization to establish rules and behaviors which support the unit both internally and externally are necessary for efficient and effective functioning. However, if the norms of a student affairs division do not also support a reasonably objective examination of the quality and impact of programs, the health and growth of the division may be impaired.

MIRROR IMAGES OF TODAY AND TOMORROW

It is difficult to accurately assess the extent to which student affairs programs and staff are currently being *adequately* evaluated. The relative dearth of evaluations reported in the professional literature suggests that few evaluations of student affairs are being conducted. This conclusion may not accurately reflect reality for at least three reasons.

First, most student affairs journals as well as journals of other professions, usually are not interested in publishing reports which were intended for use by internal audiences because the generalizability of findings are markedly restricted. A number of evaluation journals do exist which solicit such manuscripts (e.g., *Evaluation Quarterly* and *Studies in Educational Evaluation)* but they are not typically read by student affairs workers. Second, it is likely that student affairs staff, like many persons in other units in post-secondary institutions, *have been evaluating* programs and services but in a rather unsophisticated manner. In most institutions, decisions about the worth of a program tend to be based on a few opinions, on elaborate appearances without rigorous consideration of impact on students and environment, and occasionally on *post hoc* determination of program objectives to fit program activities and outcomes (see Stufflebeam et al., 1971). There are some advantages to informal assessments (e.g., time and minimal expenditure of resources) particularly when the activities to be judged are narrow in scope or have limited impact on staff, students, etc. To rely entirely on these less rigorous approaches, however, could result in subsequent evaluations being conducted by persons external to the division. Third, the pressure for disseminating the methods used in or findings from a student affairs evaluation is probably less than it is for other members of academia to share the fruits of their labors. Often there are no institutional rewards or incentives to encourage student affairs staff to publish reports on their work with students.

Some years ago, Brown (1972) suggested the profession hold up a mirror to itself to determine "not only what is, but what could be" (p. 11). As far as the state of evaluation in student affairs is concerned, the profession must attempt to:

(1) develop an appreciation and respect for evaluation as a systemic professional activity;
(2) become familiar with various evaluation techniques and strategies and apply them to evaluation problems in various

functional areas and student affairs program; and (3) share with others through professional journals, conventions and workshops, and newsletters carefully conceived evaluation designs.

This book provides a glimpse of what the future of evaluation in student affairs can be.

REFERENCES

Bishop, J. B. Some guidelines for the development of accountability systems. *NASPA Journal*, 1975, *12*, 190-194.

Boyer, J. Personal communication. March 19, 1979.

Brown, R. D. *Student development in tomorrow's higher education: A return to the academy.* Washington, D.C.: American Personnel and Guidance Association, 1972.

Brown, R. D. Implications of new evaluation strategies for accountability in student affairs. *Journal of College Student Personnel*, 1978, *19*, 123-125.

Burck, H. D., & Peterson, G. W. Needed: More evaluation, not research. *Personnel and Guidance Journal*, 1975, *53*, 563-569.

Casse, R. M., Jr., Gillis, A. L., & Mullen, J. Student services accountability utilizing a data information system. *NASPA Journal*, 1974, *12*, 36-43.

Cronbach, L. J. Course improvement through evaluation. *Teachers College Record*, 1963, *64*, 672-683.

Cross, K. P. *Accent on learning.* San Francisco: Jossey-Bass, 1976.

Dressel, P. L. Measuring the benefits of student personnel work. *Journal of Higher Education*, 1973, *44*, 15-26.

Dressel, P. L. *Handbook of academic evaluation.* San Francisco: Jossey-Bass, 1976.

Escott, S. Personal communication. March 19, 1979.

Fisher, M. B., & Howell, J. A. Evaluation and accountability. *NASPA Journal*, 1972, *10*, 118-123.

Flentje, H. E., & Sample, S. B. Statewide reallocation through program priorities. *Educational Record*, 1973, *54*, 175-184.

Freeman, J., Nudd, T. R., & O'Donnell, T. Quality control program for student personnel services. *NASPA Journal*, 1972, *9*, 279-282.

Hanson, G. R. (Ed.) Evaluating program effectiveness. *New Directions for Student Services* (Number 1). San Francisco: Jossey-Bass, 1978.

Harpel, R. L. Planning, budgeting, and evaluation in student affairs programs: A manual for administrators. *NASPA Journal*, 1976, *14*, i-xx.

Harshman, C. L., & Harshman, E. F. The evaluation of undergraduate residence hall staff: A model and instrumentation. *Journal of College Student Personnel*, 1974, *15*, 125-132.

Henderson, C. *Changes in enrollment by 1985.* Washington, D.C.: ACE, 1977. (ERIC Document Reproduction Service No. ED 140 766).

Hodgkinson, H. L. Guess who's coming to college: New learners, new tasks. *NASPA Journal*, 1976, *14*, 2-14.

Kerlinger, F. N. *Foundation of behavioral research.* New York: Holt, Rinehart & Winston, 1973.

Krumboltz, J. D. An accountability model for counselors. *Personnel and Guidance Journal*, 1974, *52*, 639-646.

Levy, S. R., & Schreck, T. C. Management effectiveness: A symposium. *NASPA Journal*, 1975, *12*, 142-211.

Miller, T. K., & Prince, J. S. *The future of student affairs.* San Francisco: Jossey-Bass, 1976.

Oetting, E. R. Evaluation research and orthodox science. *Personnel and Guidance Journal,* 1976, *55,* 11-15.

Oetting, E. R. Planning and reporting evaluative research. *Personnel and Guidance Journal,* 1976, *55,* 60-64.

Oetting, E. R., & Hawkes, F. J. Training professionals for evaluative research. *Personnel and Guidance Journal,* 1974, *52,* 434-438.

Perloff, R., & Perloff, E. Evaluation of psychological service delivery programs: The state of the art. In Author (Ed.), Evaluation of psychological service delivery programs. *Professional Psychology,* 1977, *8,* 379-388.

Provus, M. M. Evaluation of ongoing programs in the public school system. In R. W. Tyler (Ed.), *Educational evaluation: New roles, new means.* Chicago: National Society for the Study of Education, 1969.

Shaffer, R. Personal communication. March 1978.

Sims, O. S. Jr., & Kozall, C. E. A case for MBO for student development services. *NASPA Journal,* 1974, *12,* 44-50.

Stamatakos, L. C. Unsolicited advice to new professionals. *Journal of College Student Personnel,* 1978, *19,* 325-329.

Stufflebeam, D. L., Foley, W. J., Gephart, W. J., Guba, E. G., Hammond, R., Merriman, H. O., & Provus, M. M. *Educational evaluation and decision making.* Itasca, Ill.: Peacock, 1971.

Tyler, R. W. General statement on evaluation. *Journal of Educational Research,* 1942, *30,* 492-501.

Worthen, B. R., & Sanders, J. R. *Educational evaluation: Theory and practice.* Belmont, Calif.: Wadsworth, 1973.

2
KEY ISSUES IN EVALUATING STUDENT AFFAIRS PROGRAMS
Robert D. Brown

In this era of budget limitations and accountability, evaluation within student affairs programs has become almost as certain as death and taxes. Like death, evaluation is often dreaded, but nevertheless is inevitable. Like taxes, evaluation is often grudgingly accepted, but only as a necessary evil. All three: death, taxes, and evaluation also have in common a constant air of controversy surrounding them. Theologians and philosophers debate life and death issues and politicians agonize over raising and lowering taxes. Evaluators and their publics debate the relative merit of different responses to key evaluation issues. Those who are looking for pat answers to time honored evaluation questions are likely to be frustrated as the answers are not nearly as conclusive as those related to death and taxes. Nevertheless, just as individuals must make existential choices each day about life and annually on April 15th about taxes, so evaluators and program directors must confront basic evaluation questions within the context of the specific programs and situations in which they find themselves.

The purpose of this chapter is to introduce the key evaluation questions which student affairs persons commissioning or conducting an evaluation should ask. The questions will be raised within the context of a student affairs division and possible responses to these questions will be provided. Although not much can be done about death and taxes, the following discussion should provide an increased sense of internal locus of control for student affairs staff members who are responsible for program evaluation.

DEFINITIONS

Before considering the questions it is essential to have a common perspective on what is meant by the term "evaluation." There are numerous definitions of evaluation and each emphasizes a different dimension of the evaluator's role and activities and the evaluation process or product. Most definitions describe evaluation as the assessment of worth. Others suggest that the purpose of evaluation is to obtain information which can assist decision-makers (Worthen & Sanders, 1973). Assessment of worth can be independent of decision-making but in practice it seldom is. Therefore, in most circumstances, the two steps are highly interwoven. Building on the definition put forth in Chapter 1, evaluation as a purposeful intervention is defined as follows:

> To evaluate is to make judgments about the worth of a program or elements of a program. The worth of a program is ultimately determined by its impact on society as well as on its participants and those within the immediate context. Criteria for determination of worth can include the extent of the program's impact, the number of persons affected, cost-benefit analysis (accountability), and other program and person dimensions. Worth can be determined relative to the program's goals, in comparison to other programs, or to other standards. The evaluative judgments lead to decisions which have a direct impact on whether the program is continued, expanded, reduced in scope or otherwise changed. The evaluative judgment can be formal and explicit, based on an intentional and extensive data collection process and include a publicly announced decision. Because evaluation is a natural human activity, it can also be informal, based on whatever information is available at the moment, and quite private.
>
> In the strictest definition, the "evaluator" is the one who makes the judgments of worth. However, in most usages of the title "evaluator" it refers to the person planning and conducting the data-gathering who may or may not be the person actually making judgments about the program, recommendations, or decisions based on judgments. The roles and activities of the person designated as evaluator can vary. In some instances the evaluator, project administrator, and the decision-maker are all the same person.

If a dean for student affairs asks the counseling center to evaluate its assertiveness training program for women, the dean is asking for information which will help determine the program's worth. The dean may be trying to decide whether the assertiveness training program should be expanded and made available to students throughout the college. Perhaps the dean believes that the residence hall staff could be involved in presenting assertiveness training in the residence halls. On the other hand, the dean may be questioning the worth of the program in terms of staff time and the relatively few students it now reaches. The dean may think there are other programs which are more worthwhile in terms of institutional and/or society's needs at the moment. The counseling center may designate a staff member to be responsible for gathering evaluative information and this staff member could then be viewed as an evaluator even though the ultimate judge is likely to be the dean. In this instance, one of the first things the designated evaluator would want to do is visit with the dean to determine expected evaluation goals, roles, activities, and products. As a rule, the evaluator should always determine who or what group will be making the decisions, what role is expected of the evaluator in the decision-making process, and what kind of information will be needed to make the decision.

THE KEY QUESTIONS

Debates among professional evaluators are often technical and occasionally philosophical. The points of contention range from what is the nature of a true score on a multiple choice examination to what is the nature of human kind. The basic questions, however, are not particularly complex. Even though the questions may appear simple when stripped of professional jargon, they remain important. How they are answered has significant implications not only for evaluations but for the programs being evaluated. The remainder of this chapter is devoted to answering eleven questions which must be addressed when planning an evaluation for a student affairs program.

1. IS A FORMAL EVALUATION NEEDED?

It is undoubtedly heretical within evaluation circles to ask whether there is always a need for evaluation. Is not evaluation an intrinsic good which cannot be called into question? Nevertheless, the question of whether to conduct an evaluation must be taken seriously. Formal evaluations require time and money, and the benefits are not necessarily guaranteed to be proportionate to the investment. Even if there are no direct costs associated with the evaluation, staff time devoted to the evaluation activity, such as responding to questionnaires, being interviewed, and gathering data, requires psychological contributions if not a direct dollar cost. Evaluations can be intrusive, time-consuming, and sometimes counterproductive. Therefore, the question is legitimate and needs attention.

One possible response is that it is not really an issue aside from the matter of cost. This line of thinking posits that evaluation takes place all the time, is a natural activity, and therefore cannot and should not be avoided. Installation of a new career education program in the residence halls, for example, will be evaluated informally by participants, staff, and administrators, formal reactions and judgments not withstanding. Students are going to make judgments about whether the experiences were helpful in their career choice process and whether to recommend the program to other students. Staff are going to note whether professional rewards are equal to the amount of time they spend. Finally, the administrator responsible for the budget and staffing is going to decide to continue, modify, or discontinue the program. The administrator's decision will be based upon some form of evaluative evidence, if only hearsay. Thus, the question in this context is not really whether an evaluation will be made, but how it will be made — formally or informally.

However, Glass (1975) has raised a provocative question concerning the paradox of excellence. He noted that human development and excellence most often are found in a nurturing rather than a judgmental environment (Glass apparently subscribes to the Rogerian nonjudgmental therapeutic framework as a model which views persons as being able to grow and solve problems better in a setting in which they are understood and accepted rather than judged and rated). According to this approach, a student working through a family problem is assisted best by a counselor who has empathy, is supportive, fosters self-direction, and is nonjudgmental. Individuals not only solve problems best in a nonjudgmental environment, but are also more creative when they can put forth new creations without the threat of criticism. Glass wonders whether the same premise holds true for program excellence and creativity. Does the heavy hand of external evaluation get in the way of a program being the best that it possibly can be? Does the threat of evaluation inhibit creativity and therefore excellence? Is evaluation the ally of mediocrity and the enemy of excellence?

Glass posed the paradox but did not elaborate extensively on its consequences. It does raise some interesting questions, but it is not a new argument. Anyone who has been involved in directing programs which have had evaluation plans arbitrarily imposed has probably at one time or another felt that the evaluation activities were inhibiting the full blossoming of the program. For example, evaluations often necessitate a structure or framework for data collection purposes and the necessity to look at outcomes related to specified objectives. Not all evaluation models emphasize predetermined outcomes as a success criterion. However, those that do could, in this context, be viewed by some as putting the program into a straitjacket which prohibits or at least inhibits, exploration of new objectives not thought of at the beginning of the program or changing directions in other ways. Adhering to a prescribed process necessitates a good deal of work and it can be enervating. Conceivably then, a highly structured evaluation could inhibit a program from being excellent because it drains energy from potential creative activities and it reinforces a preordained set of activities rather than exploratory and potentially beneficial activities.

If it is assumed that judgments about a program will be made and that evaluation is defined as a judgmental process, then the question is not whether an evaluation should be made, but rather the degree to which the evaluation is formal and public. The distinction between an evaluation being formal and informal is helpful but it must be perceived as a continuum rather than a dichotomy. On the one end is the sometimes automatic budget decision to fund a program for another year. Thus, an implicit judgment is made when the placement center's budget is continued into the next year with a percentage increase related to inflation. On other end of the continuum is a program which faces the possibility of termination based on objective data about program effectiveness collected by external evaluators for clearly identified decision makers with the decision-moment a public event. The same might be true for an internal evaluator, but generally the external evaluator is much more threatening.

The dimensions on which an evaluation might be considered formal or informal would include: the degree to which it is public or private, whether the evaluator and decision-maker are internal or external, whether the evidence is objective or subjective, and finally whether the decision is conscious and explicit, or reflexive and implicit. Programs which are expensive and/or politically sensitive often demand a formal evaluation.

2. Is This Research or Evaluation?

Evaluation occasionally utilizes the same methodology and analytical tools as research and may be similar in other ways, but evaluation is not the same as research. As noted in Chapter 1, the purposes of evaluation are to assess worth and to provide information for decision-making. The purposes of research, on the other hand, are to test theoretical propositions and to find truth. Research attempts to be value-free, whereas evaluation is imbued with values. In most instances researchers hope to develop general laws and principles whereas evaluators attempt to understand particular events. A researcher's goal is to determine whether a specific method for reducing test anxiety is generally better than other techniques. An evaluator is concerned about whether a particular test anxiety program sponsored by the counseling center works and whether it is worth continuing.

Many times evaluation considers a broader spectrum of variables than does research and almost always takes place in a real life setting rather than in a lab. Costs and politics enter into an evaluation judgment, but not into a research conclusion. A researcher might conclude that coed suites in a residence hall are generally more conducive to fostering interdependence and social maturity among students. An evaluator, however, might conclude that coed suites are more costly than single sex suites and that they are too politically sensitive to continue.

The differences between evaluation and research are not always clear-cut. The most important distinction is their differing purposes: evaluation to determine worth and research to determine truth (Oetting, 1976; Worthen & Sanders, 1973). One of the recurring problems in evaluations is that people turn them into research projects for publication purposes because of a mistaken notion that research is better than evaluation. When this happens, usually neither purpose is served well. There are not enough controls to make the research solid and the information provided is seldom of assistance to the decision-makers.

3. What Do I As Evaluator Value?

Succinctly stated, evaluation is assessment of worth. Definitions of and criteria for determining worth are intimately related to any evaluation effort. Generally, statements about worth reflect values. Concluding that one program is needed more than another reflects values whether or not the statement is supported with statistical evidence. For example, deciding that space in the union should be allotted to a women's resource center rather than an on-campus banking center reflects the value placed on the importance of the women's resource center and related activities. This decision may be made even though the evidence indicated the center will not be self-supporting in terms of rental fees whereas the banking center would be self-sustaining, and in spite of the fact that more students supported the banking center because of its convenience than the women's resource center. The weights given to the variety of supporting evidence and the final decision reflects a value judgment, not solely an arithmetic summation of weights. Attending to political reality is also a reflection of values.

Education in general and student affairs programming in particular are imbued with explicit and implicit values. The existence of an administrative unit which is concerned with student affairs reflects a very clear value commitment. It says the institution values student concerns and needs. If a division pursues the concept of student development in programming, it communicates slightly different values which suggest that the institution expects students to mature as persons during college. Choosing between a women's resource center and a banking center is perhaps a relatively easy value choice. Suppose the choice was between space for the women's resource center and a newly expanded career placement center? Would the choice be as easy? Probably not, but the final choice would still be a reflection of values. It is critical that evaluators in student affairs be conscious of the importance of values as they are related to decisions about the worth of programs. The concerns and needs of a variety of constituencies must be considered in weighing values. What is best for students, for staff, for faculty, for society?

Gowin and Millman (1978) have posited five major forms of value

statements related to the act of evaluation. These statements include:
1. "The program is good"; an intrinsic value claim.
2. "The program is good because it results in . . ."; an instrumental claim.
3. "This program is better than other programs"; a comparative claim.
4. "This is the right program"; the decision claim.
5. "This program could be better if it . . ."; an idealization claim.

The kinds of value statements a student affairs administrator makes about a program are related to one or more of these value statements. The particular value statement chosen will affect the type of questions asked in an evaluation, the kind of data collected and the kind of conclusions drawn. It is, therefore, quite important for the evaluator and the program administrator to have a clear idea of the relevant value statement. The five statements require different kinds of evidence and therefore different kinds of evaluation.

Relatively few programs in student affairs can be justified by claims that they are intrinsically good or right without supporting evidence. Most student affairs programming is based on instrumental premises, though those with a humanist philosophical orientation (Cross, 1976) might find many of their claims to be derived from statements about what is intrinsically good. They might justify student development programming because they believe it to be necessary and growth producing and, therefore, good. Within this philosophical orientation, spending more programming money on the handicapped than on the non-handicapped students seems warranted because it is just. The same arguments are used in establishing special programs for ethnic minorities and for women's programs. Programs which are justified solely or primarily on the claims that they are intrinsically good or that they rightfully should exist are difficult to formally evaluate. Evaluation in these contexts is often viewed as a hostile activity which calls into question the premise and rationale for the existence of the program. The same might be said of many other programs which emerge with strong political support from within or outside the institution. To request an evaluation implies that the program could be dropped if the evaluation findings are negative and this possible outcome is not acceptable; therefore, evaluation is avoided. Unfortunately, this fails to recognize other possible roles for evaluators, even though it reflects political realities. That evaluation might be used to improve the program or even to assess the values of the community is seldom considered because any evaluation may be seen as threatening.

A somewhat easier task for the evaluator and a more comfortable role for the decision-maker is that of determining what a program is good for (instrumental) and whether a program is better than another (comparative claim). Many times the foci of the evaluation activities which seek to respond to these value claims in student affairs will be on student outcomes. Data will be collected about a student activities program to determine how many students participated, their level of participation, what type of activities they participated in, how they felt about the program, and whether they would participate again. If the sole or primary value claim is instrumental, this evaluation activity will probably be entirely an in-house directed venture, the goal being to amass as much data as possible to support the program.

The comparative claim necessitates a comparison group. This comparison or control group is usually a group of students not involved in the program. Counseled students are compared with those who did not use the counseling center, residence hall students are compared with students who live elsewhere, or the ratio of students finding employment who use the placement center is compared with the ratio of students finding jobs on their own. Because many student affairs programs are responding to specific student requests for services, it is not always feasible to have a matched or randomly selected control group of students who were seeking the service but can be momentarily shunted off to the side so that they can serve as a truly random control group.

Given current budget constraints, it is unreasonable to expect a student affairs division to provide two separate and different programs designed to meet identical needs and accomplish identical goals with similar students. So the possibility is highly remote that a student affairs officer would find it possible to compare directly the impact of two counseling centers or two financial aid offices. A more likely target for a quasi-experimental design would be in the residence hall complexes on the larger university settings. Because many residence units are quite similar, it is possible to provide programs with the same intent; e.g., a study skills program, but which vary significantly in format. If these opportunities exist and there are reasonably clear-cut distinctions which can be made between two programs, then this option for comparison is worth considering. However, it should not be viewed automatically as an ideal approach even if the option exists. The relative merits of the comparative approach will be discussed further in the next chapter which focuses on evaluation models and in Chapter 6.

The idealization claim (how can a program be improved?) is probably the most important value question which a student affairs administrator can ask. This is especially true for programs that have existed for some time and promise to remain an important part of student affairs. The issue becomes not whether a counseling center should exist or whether programming for student development in residence halls should be eliminated, but rather "How can they be improved?" An evaluation which focuses on discovering ways to make a program better certainly is less threatening and has a better chance of obtaining staff support.

The questions of what is of worth and value clearly are not easy to answer. Perhaps that is why they have not been attended to by many program evaluations. It would be good for the program directors to ask themselves these questions in the presence of those who will be conducting the evaluation and all those concerned about the program, including students.

4. SHOULD AN EVALUATION BE FORMATIVE OR SUMMATIVE?

One of the earliest and most important distinctions made in the evaluation literature was between *formative* and *summative* evaluation (Scriven, 1967). Formative evaluations are conducted periodically throughout the developmental phases of a program and are used to provide quick feedback to the program staff so that changes can be made to improve the program as time passes. Formative evaluations seek to identify the potential problem areas before they escalate. The audience for this form of evaluation is usually the program staff. Evaluation reports are often informal and any data analysis is simple and straightforward. The evaluation is intended to be helpful, not threatening. When the staff obtain student reactions about a study skills program in order to improve it from week-to-week, from semester-to-semester, or even from year-to-year, the evaluation is formative. If the primary purpose of the evaluation is to help improve the program, then generally it can be considered formative.

Summative evaluations are typically conducted at the conclusion of a program cycle and are intended to provide information about the program to an external group as well as the program staff. The primary audience for a summative evaluation usually consists of persons making budgetary decisions which affect the life and future scope of the program. Thus, if the counseling center staff wishes to decide whether to continue or terminate the study skills program, they would be making a summative evaluation. Some of the same kinds of information may be collected in both types of evaluations; very often, however, the formative evaluation will focus on the process of the program, whereas the summative will focus on student outcomes. Thus, if the staff in a formative evaluation want to know what needs to be changed in their study skills program, they will ask students and staff questions about the process. How much time did they spend? Were the materials helpful? Did they find the discussions pertinent? On the other hand, in a summative evaluation the ultimate criterion might well be how many students improved their academic grade point as a result of the study skills program.

Although formative evaluation usually takes place during the early stages of a program and the summative near the end, the major distinction is the intent, not the timing. Stake (1976) suggested a helpful analogy: "When the cook tastes the soup it is formative evaluation and when the guest tastes the soup it is summative" (p. 19). Summative evaluation in student affairs programs, like in the soup analogy, often includes student reactions as program consumers and their testimony often has more credibility than that of the program staff.

The distinction between formative and summative evaluation is important because too often programs emphasize designing summative evaluation activities when the focus should be on formative efforts. Summative evaluations rarely provide information which is immediately usable by program staff. When the information itself could be helpful, it is often not timely, coming as it usually does at a significant terminal point in the program.

The key determinants for choosing between formative and summative evaluation are the purpose of the evaluation and the intended audience. If the purpose is to help improve the program by providing the staff with information, then the evaluation should be formative. If the purpose is to assess the ultimate worth of the project for an external audience, then the evaluation is summative. Of course, both types of evaluations could be carried on concurrently and in an integrated fashion.

5. Do The Evaluation Results Need To Be Generalizable?

This is a very critical question and sometimes answers can be found in the nature of the program itself or in the goals of the evaluation. The evaluator must ask whether the program's design is unique to a particular setting or place, or whether the program is a pilot effort which may be expanded if successful. The evaluator must ask the decision-maker how important it is that the findings be applied to other settings, circumstances, or other students. The answer to this type of question is more likely to have a dramatic effect on the nature of the evaluation design than the response to most any of the other questions. The more the decision-maker wants to be able to generalize from the findings of one program evaluation to other programs, the more the evaluation is going to have to be quite similar to an experimental research design in terms of sample selection and a need for comparison groups (see Chapter 3).

Suppose the housing director requests an evaluation of a new procedure for hall and washroom maintenance. Students on each floor will be responsible for cleaning and maintaining their own facilities with the money saved going to other programming in the hall. This program may be viewed as risky because of cost or political reasons. In this instance, the housing director may want to see how it works on a small scale (pilot project on one residence hall floor) before considering implementing the program on a broader scale. In this example, there is a need for assurance that the pilot setting is representative of the total system so that the housing director can, in good faith, generalize the findings to other halls. The evaluator will have to consider using several research strategems such as random selection of the hall(s) for the pilot program and using other halls for comparison purposes.

On the other hand, if the program is unique and will not be extended to other settings, or for other reasons there is no need to make assertions about whether the program would work elsewhere, then an intensive case study approach may be the most appropriate and rigid controls to guarantee generalizability would be unwarranted.

6. Who Should Conduct The Evaluation?

There are several questions which must be answered before determination can be made of just who should conduct the evaluation. These questions include: a) Who will be making the evaluative judgments? b) Should the evaluator be external or internal to the program? c) What are the necessary qualifications for an evaluator? Unfortunately, these questions are seldom systematically raised and answered. Let us look at these questions in some detail.

a. *Who will be making the evaluative judgments?* In a sense, this question is asking who will be the decision-maker? Who will be deciding whether the program is to be continued or what changes will be made? Will the ultimate decision-making group be the regents, the vice-president for student affairs, the program director, or a student group? This should be determined prior to any data collection and should be shared with the person carrying out the evaluation activities. If the evaluation is to have utility for the decision-maker, it should be attending to that person's or group's informational needs and this cannot be done without communication between the evaluator and the decision-makers. If the board of regents is the ultimate decision-maker about whether to grant permission to have alcohol in the residence hall, those gathering evaluative data should know what the regents would consider as evidence. The relative importance and credibility of certain data may be quite different among the student government, the student affairs staff, and the regents. Time and energy can be wasted collecting information that carries little weight with the ultimate decision-maker.

A related and equally important question is how much of an evaluative judgment role should be expected from the person responsible for carrying out the evaluation activities? If the title "evaluator" has precise meaning, it implies that evaluators are doing more than actually collecting data; they are also involved in making judgments about the program. In practice, there is a great amount of variability.

Some evaluators function as technical data collection and analysis experts without making judgments, and others assume roles in which their recommendations carry essentially the final authority. There are, of course, numerous variations in between. This issue is also a point of contention among those who consider themselves evaluators as some characterize their role solely as data collectors, others as interpretors and clarifiers of issues, and still others as being responsible for making judgments.

This rather basic issue should be resolved early in the evaluation process and continually clarified, if need be, as the evaluation continues. The level of experience and expertise of the evaluator would certainly influence how much credence a decision-maker would want to place in the judgments and recommendations of the person conducting the evaluation. It is important to remember that the process of collecting evaluative data often puts the evaluators more intimately in touch with the true nature of the program; therefore, their reactions and judgments should not be completely ignored.

It should also be noted that even in most instances in which the evaluator is primarily a data collector, there are hosts of value judgments being made that subtly or directly impact on the nature of the eventual decision. The evaluator's judgments enter in constructing questionnaires, conducting interviews, and interpreting findings.

b. *Should the evaluator be external or internal?* Should the person conducting the evaluation be a member of the program staff or someone outside the program? The answer to this question is sometimes dictated by the nature of the program. A federally funded program for special programming for ethnic minorities, for example, may carry with it explicit guidelines as to what information is to be reported and who will make the evaluative judgments. All that is necessary is designating someone to be responsible for processing the forms. Quite frequently, federal funding agencies require a description of the proposed program's plan. The decision regarding the quality of the total proposal is influenced by the quality of the evaluation plan and the expertise available to carry it out. At the other extreme might be a student-funded day care center which has no mandate to conduct an evaluation. The decision of whether to conduct an evaluation is left to students. If given the choice between an external or internal evaluator, the program administrator must weigh the advantages and disadvantages of each.

There are at least two possible advantages of having an external evaluator: (1) unbiased view of the program and (2) credible evaluation results. Although there is no guarantee, the odds are that an external evaluator, whose job is not contingent upon the success of a particular program, is more likely to be unbiased than an evaluator who is also a staff member of the program. This choice also enhances the credibility of the evaluation results, especially for an external audience.

The findings of an external evaluator are more likely to be accepted as unbiased.

These advantages are counterbalanced, however, by several disadvantages. The external evaluator is generally less familiar with the project. Start-up time is necessary for the evaluator to get a sense of the program and to become familiar with staff and program needs. Whereas the external evaluator's efforts have more credibility with external program audiences, quite often, external evaluators, because of unfamiliarity with the program, overlook important dimensions of the program. Program staff often find external evaluators provide little information that is directly helpful to them and, of course, external evaluation can be more costly.

The opposite holds true for the internal evaluator. Program staff conducting their own evaluation usually attend to factors most salient to their own concerns. The cost of the evaluation is substantially less but so is external credibility.

Considering the advantages and disadvantages, the choice between the external or internal evaluator depends upon the specific purpose of the evaluation and the need for credibility with external audiences. If the evaluation findings are reported to external groups who will be making important decisions/judgments about the program, then an external evaluator would be more appropriate. On the other hand, if the purpose of the evaluation is primarily to improve the program and the evaluation findings are mostly for an in-house audience, then an internal evaluator is the best option.

c. *What skills should the evaluator have?* Ideally, the evaluator should possess knowledge and skills in three areas: 1) compentency in a variety of measurement techniques including statistics, 2) awareness of evaluation techniques and research designs, and 3) skills in observation and consultation processes. The first provides the evaluator with the analytical tools to develop appropriate assessment procedures and to process results. Knowledge of evaluation strategies as well as research designs should provide the evaluator with the flexibility to adapt strategies to the particular needs of the evaluation. Finally, consulting skills provide some guarantee that the evaluation will be relevant, the data-gathering a cooperative venture, and the results utilized. All three of these competency areas are important if the evaluator is to be successful in providing a service which has real utility for the administrator.

The student affairs administrator might try several ways of obtaining access to these skills. A team approach is certainly a viable one; the expertise may be available within current staff, but scattered across individuals. Several universities have organized research and evaluation units within student affairs. A reasonable goal should be to develop skills within the unit of student affairs through staffing and inservice training so that staff are eventually capable of conducting their evaluations with a minimum of outside consultant help.

7. Is There a Need for a Needs Assessment?

Evaluation is subject to its share of fads. A current trend is to conduct a needs assessment (a survey of the clientele to determine their needs) prior to designing a program and evaluation. A major problem with such efforts is that many "needs" assessments are really "wants" assessments (see Chapter 14). Surveys are sent out to determine what students have to say about various aspects of campus life. These in turn are interpreted as needs, when they are really wants. There is a belief that numbers and percentages will answer all the questions about needs if the available information is entered into an equation. Determination of need is a much more complex issue than surveying wants as the latter is only one component of needs. For example, students may have indicated that they want alcohol available in the residence hall. Should this then be considered a need?

Student affairs officers are particularly vulnerable to this misinterpretation. Because of the profession's traditional humanistic perspective on the student experience and the desire to be responsive, it is only natural that student affairs would be particularly interested in the concept of needs assessment as a necessary precursor to program planning. This issue directly influences the perceived role of the student affairs officer. Though seldom this clearcut in an actual situation, it does become a question of whether student affairs gives students what they say they need (want) or provides what they really need. Of course, the next question is how is authentic need determined? This cannot be answered through a survey; true need is a reflection of values. Determination of whether money should be spent on training residence hall floor assistants in career planning or in first aid can only be made after weighing different needs and values. There is no equation available.

Surveys, however, can be utilized to assess different groups' perceptions of needs and the weight or value they give them. This can be helpful information before a decision is made and should really be part of a total needs assessment. Chapter 14 addresses these and related needs assessment issues in more detail.

8. What Are the Policies of the Situation?

There are times when evaluation is required because of political necessity (Weiss, 1973). This is often the case for new student affairs programming. Changes in living arrangements with residence halls or in student conduct regulations can be sensitive issues with the general public and within the college community, and an evaluation is prudent even though not mandated. For example, a change to coed residence halls can be labelled an "experiment" if the governing board requests the chief student affairs officer to present one year later evaluative information about the new living arrangement. However, the board will undoubtedly want to know more than the degree to which students were satisfied with the arrangements. In this instance, the board's interest may be as much in the concerns of parents as in the concerns of the students. A dramatic change in alcohol policies, such as making alcohol available in the union or in the residence hall, may require not only an assessment of the new policy's impact but may also require the establishment of an alcohol education program, which also will need to be evaluated.

Political necessity may be one rationale for evaluating many other new programs. Generally, the installation of new programs results in reallocation of expenditures previously alloted to other programs and in the final analysis may even result in the termination of other programs. Thus, a new program represents a new budget item which needs justification. New programs may also entail personnel shifts which, in turn, require changes in how staff spend their time, who they interact with, and what rewards are available to them. This makes the programs vulnerable to criticism from internal staff who may not welcome the change. Involving these staff in planning the evaluation as well as the program itself can diffuse hostility and fear.

9. Is There A Need To Specify All Objectives In Detail?

For years professional evaluators have been encouraging program administrators to be thorough in program and evaluation planning. It was believed that the objectives of the program should be described in detail in advance and that criterion measures and evaluation strategies also needed to be clearly articulated before a program was implemented. Evaluators demanded program administrators "operationalize" program objectives in behavioral terms; e.g., "Please describe in behavioral terms what you expect students to be like after they participate". Once the objectives were on paper, it was believed that the rest of the evaluation would systematically follow.

This approach is still a frequently used evaluation strategem. It has its limitations, however, particularly for innovative programming in higher education. It is not always possible for bold new programs in student affairs to specify in great detail what outcomes are expected as not every possible outcome can be anticipated. Often innovative programs are implemented with intuition as the guide rather than specified objectives for a roadmap. To force a program to specify its objectives and relate them to specific dimensions of the program prematurely may stifle program creativity. Some latitude should be provided for changes in program objectives after the program has begun. Without such flexibility there would be no room for serendipity, the mother of many successful innovations. This is not to suggest that new programs should be left alone to flounder, or that they should change directions on a whim, but rather that planned objectives and evaluation strategies should be flexible and responsible to the changing needs of the program.

10. SHOULD THE EVALUATION FOCUS ON THE PROCESS OR THE PRODUCT?

Student affairs programming generally has one primary product that can be attributed to programs: the development of students. It may be an improved grade point resulting from participation in a study skills program, new leadership skills acquired as a result of involvement in assertion and leadership training programs, or selection of a satisfying career choice after participation in a life planning workshop. There are, however, other products. These can be the packaged programs themselves — the materials and formats utilized. This can be a focus for the evaluation and one that should be assessed as well as student outcomes.

Student affairs programmers are seldom remiss in obtaining feedback on process; in fact, many evaluations focus exclusively on process. Sometimes, however, the wrong kind of process is assessed. Assessment is often centered on the question of whether everyone had a good time or enjoyed the process. Enjoyment is important, but attention must be given to other dimensions of process, including the efficiency and effectiveness. How long do students seeking assistance in the financial aids office have to wait before they see a staff member? Is the residence hall advisor available during office hours? Is the registration staff helpful in providing directions? Are the forms understandable? These are examples of process questions which need attention.

11. SHOULD THE EVALUATION BE OBJECTIVE OR SUBJECTIVE?

Most evaluators would assert that evaluations should be as objective as possible. Program goals should be specified and phrased in measurable terms. Instruments should be utilized which have proven reliability and validity to assess how well the objectives have been achieved. What then is at issue? The truth is that the area of evaluation and, in particular, assessment of change in individuals has not yet reached a point where anyone can feel very comfortable with the measurements. Fewer measurement specialists today are confident in asserting "if it cannot be measured, then it does not exist," which was a popular statement a decade ago. They recognize, or are at least willing to admit more readily now, that there are outcomes which are currently quite difficult, if not impossible to measure. Programs may have an impact on students which is not readily observable. In fact, some programming may not result in an observable influence until some distant point in the student's future.

Much of the evaluation within student affairs has been at one end or the other of the two extremes. Decisions about programs have seldom been data-based and heavy reliance has been placed on student opinion and feelings. Yet, when programs are formally evaluated, there is a tendency to attempt to emulate a research model (see Chapter 3). Naturalistic inquiry promises to provide an alternative approach to evaluation in student affairs (Guba, 1978). Too often, objective is viewed as synonymous with scientific, and subjective with unscientific. This view clearly does not have to be the case (Scriven, 1967). The tactics of the anthropologist or the ethnologist can hardly be called unscientific.

CAVEATS

Successful evaluation can only be assured by avoiding problems which typically arise during the process. There are at least seven common pitfalls which deserve to be reemphasized.

1. *Poor planning.* Evaluation cannot be tacked on to a program. Because it must be included in the program process, the evaluator should take part in planning sessions.
2. *Too much complexity in the evaluation design.* Student affairs programs provide a rich environment for the collection of data; therefore, evaluators must be cautious of a tendency to over-evaluate. If the evaluation does not produce pertinent data for decision-makers, then they are of little use. The evaluation goals are most important and should not be compromised to correspond to a particular theoretical evaluation model.
3. *Administration cooperation.* Unless careful attention is given to all the details surrounding data collection, the most sophisticated evaluation design will fail. Staff members and evaluators must cooperate to insure that the necessary materials and data collection activities are well coordinated.
4. *Inexperience.* Lack of experience in designing and implementing evaluation procedures can cause two types of problems for student affairs staff. First is a tendency to be awed by evaluation expertise and not ask pertinent questions because they may appear to be irrelevant. The second problem focuses on the lack of experience on the part of evaluators in actual program planning. Staff members must share their specialized program expertise with evaluators. It is necessary to confront issues when implementation is assured of failure because of program constraints.
5. *Failure to use data.* Often elaborate procedures are designed

to collect evaluative feedback and then nothing is done with the information collected. Collection of data without a clear plan for utilization is not justifiable in terms of financial and personnel resources.

6. *Territoriality.* Fear of failure often causes a reluctance to expend full resources on the design and implementation of an evaluation system. Program protection instead of program improvement becomes the primary goal. Evaluation should not be viewed as an invasion of territory by others. As Kuh has indicated in Chapter 1, attitudes need to be changed regarding the use and purpose of evaluation.

7. *Poor presentation of results.* Evaluation data must be presented in ways that will be of maximum benefit to those receiving the data. Not all the data need to be presented to all audiences. Selective presentation of data that will provide specific assistance to decision makers, presenters, and staff members is strongly encouraged. Short, succinct presentations are more likely to be read and utilized than lengthy statistical reports. It is crucial that a complete data file be maintained and made available to those who wish additional information (Barr, Justice & Yancey, 1979).

CONCLUSION

These foregoing questions and caveats can serve as a useful checklist for student affairs administrators considering commissioning an evaluation as well as to staff planning to conduct an evaluation. They illuminate helpful procedures while providing both the administrator and the evaluator with a useful checklist of critical issues which need to be examined.

There are several mistakes that evaluators and those commissioning an evaluation make. Both are at fault. The most frequent error made by persons commissioning an evaluation is to assign an evaluator, abdicate any further responsibility for the task, and avoid further contact with the evaluator. Most administrators are very busy people, but somehow their priorities are inappropriate if they cannot afford to discuss with the evaluator some of the key issues raised in this chapter. If the administrator knows that decisions will be made independent of the data collected, then it seems even more important that the questions and issues be addressed. Going through the motions in an evaluation is not a rewarding professional exercise for anyone's credibility.

The mistake most often made by the person conducting the evaluation is not to demand more consulting time from the administrator. Very often the evaluator is aware of the administrator's busy schedule and is somewhat fearful that the request for more of the administrator's time is an intrusion and may reflect negatively on the evaluator's competence. As a result, evaluations become interesting, but frustrating exercises because they fail to attend to the real programmatic issues and gather the wrong sort of data.

The list of 11 questions should give the evaluator and the administrator some important issues to consider before embarking on an evaluation effort.

REFERENCES

Barr, M. J., Justice, S. H., & Yancey, B. D. Personal communication. February 13, 1979.

Cross, K. P. *Accent on learning.* San Francisco: Jossey-Bass, 1976.

Glass, G. A. A paradox about excellence of schools and the people in them. *Educational Researcher,* 1975, *4,* 9-13.

Gowin, D. B., & Millman, J. Can meta-evaluation give direction for research on evaluation? Paper presented at Annual Meeting of the American Educational Research Association, Toronto, 1978 (mimeo).

Guba, E. G. *Toward a methodology of naturalistic inquiry in educational evaluation.* Los Angeles: UCLA Center for the Study of Evaluation, 1978.

Oetting, E. R. Evaluative research and orthodox science. *Personnel and Guidance Journal,* 1976, *55,* 11-15.

Scriven, M. The methodology of evaluation. In R. E. Stake (ed.), *Curriculum evaluation.* American Educational Research Association monograph series on evaluation, No. 1, Chicago: Rand McNally, 1967.

Stake, R. E. *Evaluating educational programmers: The need and response.* Paris: Organization for Economic Cooperation and Development, 1976.

Weiss, C. Where politics and evaluation research meet. *Evaluation,* 1973, *3,* 337-345.

Worthen, B., & Sanders, J. *Educational evaluation; Theory and practice.* Worthington, Ohio: Charles A. Jones Publishing Company, 1973.

3
EVALUATOR ROLES AND EVALUATION STRATEGIES: A CONSUMER'S INTRODUCTION
Robert D. Brown

There are at least as many program evaluation models as there are major brands of beer. Like beer drinkers, every evaluator has a favorite brand, though they may partake of a variety upon occasion. Researchers tell us that when put to a taste test, few beer connoisseurs can distinguish among beers, even failing to identify their favorite (many beer drinkers disagree and some protest loudly!). Evaluators have not yet been put to that sort of test, though some theorists would suggest that many evaluation models have more in common than their advocates would admit. Several attempts have been made to find a suitable framework for synthesizing the models (Worthen & Sanders, 1973; House, 1978; Stake, 1977) and the serious student of evaluation should examine these efforts. As yet, however, no one synthesis has been accepted as the best framework for a consumer guide. The models overlap in varying degrees in their purposes, methodologies, and definitions. It is not possible, therefore, to present a flow-chart which would make it possible for the evaluator or the student affairs administrator to select a model or the most appropriate evaluation approach for a particular program evaluation.

This chapter is organized around the several significant roles which an evaluator can assume. The roles are not necessarily mutually exclusive. Some roles are generally associated with only one evaluation model, other roles are compatible with several evaluation approaches. By knowing something about the roles of the evaluator, however, it is possible to obtain a more direct insight into the functions, activities, and perspectives of an evaluator than by examining the theoretical concerns of each of the evaluation approaches. The five evaluator roles discussed include: systematic planner, issue resolver, reporter, experimental researcher, and unbiased judge.

SYSTEMATIC PLANNER

The primary focus of educational evaluation for many years was on specifying program objectives and determining (usually by administering tests to students) whether these were accomplished. The role of the evaluator was to assist the program director in defining, classifying, and stating objectives in behavioral terms so that measuring techniques could be developed to determine whether the objectives had been accomplished (Tyler, 1942). Because many programs had vague objectives, it was often a difficult task to get directors and staff to define their objectives in more specific terms. It was, therefore, a major step forward for programs to have explicit statements of goals, objectives, and indications as to whether students in the programs had reached these targets. However, specifying and measuring objectives fell short of meeting program planner needs. There was still a large gap between what happens in the beginning of a program when the goals are established and assessing how well the students had accomplished them at the very end of the program. Questions which needed attention included: Was the program really needed? Were all the program dimensions implemented? Did the program last as long as intended? Was the staff properly trained?

One of the objectives for residence life programming can be to reduce hall damage. Tabulations of damage figures at the end of the year can be a helpful index. However, what is lacking is an indication of what happened in between to affect the amount of damage. Was a special programmatic effort to reduce residence hall damage implemented? What were the characteristics of the program? Was it the only option available?

It seemed inevitable that sooner or later evaluation would become a part of the intermediary steps involved in program planning. Program planners need more help in making the decisions which have to be made as a program is planned, implemented, and maintained. New models of evaluation focused on the broad range of decisions which have to be made about a program, ranging from the minor day-to-day decisions to those which affect the ultimate fate of the program. Generally, these models, sometimes referred to as systems models, carefully delineate the decision steps and the alternative responses in program development, along with the accompanying criteria for making each decision and a description of the steps which follow each outcome and each decision. The resulting flow-chart serves as a program development guide and management tool, as well as an evaluation plan. The systems approach is particularly suitable for complex programs which require extensive planning to ensure coordination of a large number of subtasks and personnel. A multi-faceted new student orientation program is an example of a program which involves coordination of material development, a variety of faculty and staff, and program elements.

One of the most prominent systems approaches is the CIPP model devised by Stufflebeam et al. (1971) (see Chapter 15). Another useful systems approach to evaluation, the Discrepancy Model, was put forth by Provus (1973). In this approach, the evaluator assists program developers in examining the differences between expectancies (stated as standards or objectives) and actual accomplishments. The evaluation process necessitates: (1) agreeing on and establishing program standards, (2) collecting information to determine whether a discrepancy exists between the standards and the accomplishments, and (3) feeding these data back to the program developers so that changes can be made. The information can be used to improve, maintain, or terminate a program.

Provus outlined four major developmental stages for programs during which evaluation information can be collected: (1) *program definition,* (2) *program installation,* (3) *process,* and (4) *product.* The goal of evaluation is to collect information as the program moves through the stages, provide feedback at each stage relative to the match of standards and accomplishments, and assist in the development of new standards, if necessary, for future comparisons. Each stage requires a decision. The decision may be to go on to the next stage, to modify the current stage, or possibly to terminate the program.

Provus clearly distinguished the role of the evaluator in the process. The evaluator is to ask the questions at each stage (e.g., Stage I, "Is the program adequately defined?"). The standards by which to judge whether the question has been adequately answered are determined by the program administrator. Determination of what evaluative information will assist in answering the questions is a joint responsibility of the evaluator and program staff. The decisions to be made are outlined by the evaluator, but the choice among the alternatives is the province of the program administrator.

The role of the evaluator and the orientation of the evaluation is generally similar to a problem-solving approach. There is less emphasis on determining worth and more emphasis on determining what works, what does not work, why, and what will work. There is also greater emphasis on a team approach for evaluation than in some other models. Provus recognized that it takes a variety of skills to conduct a worthwhile evaluation, and he intimated that few individuals have all of these skills. Among the skilled individuals needed for an evaluation team are: (1) group process facilitators, (2) psychometrists, (3) research design specialists, (4) technical writers, (5) data processing specialists, and (6) experts on the program being evaluated. Clearly using the team approach to conduct a single program evaluation would be expensive. However, for student affairs decisions at large universities, this model warrants serious consideration for determining the staffing needs of a research and evaluation unit.

A brief description of the stages of the Discrepancy Model as it might be applied to a student affairs program follows. Consider the establishment of a series of cultural programs for a residence hall setting as an example of a new program. During stage one (definition), the evaluator would raise key questions related to the program description. What is defined as a cultural program? For example, does the definition include folk music as well as chamber music? Who is responsible for the planning of the program? For how long is the program scheduled? Does the staff have the necessary skills and information to organize the program?

At this stage, the evaluator is interested in whether there are some short range and enabling skills or objectives which must be accomplished prior to moving to the next stage? These might include staff skills, environmental constraints, or the readiness of students for this type of programming. Included in the definition stage are expectations concerning what kinds of students are expected to attend these events and what is likely to happen to them as a result. Basically, these can be summarized as: intended outcomes, intended program activities, and intended participants.

During stage two (program installation) the evaluator is concerned with whether the intended program activities actually occur. How many cultural events were planned and how many were held? Were they held in the intended setting? Did the performer(s) do what was expected? Were there any unintended activities? The focus is on comparing the intended activities with the actual activities. In this instance, it is possible to obtain relevant information after each event. The discrepancies can be noted and the program staff can make decisions about continuation of the program or determine how they might change the program. They might even revise the standards.

In stage three (process), the evaluator would be interested in what is happening to students as a result of the cultural programming. There may have been some objectives established in terms of the kinds of students who attended, whether the same students attended all the activities, whether they liked the event(s), whether they thought the program should be implemented in other residence halls, or whether it should be continued within the same halls. This information would be obtained early in the process so that it can be fed back to the program planners in order that the program might be revised if necessary. It might be, for example, that students are quite excited about the chance to ask questions of the performers after the event. This opportunity may have occured serendipitously with one particular performer, and as a result of the feedback, the staff might decide to schedule post-concert conversation as a regular part of the program. Negative reactions to program length, time of day, and related information would also be used to revise the future program events.

Finally, at stage four (product), the evaluator and the program developers consider information which is summative in nature. Questions at this stage are phrased as concerns for the program as a whole. Was the climate of the residence hall substantially affected? Did students continue to attend throughout the length of the program? Did the program broaden the awareness of students in the arts? Are more students attending other cultural events on campus as a result?

These are examples of "product" questions which might be raised. At this stage, decisions have to be made whether the program should be continued. Other information may bear on this decision (e.g., cost). Did enough students attend to make it worth the time or money required to provide the program? The program might be a success in many ways, but financial realities may have a negative impact on whether the program is maintained, revised, or discontinued.

These stages have been briefly and informally described in this chapter. For more complex programs, flow-charts which include critical decision points would more clearly specify what must be decided when, and what information is needed to make the respective decisions. Utilizing a systems approach helps to prevent decisions from falling in the cracks by providing helpful information at timely intervals. The system planner role requires that the evaluator be well-organized, have a good understanding of how organizations work, and be able to work well with administrators.

ISSUE RESOLVER

Many of the evaluation models and the activities of evaluators assume that the decision making process is highly rational and if the evaluator can collect appropriate data, the decisions will be easier to make. Ideally, the decision elements and the performance of the program could all be put into an equation with only the need to substitute actual program information in order for the best decision to be made. Unfortunately, decisions are not that simple. Politics, values, and personal preferences all play an important role in even the most minor program change or addition. There are traditions which influence the reactions to change and there are loyalties which affect responses to new programs. Evaluations which fail to take these factors into consideration are doomed to have limited impact and this has been a major source of frustration for evaluators for years.

"Why do administrators ignore the evidence from the data?" is an oft-repeated cry of woe heard across the land from evaluators. The answer is that the evaluator assumed the wrong role and collected the wrong type of information. There are several evaluation models which propose to enhance the relevance and utilization of evaluations. The two discussed here, the responsive and transactional approaches, each call for different roles and activities for the evaluator. Both propose that the evaluator focus on the values and issues involved in each program decision.

Responsive Approach

Stake's (1975) responsive evaluation approach is designed to assist program staff, administrators, and participants, in identifying the issues which are important in program decisions and to provide useful information related to the issues and the decisions. In contrast to evaluation approaches which concentrate on program objectives and student outcomes, the responsive evaluator: (1) focuses on program activities, (2) seeks out and responds to a variety of people's needs for information, and (3) considers the different perspectives on the issues when reporting on the evaluation findings. Stake contrasts this approach to "preordinate" evaluations which emphasize development of goal statements, place heavy reliance on objective tests and questionnaires, and present results in a research report format. In many instances preordinate evaluation plans are specified in great detail even prior to the initiation of the program. The responsive evaluation, on the other hand, emerges as the evaluator discovers more about the program and the issues. As the issues change, so does the evaluation. There is less reliance on formal questionnaires, and reports may be informal and take a variety of forms.

At first, the responsive approach appears to be unstructured with no focus and mostly an informal methodology. There is a definite structure, however, in the responsive approach, even though the particulars cannot be specified in advance. The evaluator is constantly attempting to determine the underlying issues surrounding a program which are the concerns of staff, administrators and all others who may be affected and may play a role in determining the fate of the program.

Stake has identified twelve major evaluation activities in a responsive evaluation:
1. *Identification of program boundaries.* What does the program encompass? Is the evaluation of an entire agency, a subunit, or a specific agency program? The evaluator drafts a brief description of the program and verifies this description with the programs staff.
2. *Discuss program with clients, program staff, audience.* The evaluator collates the varying viewpoints and perspectives of these people and compares them to the program intents and activities.
3. *Observe the program for an overview.* The evaluator obtains a direct view of the program and gets acquainted with the personnel who are directly involved in implementing the program. This overview is shared with others verbally or in writing.
4. *Discover rationale, intents, standards, hopes, and fears.* At this point the evaluator assesses what is important to the people involved, what rewards are they getting from involvement, what are the territorial battles, the hopes as well as fears that people have.
5. *Conceptualize issues and problems.* The evaluator attempts

to determine the major issues which have been voiced and the potential problems, and puts them into some organized framework.

6. *Identify data needs for issues, problems.* Now that the issues have been identified, the next step is determining what are the sources of information which relate to these issues. The evaluator must choose appropriate data collection procedures.

7. *Observe designated antecedents, transactions, outcomes.* The evaluator gathers information on the intended and actual *antecedents* (Who was the program designed for? For example, did a reading improvement program attract only those who already read above average? Did a life planning workshop have any participants who were vocationally undecided?), *transactions* (What was the program expected to be like? Did the planned program events actually occur? Did students actually work through the entire sequence of a programmed career education module?) and *outcomes* (What were the students expected to be like after the program? How many were expected to make a career choice or visit a professional person in a field related to their job choice?).

8. *Make records of observations.* These records include responses to questions, observational records, scores on tests, or narrative descriptions.

9. *Thematize records and find contingencies.* The evaluator organizes data around the identified issues or some other appropriate structure and seeks relationships between data, notations, and observations and the themes.

10. *Winnow, choose reportable issues.* Not all of the issues may need attention at this moment or all of the evidence may not be in which addresses itself to these issues. The evaluator must select the prime issues.

11. *Prepare formats for reporting, discussing.* The evaluator puts together the report which may be an informal oral report, a formal presentation to a board, a written report, or some combination. Usually, a draft copy is prepared and corrections made after feedback.

12. *Issue formal reports, if any.* Stake places a great deal of emphasis on communicating evaluation results in a timely and informative fashion.

Stake suggests that these events not be considered as sequential. They may occur in any order and throughout the evaluator is continually checking the accuracy of his or her perception of needs, the relevance of the information being collected, and the emergence of any new issues and informational needs.

This approach to evaluation does not ignore outcome or product information, but it places a greater emphasis on determining what the real issues are in the decision making process and gathering related information. The future, for example, of a new arrangement for providing student health services may not be dependent directly upon the effectiveness of those services, but rather may be more dependent on the concerns of the physicians providing those services, their professional integrity, and their concern for the response of other local physicians. The evaluator is not being responsive to these issues if they are ignored and only student opinions about the new services are gathered.

Transactional Evaluation

The transactional approach (Rippey, 1973) suggests an even more active role for the evaluator working on resolving program issues than does the responsive approach. The transactional evaluator not only identifies the key issues and collects related information, but the evaluator also seeks to assist in the resolution of the issues. In this role, the transactional evaluator is less a judge than a facilitator of change and issue resolution. The distinguishing task is perhaps not unique; all evaluations which focus on process in a sense are serving a facilitation role. However, the emphasis given to the facilitator role in a transactional evaluation is unique and for this reason makes it of particular interest in the area of student affairs.

From the perspective of the transactional approach, every new program is imbued with elements of change which are accompanied by conflict. The very suggestion of developing a new program implies that the old program is not meeting current needs. A proposal to develop occupational information files in the residence halls reflects on the adequacy of the libraries available in the counseling and placement centers. Perhaps these agenices would prefer to have their budgets increased so that they could improve their resources rather than see the money go elsewhere. If a counseling center develops a crisis intervention service, what impact does this have on a similar service that the health center was planning, but had not yet implemented? These are just a few examples of how new programs reflect on currently existing efforts and how the seeds of conflict are unconsciously sown.

New programs often represent threats to individual personnel as well as agencies. Unless funded externally, new programs will be staffed internally by personnel already on board. Some staff involvement will be voluntary. Other staff will be stimulated by being involved in something new. For others, however, involvement in a new program may mean an involuntary assignment change and perhaps even more work on top of current responsibilities. At a minimum, it will result in changed roles, expectations, and rewards. These changes may result in lack of acceptance of the new program or overt hostility toward it.

Transactional evaluation recognized these two sources of resistance as major threats to the success of new programs. Unless these threats are handled properly, they could easily result in the demise of the innovation as many or more programs fail because of these conflicts than because of ineffectiveness. It would be interesting to check on the lifespan of innovative student affairs programs which have been presented at conventions or in a variety of professional publications. How many had very positive results and yet are no longer in existence?

The transactional evaluator confronts the conflicts with the hope that the energy that would have been expended to resist the program will be transformed into activity which will facilitate the program's implementation. The transactional evaluation focuses on the system undergoing change rather than the program's outcomes. The information obtained is intended to serve almost exclusively a formative function; i.e., to improve the program.

One of the first tasks in transactional evaluation is the identification of the sources of conflict. Who are the opponents of the program? Who are the program's protagonists? What are the issues? Who are the people most likely to be harmed if the program succeeds or if the program fails? These questions may be answered through interviews, questionnaires, and other means. Once the sources and issues have been identified the evaluator must design an evaluation which will attend to the issues and satisfy the program's antagonists as well as protagonists. What type of evidence would convince those most negatively biased toward the program that the program does work?

A transactional evaluation is much different than the traditional process evaluation. The success of the evaluation is judged by the success of the program. The evaluator must be willing to work within the system and to study the system rather than the outcomes (Walberg, 1973). The role merges with management and planning. This type of evaluation calls for someone who is willing to spend time working with the people in the program and those affected by the changes brought about by the program. The evaluator must possess a high level of interpersonal skill, in particular a tolerance for divergent viewpoints and the ability to get people to work together. The role merges extensively with program management.

The foci on the system and the process are not to exclude the importance of monitoring what the ultimate effects of the program might be on students. These effects remain important. However, the emphasis is on assuring that the program succeeds rather than in proving that one system is better than another. The success of a transactional evaluation depends upon the extent to which it is timely, attendant to appropriate issues, and produces observable effects on the program.

The responsive and transactional approaches to evaluation are particularly suitable to innovative new programs and programs which may be controversial. Both call for a high degree of interaction between the evaluator and the program staff and management. They are probably most appropriate for a student affairs organization which is open to a participatory administrative style. They appear to be quite compatible with the management approaches which focus on organizational development (Blaesser, 1978).

REPORTER

This approach to evaluation has been articulated less frequently as a particular approach than as an element of several other models, particularly the responsive approach. Nevertheless, it can stand alone as having a unique orientation and methodology. This is especially true as more serious attention is given to naturalistic observation as an evaluation strategy.

The basic rationale for this approach is that the best aid for decision making and for making judgments is having a complete picture of what the program is like. According to this approach, the most damaging or most supportive information which could be provided about a program might be a simple description of what the program is like and what the products, if any, are like. Such a description could be multifaceted, presenting the program as seen through the eyes of the staff, the participants, and significant outsiders.

The reporter describes an event as accurately and as fairly as possible. The investigative reporter digs under the surface of a story, but the goal is still truth. The assumption is that the reader of the news article needs to be informed and is capable of formulating opinions. Supposedly, the personal views of the newspaper person are reserved exclusively for the editorial page.

At its best the news story makes the reader a vicarious participant in the story event. Carried to its extreme, this form of evaluation would have all decision-makers be participant observers in the program being evaluated. Thus, the decision-makers would participate in a value-clarification workshop, attend an orientation program, go through the process of registering for courses or applying for financial aid. There is no doubt that role playing has value in gaining an understanding of how a program participant feels and how different facets of the program affect students' perceptions of self and campus life. Living in the residence halls for a short time can present to the decision-maker the paradoxical loneliness of the long corridor halls that coexist with the lack of privacy in the paper-thin walled rooms. Having to stand in the wrong line to drop and add courses can vividly bring home the impersonality of computer-based registration processes. There is no doubt that having the decision-makers actually participate in the program has immense value and certainly it is a valuable data gathering tactic for the evaluator.

A more intensive role than that of participant observer is suggested for the phenomenological evaluator (Stone, 1978). This evaluation approach encourages evaluators to report their own feelings and clinical judgments about events as well as reporting events and the feelings of other participants. Rather than trying to pretend that observations and reports are completely objective, the phenomenological evaluator recognizes his or her feelings and readily reports them as well as judgments.

There are problems with this approach. There are relatively few programs for which it would be possible for the decision-maker to truly be a full participant. For the most part, it would be role-playing and while this provides a helpful perspective, it would never be the same as being a student. Also, each participant observer would be an n of 1 and would have to assume that their perceptions and experiences were the same as others. The risk of overgeneralization would be present as it would for any study based on a limited number of data sources. Another problem would be to find the time for the administrators to assume full participant roles. Not many would be able to free their calendars for this level of participation.

The next best strategy for the evaluator as reporter is to provide a program description which provides the decision-maker with a sense of what it is like to participate in the program. Besides the participant observer role, the evaluator might study one or more students intensely as they go through the program. The case study approach has been utilized extensively by reporters to provide their audiences with a vicarious sense of participation. On-site interviews and following the trail of one or two actors in an athletic, political, or other significant event is used in many news stories and in television documentaries. The case study has long been a useful technique for anthropologists and ethnographers and has received attention from evaluators as a primary methodological technique as well as a supplementary evaluation tool (Guba, 1978).

Whether naturalistic inquiry or participant observation are used to gather data is essentially the evaluator's preference. Most important is to select a technique which will result in a report which fully describes the program for the decision-maker. Reporting represents a critical juncture for most evaluations. Evaluators have frequently emulated their research brethren in designing evaluations. Unfortunately, they have also used research report writing styles for evaluation reports. Too often the evaluator writes an evaluation report for an audience of research colleagues rather than a report which can communicate fully with a variety of audiences. This has resulted in evaluation reports becoming compilations of data and statistical tests, sometimes taking up to a hundred pages to report insignificant results. It is doubtful whether evaluators will have a meaningful impact on decision making until they learn how to communicate effectively to different audiences (Brown, 1978). Ideally, program participants should be able to recognize their program in the report. If the objective of the evaluator is to report in a descriptive fashion what the program was like so that the decision makers can make up their own minds about the program, the first goal is to obtain a clear understanding of the program, but a close second is to devise a reporting technique which will communicate that understanding to the variety of evaluation audiences. Use of executive summaries, slide presentations, and case studies are helpful communication devices and rich supplements to the more typical technical report which generally gathers dust on a shelf.

EXPERIMENTAL RESEARCHER

As mentioned in the earlier chapters, evaluation is concerned with assessing worth and research is concerned with drawing generalizable conclusions. Though many would say that the primary flaws in evaluations in the past have been due to evaluators trying too hard to emulate research models, there is still strong support for the research model (Campbell & Stanley, 1965) and the advantages and disadvantages of this approach should be considered if it is appropriate and possible.

Campbell and Travis (1975) has proposed an experimenting society which would utilize an experimental research model whenever possible for evaluation of major social programs and innovations. Ideally, a true experiment entails a comparison group, often called a control group, and random assignment of subjects to the two groups. By assigning one group to the program (treatment condition) and identifying a similar group not participating in the program (control condition), it will be possible to determine with a high degree of certainty that differences noted after the program can be attributed to the impact of the program, provided that other sources of error are controlled.

To utilize a true experimental design for assessing the impact of an assertiveness training program for undergraduates, one half of a group of interested students would have to be randomly assigned to the training program and one half would be denied participation, at least until the experimental group completed the assertiveness training program. The group receiving the training would respond to a measure of assertiveness prior to and after the training. The control group (those not in the training program) would also complete the assertiveness measure at the same times. The assumption is that if the pre-post differences of the trained group are statistically significantly different from the pre-post differences of the comparison group, it must be due to the effectiveness of the training program. If large numbers of students are involved, the experimenter may feel comfortable in not administering a pre-test and simply comparing the two groups on the post-training measure of assertiveness. A good researcher would probably want some other measure than simply a paper and pencil self-report questionnaire. Data might be collected from direct observation of behavior and reports of peers.

There are a number of problems with applying the strict true experimental designs to program evaluations in student affairs. A basic practical problem is finding an appropriate way of having a comparison group. This is especially true in the area of services or in program areas which are available to students who show interest. Could the assertiveness training be denied some students (a control group) if it was advertised and they stepped forward? One justification would be if the program would be offered at a later date and there was some credible rationale; e.g., not enough trained leaders for offering it to all students at the same time.

Most of the programs of this nature in student affairs are volunteer programs. Students who participate in activities, floor government, counseling center programs, and other student affairs programs do so on a volunteer basis. There is sufficient evidence indicating that students who self-select themselves into self-help programs, for example, are different from students who do not (Rosnow, 1973). This means that the results of an experiment involving only volunteers can be generalized only to students who would volunteer.

A more likely source for utilizing the experimental research model is in the residence halls. It may be possible to initiate a unique program in one residence hall, but not in another. Students in the comparison (control) residence hall may not even know what is being done in the program (treatment) hall. It may even be possible to establish experimental programs on different floors of the same residence hall, though there is greater danger of students on the comparison floors participating in the program or hearing about it and, therefore, not being a true control group. However, the major flaw in all these options could be that each student was not randomly assigned to the hall or floor. Whatever played a part in their selecting or being assigned to the residence might be related to the variable being studied and, therefore, the results would not be conclusive.

There are other problems with the experimental approach. One concern is related to the "Hawthorne effect"; i.e., the very fact that students know they are involved in an experiment may prompt them to behave in certain ways. Usually the students or staff involved in an experiment will be more highly motivated, more curious, and generally work harder to achieve the effects which the experimenter hopes to achieve. This often results in very positive findings for the experimental program. Unfortunately, when the program is implemented elsewhere, the aura of innovation is likely to be diminished and students are less enthused. In many instances, the results are seldom as positive as they were with the experimental group. This same effect, of course, happens in the installation of many new programs whether they are being evaluated with a research design or through some other method.

The experimental research approach is also criticized because it often is rather rigid, permitting few changes as the program progresses, and also because the research findings are reported after a decision has had to be made about the future of the program. It is true that these are often accompanying features of an experimental research model, but they are not necessarily an inherent feature.

If it is possible to randomly assign subjects and to have a control group, then the research model should be explored as a viable evaluation model. But this decision should not be independent of the nature of the project. Cost and time are just two of the factors which need to be considered. The politics of the situation and the complexity of the program may dictate some other evaluator role.

AN UNBIASED JUDGE

There is always the fond hope that like courtroom judges or the disinterested researcher, the educational evaluator will be fair, objective, honest, and in all forms an unbiased observer and judge of a program. It is important that the evaluation report be credible and that it reflect the true nature of the program and people's response to it, and not the particular views of the person collecting the data and making the report. A disinterested evaluator is hard to find. Brickell (1976), in a candid discussion of the issue, admits that the politics of the evaluation circumstances always play a role in what is written in an evaluation report. Even an external evaluator, who has no ego investment in the success or failure of a given program, may be co-opted in subtle ways. Like most persons, an evaluator who is treated kindly has difficulty reporting negative findings about the person who offered the kindness. How then can evaluations have any credibility if the evaluator is subject to human foibles? Two responses to this concern will be explored here as alternative evaluation approaches: goal-free evaluation and the adversary approach.

Goal-free Evaluation

Scriven (1972) has suggested that one of the major sources of evaluator bias is familiarity with the program's goals. Knowing a program's goals is like being told what to look for in a program. If told what to look for in a program, the evaluator will probably see it if there is any faint possibility that the outcome was produced. For Scriven, this is like putting blinders on evaluators. They have only so much time and if told what to look for, then that is what they are going to look for, often to the exclusion of other possible outcomes. Out of the universe of possible program outcomes the evaluator will most likely focus on those which relate directly to the program's objectives. If a values clarification workshop intends for students to carefully examine their value system, the evaluator is going to utilize or design an interview schedule or a questionnaire to determine how many students did reexamine their values. This certainly is a difficult task in itself. There may however be other possible effects not intended by the value clarification workshop developers. These effects may be positive or negative. For example, suppose the evaluator, after interviewing the students who participated, found that 85% reported they had carefully examined their basic values and a pre-post questionnaire indicated that a sizeable number had changed their values. This suggests that the program was very effective. There could, however, be any number of other effects. Suppose those who changed their values as a result of the workshop found themselves in greater conflict with their parents and were not prepared to cope with this conflict. What about those who did not succeed in clarifying their values and, in effect, became more uncertain and concerned? Or what about the students who made no change or did not feel that their values were any clearer, but did take several positive steps such as visiting a counseling center to explore career choice options and taking a philosophy course. The goal-based evaluation might overlook these side effects.

The goal-based evaluator is prone to bias in at least two ways. By knowing the goals of the program, the evaluator is: (1) subject subtly or directly to influences which would suggest that the program is accomplishing its stated objectives; and (2) likely to limit the primary focus of the data gathering on outcomes related specifically to the specified goals. As a result, potential side-effects may be overlooked.

Unlike the goal-based evaluation which designs its data collection procedures so that they compliment the project's stated objectives, the goal-free evaluator will go to great lengths to be unaware of the program's specific goals. Please note that it is the evaluator who is goal-free, not the program. The program might have quite an elaborate and detailed set of goals and objectives (Brown, 1978). Through examination of materials and direct observations of the program the evaluator devises an approach which will obtain information on a broad range of possible outcomes. The goal-free evaluator is trying to determine the actual impact of a program, independent of the rhetoric of the stated objectives.

Goal-free evaluation can be quite time-consuming. The evaluator must get to know the program fairly intimately and must have available a broad array of knowledge and skills for assessing a multitude of potential student outcomes. Scriven suggests that goal-free evaluation not be used as the sole approach to evaluation, but rather to compliment goal-based evaluation efforts. Adding a goal-free component to an evaluation would substantially increase the cost of the activity.

Adversary

An interesting new evaluation approach has the evaluator serving directly as an advocate or adversary of a program. This approach has been carried to the extreme of having a judicial hearing on the program with one evaluator presenting the evidence for the program, one evaluator presenting evidence in opposition to the program, and a jury or panel determining the fate of the program (Wolf, 1975; Levine, 1973).

This approach takes evaluator bias into consideration by asking the evaluator to focus on only one side of the case. The evaluator gathers relevant evidence to either support or oppose the program. The jury, a panel of participants or knowledgeable experts, is responsible for sifting through the evidence and making a judgment or recommendation similar to the manner a court jury performs.

The adversary approach provides a definite focal point for the evaluator during the data collection, interpretation, and presentation of results. In these phases of the evaluation effort the evaluator expends little energy remaining objective. However, there is some fear that evaluators will become performers and that juries will be more influenced by histrionics rather than the evidence. In any case, in an adversarial evaluation, the decision moment becomes a very definite event and the jury plays a prominent role. Given that the judicial system in the United States has survived for hundreds of years in spite of various problems, this approach to evaluation in student affairs deserves consideration.

Other Roles

There are numerous other roles the evaluator can assume in the course of conducting evaluations. The expert role, for example, has a long tradition. External consultants, special committees, and blue ribbon panels are as old as educational institutions. The accreditation approach places the evaluator in basically an expert role. It is interesting that the expert role is undergoing a renaissance in the form of a proposed connoisseur role (Eisner, in press). It may be that evaluation has swung full circle from reliance on experts to objective data, from systems analysis to issue resolver and back again to the connoisseur.

SUMMARY

There are at least five major roles for the evaluator in student affairs. These include: *issue resolver, systematic planner, reporter, experimental researcher,* and *unbiased judge.* Each of these roles requires different sets of skills and each is particularly applicable to different evaluation questions and contexts.

The *issue resolver* role would be best for the evaluation of a program which is highly controversial or for one which could dramatically affect the lives of a significant number of people. This approach to evaluation would require that the evaluator act as a facilitator; therefore maturity and a high degree of interpersonal skill would be expected of the evaluator. The *systematic planner* approach would be quite suitable for a complex program in which there are numerous potential decision points during program development and implementation. It calls for an evaluator with highly developed organizational skills. The *reporter* role could be very helpful when it is necessary to describe a program to outsiders who may not be familiar with the program. Student affairs staff conducting this kind of evaluation need to have good expository skills as they must be able to describe events and activities in a manner which will be understood by those not intimately acquainted with the program. The *experimental researcher* is appropriate when it is possible to implement a program in phases, or in some areas of the institution and not others. The context should also be one in which it is not necessary to change the program while it is in process and the decision will be based primarily on behavioral outcomes rather than political or cost dimensions. The *unbiased judge,* or goal-free evaluator, is helpful when credibility is a sensitive issue and when it is more important to convince a decision-maker of the value of the program than it is to improve the program while it is in process.

Evaluation is a field that is in a high flux state. New models and perspectives are presented with increasing frequency. There are contrasting philosophical orientations which make some models more attractive than others to some evaluators. The student affairs administrator, however, is generally close to the trenches, is often forced to make highly pragmatic decisions, and needs information that will assist or support those decisions.

In actuality the evaluator roles discussed in this chapter are not necessarily mutually exclusive. In some contexts, it may be useful to have a combination of talents available. A closer look at the various models will reveal substantial overlap. They have been presented here not necessarily for consideration as distinct approaches, but in terms of their various emphases. It is hoped that these distinctions expand the role expectations for student affairs evaluators so that ultimately the student consumers will benefit.

REFERENCES

Blaesser, W.W. Organization change and student development. *Journal of College Student Personnel*, 1978, *19*, 109-118.

Brickell, H.M. The influence of external political factors on the role and methodology of evaluation. *Evaluation Comment*, 1976, *5*, 1-6.

Brown, R.D. Implications of new evaluation strategies for accountability in student affairs. *Journal of College Student Personnel*, 1978, *19*, 123-126.

Brown, R.D. How evaluation can make a difference. In G. Hansen (ed.), *New directions for student services*. San Francisco: Jossey-Bass, 1978.

Campbell, D.T., & Travis, C. The experimenting society: To find programs that work, government must measure its failure. *Psychology Today*, September 1975, p. 476.

Campbell, D.T., & Stanley, J. *Experimental and quasi-experimental designs for research*. Chicago: Rand McNally, 1966.

Eisner, E.W. *The design and evaluation of educational programs*. New York, NY: Macmillan, in press, 1979.

Guba, E.G. *Toward a methodology of naturalistic inquiry in educational evaluation*, Los Angeles: UCLA Center for the Study of Evaluation, 1978.

House, E.R. Assumptions underlying evaluation models. *Educational Researcher*, 1978, *7*, 4-12.

Levine, M. Scientific method and the adversary model. *Evaluation Comment*, 1973, *4* (2), 1-3.

Provus, M. *Discrepancy evaluation*. Berkeley, CA: McCutchen, 1973.

Rippey, R.M. *Studies in transactional evaluation*. Berkeley, CA: McCutchan, 1973.

Rosnow, R.L. More on the social psychology of the experiment: When compliance turns to self defense. *Journal of Personal and Social Psychology*, 1973, *27*, 337-343.

Scriven, M. Prose and cons about goal-free evaluation. *Evaluation Comment*, 1972, (4), 1-3.

Stake, R.E. *Evaluating the arts in education*. Columbus, Ohio: Merrill, 1975.

Stake, R.E. *Evaluating educational programs: The need and response*. Paris: Organization for Economic Co-operation and Development, 1976.

Stone, J.C. e-value-ation. In S.B. Anderson and C.D. Colesled, (Eds.)*New directions for program evaluation: Exploring purposes and dimensions*. San Francisco, CA: Jossey-Bass, 1978.

Stufflebeam, D.L., et al. *Educational evaluation and decision-making*. Itasca, Illinois: Peacock, 1971.

Tyler, R.W. General statement on evaluation. *Journal of Educational Research*, 1942, *35*, 492-501.

Walberg, H. Transactional evaluation. In R. Rippey (ed.), *Studies in transactional evaluation*. Berkeley, CA: McCutchan, 1973.

Wolf, R.L. Trial by Jury: A new evaluation method. *Phi Delta Kappan*, 1975, *57*, 85-187.

Worthen, B., & Sanders, J. *Educational evaluation: Theory and practice*. Worthington, Ohio: Jones, 1973.

4
ADMISSIONS

L. J. Abernathy

The admissions office provides many prospective students with their first glimpse of the institution. The office not only provides information, but also strongly influences the perceptions which students develop about the institution. From an economic standpoint, admissions is directly responsible for generating a substantial portion of institutional income in the form of tuition.

The office directly influences institutional size and enrollments in particular departments or majors. The staff is responsible for communicating the benefits afforded by the university and, more specifically, the benefits associated with each school and department within the institution. Thus, the admissions office directly affects students' decisions to pursue studies in a particular department or school (Gleazer, 1976).

The perceived role of the admissions office is quite different today as compared with its image of a few years ago. In most instances, the admissions function has an important and necessary role in maintaining the health and viability of the institution. In the past, the admissions office was primarily responsible for collecting information from students who would, more or less, voluntarily come to the institution. The admissions office is now perceived to be that arm of the institution responsible for important recruitment responsibilities related to the overall mission of the institution (Witmire, 1978).

The changing perception of the role and function of the admissions office has increased the importance of its activities. This fact is best exemplified by the increase in budgetary support provided to admissions offices throughout all strata of institutional size and type resulting in more staff and more resources assigned for new and different admissions activities (Curry, 1977).

The admissions office is considered as the repository of important data for use in institutional planning. This information function includes defining and describing the students attracted to the institution. Other important functions include collecting, analyzing, and interpreting information relative to application trends and making projections about the size of future applicant groups. Such projections must, of course, be quite specifically related to the goals of the institution in order that the data will provide reliable estimates for planning (Kuh, 1977). The office of admissions is becoming increasingly involved in policy decisions at the upper administrative levels. In fact, admissions directors are often included as a part of the administrative team responsible for determining long and short range institutional goals. One of the most important responsibilities of planning is the accurate interpretation of information. The office of admissions is in a position to collect and analyze information from prospective and currently enrolled students (Abernathy, 1976).

Generally speaking, most admissions offices are operating in a recruitment mode rather than a selection mode (Tilley, 1977). That is, most institutions could serve even larger numbers of well qualified students than are typically applying for admission. Such institutions probably make up the majority of institutions nationally, and this phenomenon has necessitated using a larger proportion of the admissions budget in recruitment or marketing activities including media, direct mail, and increased travel to expand the geographic area from which students come (Leach, 1977).

Increasing emphasis on recruitment has been brought about by many factorsb; shifts in population centers; changes in patterns of college-going; marked decline in birth rate; the economy; military actions; and the general social climate as interpreted by the college-going population. Most institutions have made changes in the functions of their admissions offices to effectively cope with the projected steady state in admissions (Marsee, 1978). The market economy suggests that the admissions office must be more aware of and responsive to these factors if the institution is to remain viable and survive. In many instances, the admissions officer does not have the time or the skills required to design studies to address these salient concerns. Because of the pressure of day-to-day responsibilities, the evaluation of current efforts is rarely conducted. Given the current situation, evaluation is imperative.

AN EVALUATION MODEL

Much discussion has centered around the value of high school visitations by admissions office staff (Peterson, 1969). This activity often utilizes a significant portion of budgetary resources including the expenses related to travel and staff time. Surprisingly little is known about the efficacy of such visits (Kuh, 1977). Needless to say, it is quite important for each institution to evaluate the effectiveness of their own particular visitation program. Such an evaluation, while carefully done, need not necessarily be an extensive or complex effort. It can only be accomplished, if appropriate information has been recorded.

The information needed for thorough evaluation in this area will be available if activities have been carried out according to a pre-determined plan with specific objectives and goals delineated (see

Chapter 3). A straightforward evaluation activity would be to ascertain if these specific goals had been reached. That is, were the planned number of high school visitations made in the particular regions, states, or cities as dictated by the overall plan? Were the planned number of student contacts completed?

The second level of evaluation in this particular example would be to assess the effectiveness of those activities. Were more applications for admissions received from schools that were visited than from similar schools which were not? Was there a differential response in the number of applications received relative to the number of visitations made at a particular high school? Was there a differential response as shown by the number of applications received from different schools visited by different staff members? Did various follow-up procedures result in differences in the number of applications for admission received (i.e., after students had been contacted at the high school, did it make a difference if they subsequently received a letter, a phone call, specific kinds of publications, or an invitation to visit the campus)? Generally speaking, these suggestions result in rather straightforward accountability indices of the effects of a particular activity. Such efforts do not require complicated data collection and analysis.

Admissions activities are not usually simple and uncomplicated. Institutions which conduct a rather extensive number of high school visitations are often involved in other intensive admissions activities such as work with high school counselors, extensive use of the media, and direct mail activities. Evaluation becomes more complex when a plethora of activities must be assessed. It is quite likely that a student might be visited in high school, the student's counselor might have participated in a meeting sponsored for recruitment purposes by the college, and the student might have seen advertisements placed by the institution on television or in a youth-oriented magazine (Stear, 1977).

The overlap of multiple contacts can be addressed by carefully monitoring admissions activities and collecting information which documents the overlap. If the effects of high school visitations were to be evaluated, it would be necessary to identify particular schools to be visited and a similar set of schools that would not be visited. Such an evaluation has some inherent risks and perhaps should be conducted with a limited sample of matched schools. The smaller sample could provide important information to be considered in future evaluations and planning activities. It would also be necessary to control for other intervening activities such as particular follow-up programs or other concurrent recruiting activities that might have influenced the effect. If the findings indicate no substantial differences in the numbers of students applying from those schools which were visited compared with those that were not visited, expending resources for extensive recruitment through visitation could be questionable.

If resources are assigned for new recruitment activities, such as development of specially prepared publications, an evaluation based upon representative samples could be very helpful. This would mean that particular groups of students could be identified or representative high schools selected to participate in the evaluation. In this instance, it might be easier to work with a particular set of schools rather than having to identify the appropriate numbers of individuals.

If several different publications were to be evaluated, it might be possible to field test each of the alternatives to see if, in fact, particular response patterns were evident. An important part of such an activity would be the general reaction to the published materials. Reactions could be gathered in brief, structured interviews with small groups of students. Such activities have proven to be most helpful in aiding in the development of publications intended to meet student needs for information related to their post-secondary school decisions. In this example, it might also be desirable to include a control group in order to evaluate any differential response.

ENROLLMENT PROJECTION

Enrollment projection is an important activity related to budgetary needs and goals. To accurately project enrollments, the admissions office must identify the group of students (recruitment pool) likely to be served by the institution and its programs (Parker, 1977). A college with a small recruitment pool will need to attract a larger proportion of that pool than would be true for a college drawing from an extremely large pool of students. For example, a large public institution might legitimately consider every college-bound student in the state as comprising its major recruitment pool. If that pool contained a total of 50,000 college-bound students, and if the institution's goal was 2,500 in-state students, then enrolling only 5% of the pool would meet the goal. In a small, private, church related women's college with a limited curriculum, it is possible that the total pool which might be drawn from several states consists of only 1,000 students. If the goal is to enroll 200 students from that pool, the institution would have to enroll 20% of its potential recruitment pool.

Several important tasks are involved in projecting freshmen enrollments. One particularly revealing analysis is the review of information about those students who have enrolled during each of the preceding two or three years. This analysis should identify important sub-groups of students which comprise the cohort enrolled each year. While sub-groups such as those from important feeder high schools and from urban areas are usually given closest scrutiny, other less conspicuous sub-groups are also worthy of careful review. These might include students with particular major or career interests and those with special abilities who are attracted to the institution because of particular curricular or co-curricular offerings.

The types of sub-groups reviewed in depth will, of course, vary by institution; however, categorization by ability level and residence are suggestive of levels at which to start. As these techniques become more sophisticated, more sub-groups will be recognized for review at various institutions.

The purpose of this activity is to determine whether different sub-groups enroll at variable rates compared with the overall enrollment for the institution. In addition, this activity can help to define and quantify the general recruitment pool for the institution. The success of this activity will be determined by the extent to which it results in more reliable enrollment estimates and provides a clearer description of the recruitment pool and the sub-groups that comprise it. If the recruitment pool can be described in this manner, estimates can be posited as to how many of these students are likely to want to attend an institution such as the one in question (i.e., public or private, large or small, located in a large city or small town, etc.). All such factors must be taken into account in evaluating the size of the recruitment pool from which the institution can realistically expect to attract applicants.

YIELD ANALYSIS

In projecting enrollment, it is often helpful to estimate the yield obtained in admitting recent classes from the recruitment pool. Past yield performance can provide the basis for subsequent projections of yield for planning purposes. Such yield projections must necessarily be made from a carefully defined recruitment pool which has been stratified into as many significant subsets or specific groups as is meaningful.

An example would be to ascertain the number of students in the recruitment pool from a particular geographic area (e.g., a state). Of the proportion of those students with whom contact had been made, how many of those contacts and other activities resulted in applications for admission? A meaningful evaluation could be made by comparing the proportion of students contacted in other geographic regions with the proportion who applied for admission from the particular state (Table 1). It is also possible to determine whether resources expended in one area are generally more productive than resources spent in other areas.

Using this kind of model, it is also possible to identify the number of students in the current recruitment pool who were interested in pursuing particular college majors. Yield comparisons could then be made across major areas of study; large differences can be indicators for further evaluation of student perceptions and interests.

More comprehensive evaluations can be conducted by combining particular variables of interest into two-way or three-way analysis of yield. An example of this might be to evaluate the yield among students contacted from the current recruitment pool who were in the upper quarter of their high school graduating class and whose entrance scores were above the 70th percentile and who lived within 100 miles of the institution. Yield analysis of this type can assist in making decisions about targeting resources for recruitment of particular groups (e.g., students with special abilities, interests, etc.).

EVALUATION OF COMMUNICATIONS ACTIVITIES

Analyzing the characteristics of students applying for admission to the institution is a relatively simple method of evaluating how well the expectations of the institution have been communicated to the applicant pool. That is, are students who are applying for admission eligible according to the published criteria? Are they eligible for admission to the school or major field to which they aspire? If an institution is selective in its admissions policies and the majority of applicants meet the selection criteria, this indicates that the institution's image is salient and is being adequately communicated. However, if substantial numbers of students in the applicant pool are not eligible for admission, the messages being disseminated by the institution should be carefully evaluated.

The size of the group of students accepted for admission is, to a large extent, controlled by the institution through its selection procedures and through the implementation of its admissions policies. To determine the efficacy of these policies and procedures, demographic characteristics comparisons can be made between the students applying for admission to the institution and those that are accepted. Do the applicants exhibit desirable characteristics compatible with the institution's goals? Do the candidates have the ability as indicated by high school grades and other predictors to succeed academically? Do the candidates indicate interests in academic areas in which the institution has strength? Does the group of students admitted reflect other desirable factors and traits such as geographical representation and sex balance?

Many factors affect the yield between the group of students accepted for admission and the group that matriculates in the fall. College choice is, at best, haphazard (Kuh, 1977). It is not uncommon for a student to apply for admission to several colleges. It is especially important for an institution to carefully evaluate the yield at this stage since this number is the most critical to institutional vitality.

Varying yields between institutions at the final stage of comparison (accepted vs. matriculated) are not uncommon. The higher the yield, however, the more efficient admissions office activities have been.

That is, at the highest level of efficiency an institution would have to admit only one student for each opening in its freshman class. At the 50% efficiency level an institution must admit two students for every opening in its freshman class. An evaluation of efficiency can provide important information relative to the activities which will likely be required in a subsequent year (see Table 1).

The use of yield analyses results can be of interest to a variety of units. Certain of the findings from the early stage analyses will be of use in planning admissions office strategy for the coming year and for use by academic departments in predicting staffing needs, curriculum planning, and allocation of resources for the services needed by the incoming group of students. Therefore, yield analyses should be conducted as early as possible in order that findings can be evaluated and results shared across the institution.

TABLE 1
Admissions Yield Analysis

	Recruitment Pool	Applicants	Yield	Accepted	Yield	Enrolled	Yield
Total	2766	439	16%	367	84%	134	86%
State #1	1243	263	21%				
State #2	747	134	18%				
Men	2044	273	13%	215	79%	176	82%
Women	722	166	23%	152	92%	138	91%
Ability (HSR):							
Upper ¼		311		294	95%	276	94%
Lower ¾		128		73	57%	38	52%

AN IMPORTANT TASK

Evaluation is of considerable importance for making decisions and establishing policies. Many useful data are available in the office of admissions. Sharing these data with others in the institution will increase the visibility of the admissions office and favorably influence colleagues' perceptions of the activities conducted by the office.

At present, the admissions office is in an influential position in post-secondary institutions. Through frequent contacts with important constituent groups such as students, counselors, and parents, the admissions office can provide valuable information for institutional decision-making. Careful evaluation of the meaning and significance of these data, both for their implications for the admissions function as well as for the overall mission of the institution, are several of the more important activities of the office. The admissions function can no longer depend upon anecdotal testimony to support requests for resources. Carefully considered plans coupled with thoughtful and through evaluation will provide a firm foundation upon which other admissions activities can be built.

REFERENCES

Abernathy, L. Highlighting what's new in admissions. *The College Board Review,* 1976, *100,* 29-35.

Curry, M. K. What a president expects of the admissions officer and what a president owes to the admissions officer. *The National ACAC Journal,* 1977, *21* (4), 17-19.

Gleazer, E. J. Positioning the community college. *The College Board Review,* 1976, *99,* 1-4.

Kuh, G. D. Admissions. In W. T. Packwood (Ed.), *College student personnel services.* Springfield, IL: Thomas, 1977.

Leach, E. R. Implementing the marketing process. *Community and Junior College Journal,* 1977, *48* (4), 20-24.

Marsee, S. E. Twenty issues for '78 and beyond. *Community and Junior College Journal,* 1978, *48* (7), 42-43.

Parker, G. G. Endangered species: Enrollment prospects and institutional implications. *The National ACAC Journal,* 1977, *22* (1), 1-4.

Peterson, D. W. How high school visits influence college admissions. *The College Board Review,* 1968, *68,* 8-18.

Stear, C. A university measures the effects of its advertising. *The National ACAC Journal,* 1977, *21* (3), 7-9.

Tilley, D. C. Dealing with not enough to go around: Past 1980 enrollments? *The National ACAC Journal,* 1977, *22* (1), 5-8.

Witmire, D. E. The admissions office: A study of change in the profile, status, and professionalism of a higher education administrator. *The National ACAC Journal,* 1978, *22* (4), 4-7.

5
ORIENTATION
Margaret J. Barr, Sharon H. Justice and Bernard D. Yancey

Entering a new college or university involves many of the same problems as traveling to or establishing residence in a foreign land. A new cultural milieu must be understood, an unfamiliar environment negotiated, and vast amounts of new information must be processed and assimilated in order to insure success. These are not new problems and college students have faced them for many years. In the 1970's, however, with increasing numbers of older, minority, handicapped and other non-traditional students entering college, more attention must be given to the manner in which all students become acclimated to the environment.

In order to ease the transition from high school, home or work to college, orientation programs have been developed to assist new students with this process. Van Eaton (1972) reported that 89% of the four-year colleges under 10,000, 85% of the junior colleges, and 80% of the larger institutions had implemented some type of orientation program. In an era of diminishing resources, the value and utility of orientation activities must be documented in order to assure continued institutional support. Evaluation of orientation programs is no longer a luxury, but rather a necessity.

Since orientation can be viewed from a variety of perspectives – it is important that clear program goals be established on each campus (Dannells & Kuh, 1977). Butts (1971) conducted a national survey of orientation programs and identified the following common goals for orientation: completion of the registration process, dissemination of information, building awareness of educational opportunities, exposure to career resources, and relationship building. Each institution will have other unique priorities for the orientation program. Before any program is designed and any attempt is made to evaluate program effectiveness, a clear statement of institutional and program goals for the orientation process should be developed. This process is crucial even if an orientation program is already well established on campus. Goal delineation at the beginning of any phase of program development in orientation is essential. Goals for orientation programs often fall into two categories which are: (1) institutional goals, and (2) personal growth goals of the orientee (Barr, 1972). Institutional goals can range from the completion of certain essential pre-enrollment procedures (e.g., testing and registration) to the careful exposure of the new student to the broad educational philosophy of the institution. Personal growth goals can range from system survival skills to self awareness of ethical and moral issues. Both types of goals are legitimate but must be articulated and agreed upon by all those concerned with the orientation process before any program plan is implemented.

It is only when program goals are clearly delineated that a useful evaluation procedure can be designed. The orientation evaluator must focus on five questions compatible with those introduced in Chapter 2 in order to produce evaluative data which is appropriate and useful within the institutional setting. These questions are:

1. What should be evaluated?
2. Who should evaluate?
3. Who should provide evaluation data?
4. When and how should evaluation occur?
5. How is the evaluation data to be used?

The specific procedures for answering these questions may vary. However, each one must be addressed in any orientation evaluation design. In order to answer these questions it is imperative that the evaluation process be integrated into the total planning procedure.

WHAT SHOULD BE EVALUATED?

An orientation program is composed of a wide variety of procedures, programs, activities, staff members and policies. All of the following facets must be considered as part of the evaluation design, and each may generate specific sub-questions for inquiry.

PROCEDURES

If residence life, food service, registration, testing, and other activities were involved in orientation, were their contributions complementary and satisfactory? Are there more efficient ways to accomplish these same tasks? Are there specific changes which could be made to ease the transition from the pre-college setting to college? What students and how many attend the program? Are certain populations underrepresented due to scheduling and procedural difficulties? Evaluative feedback from the orientee regarding routine processes and procedures can often assist the orientation planner in creatively exploring new solutions to old procedural problems. For example, advanced placement testing can consume an inordinate amount of orientation program time. Assessment of the test-taking experience of orientees often will indicate that a revised testing schedule is possible. Rescheduling of tests, will reduce the total time allocation for this activity in the program while still meeting the student and institutional needs.

Specific Programs And Activities

Orientation activities, whether in the form of a freshman week, summer residential program, continuing orientation or workshops at the beginning of each semester, are composed of a number of distinct activities within programs or sub-programs. A number of evaluation questions should legitimately be raised regarding the value, utility, and impact of each of these activities. As the student population changes (e.g., transfers, older, minority and handicapped individuals), constant appraisal of sub-programs for specific student groups becomes a necessity. Information and issues which were appropriate and useful for the traditional college student of several years ago may have to be re-examined in light of evaluation data provided by non-traditional students (Dannells & Kuh, 1977).

Many times such programs and activities are not in the direct control of the orientation staff but are presented by other campus agencies or faculty members. Formal evaluative data regarding contribution by non-orientation staff should not be collected without the full knowledge and consent of the participating parties. In addition, strategies for the dissemination of such evaluative data need to be determined as part of the evaluation design. One effective strategy is to design individualized agency evaluation reports. Such reports should contain evaluation data related to their specific presentations. This approach permits the agency to focus on their contribution to the program and avoids the pitfall of data overload.

Assessment Of Staff

Many orientation programs select students to serve in paraprofessional or volunteer positions to assist new students. Often these students are the only individuals who have direct, sustained interaction with the new student during the orientation processes. Therefore, their skills, attitudes, and abilities become crucial to the success of the total orientation program.

Evaluation of student advisor performance involves a number of variables: the ability to communicate needed information, the accuracy of information presented, the interpersonal skills exhibited by the student staff member, and staff sensitivity to the concerns of the new student. Evaluation data on student advisor performance can be used immediately as a supervision and staff development tool. Long range application of such evaluative feedback can provide insight into the appropriate selection and training procedures for student paraprofessionals. For example, in response to a need to find better ways to choose effective orientation advisors, a study conducted at the University of Texas at Austin (Aiken, Barr & Lopez, 1976) focused on specific attributes of advisors that were seen as facilitative for new students. New students saw advisors as helpful when they had higher GPA's, were perceived as reserved and subordinate in interpersonal relationships, and displayed sensitivity to their own stress and that of the new student. These conclusions were then used over the next few years in designing the training and selection process for new advisors.

It is essential that timely, useful feedback on the level of performance be provided to the student advisor during the orientation process and that these data be used subsequently to assess selection and training needs.

PROGRAM IMPACT

Assessment of student development is a complex issue (see Chapter 14). Therefore, the evaluation of the impact of the orientation experience on student development requires careful thought and planning. Hypotheses should be generated about the direction and degree of impact which might occur developmentally from participation in the orientation process. Evaluative data can then be used to test these hypotheses. The results of some efforts (see Mitchell, 1967 and Bonner, 1972 below) to answer this question have been contradictory. Ayers and Wood (1975) reported that students who attended a five week summer orientation program exhibited more realistic expectations of their intended institution of higher education (a specific program goal) than they did at the end of their junior year of high school. Impact of orientation on the self-image of orientees was explored by Terranova (1976). She found that attitudes about self and others became more open and the self-image of orientees declined as a result of participation in orientation.

Mitchell (1967) reported that students experiencing orientation have higher GPA's for the first semester than non-participants. Bonner (1972), on the other hand, found no significant differences on the *College and University Environment Scale,* first semester GPA, and enrollment status for the second semester between students attending a traditional orientation program, students working with trained peers, and students who did not participate in orientation. When McCannen (1975) studied an older student population that had participated in an orientation and counseling program, the results indicated that participants had significantly higher GPA's at the end of the first semester than non-participants. Other studies have reported similiar diverse results on the impact of the orientation experience on academic performance. With such lack of clarity regarding academic impact of the orientation process, this area merits further investigation.

Evaluation of general program impact is a complex question and involves a commitment on the part of staff members to sustain this line of inquiry over an extended time period. Orientation planners need data on such long range efforts of orientation if they wish to use this rationale for continued institutional funding and support.

Policy

Many times the policies surrounding the orientation process are ignored in the evaluation effort. Policies often evolve without careful attention or evaluation through tradition, convenience, or the educational philosophy of the orientation staff. In order to make sound policy decisions, data are needed concerning the impact of policy on program design and available orientation services. Decisions regarding costs, services offered, and regulations imposed can have significant consequences for the new student. Evaluation of current policies provides data to assess the potential impact of policy changes. A conscious decision must be made by evaluators and planners to gather such data or this set of crucial issues will never be explored.

For example, at the University of Texas at Austin, large numbers of older students had not been participating in the Summer Orientation Program. General orientation policy required all orientees to live in the residence halls. Evaluative data indicated that this requirement was a major barrier for older students. Therefore, the restriction was waived for this group and increased numbers of older students subsequently have participated.

WHO SHOULD EVALUATE?

There is considerable debate over the relative merits of internal and external evaluators for orientation. Both have merit and the decision about the use of internal or external evaluators is often predicated by specific campus conditions and available resources (see Chapter 2). Cost is certainly a factor and as decisions are made to move from internal to external evaluators, the financial impact on the budget for the program increases.

A combination of external and internal evaluators appears to be the most satisfactory solution to the problems. One or more orientation staff members can be charged with liaison responsibility to an external evaluator or an outside consultant. If financial and time constraints do not permit the use of an external evaluator, consultation on the evaluation process and procedure can be sought from appropriate academic units within the institution. The focus of such a relationship should be on the evaluator as a consultant with an emphasis on improving the staff member's effectiveness (Keating & Hurst, 1978). Orientation staff members can and should be able to learn and use evaluation as an effective tool for program improvement.

For example, the orientation program and the Research and

Evaluation unit at the University of Texas at Austin are both located within the Dean of Students Office. It is the responsibility of the Research and Evaluation Unit to conduct or provide technical expertise for all internal evaluation efforts. Because there is no staff overlap, the planning and implementation of the evaluation effort is shared by both units. The evaluation data are collected by the orientation staff with instrumentation designed by or with input from the Research and Evaluation staff. Subsequent analyses and interpretations are then provided to the orientation staff by the Research and Evaluation Unit.

WHO SHOULD PROVIDE EVALUATION DATA?

Informal and formal evaluation procedures should seek information from all consumers, staff members, and other participants in the orientation process. Each subgroup brings a unique perspective to the orientation program which should be reflected by the final evaluation report. The aggregate of these different viewpoints is helpful in understanding the impact and relative strengths and weaknesses of the orientation program.

STUDENTS

Participants in the orientation process can provide useful subjective and objective comments regarding the orientation process. The evaluation procedures must be designed not only to assess reactions to program components, but also to identify the responses of special subgroups. Particular attention should be paid to the responses of older, minority, graduate, transfer, and handicapped students.

STAFF

Student paraprofessionals and professional staff associated with the program are rich sources of useful, pertinent evaluation data. Staff members routinely provide informal feedback on the general program and the orientee's response to them. Systematic collection of these informal observations can provide valuable insight into daily program operations.

It is equally important, however, to collect formal evaluation data from staff members at the conclusion of the orientation procedure or program. Such a formalized system of program evaluation by staff can provide evaluation data not only about the actual orientation program, but also about needed modifications in the training, selection, and pre-program preparation phases of the orientation process.

PARENTS

Many orientation programs have designed and implemented formal orientation procedures for parents of incoming students. Several recent studies have concentrated on the effect of these programs on the attitudes and concerns of parents. Conrad (1976) reported that parents, after participating in orientation, indicated that they had a more liberal perspective, particularly in the area of student self-responsibility. This study supported the program planners' hypothesis that issue-oriented discussion can effect parental attitudes.

Parents can provide a base of support for new students. An orientation procedure directed toward parental concerns can assist in clarifying the institution's relationship to both parents and their children (students). The parents' orientation programs at Colorado State University, the University of Maryland, and Wichita State University have developed evaluation designs to solicit feedback from parents about their perception of the orientation program and the institution. These efforts may serve as models for other evaluators.

OTHER PARTICIPATING STAFF, FACULTY AND AGENCIES

Since most orientation programs are an amalgamation of a number of discrete sub-programs, many other staff members and campus agencies are involved in the direct delivery of orientation services. Any evaluation design should provide a mechanism to collect and synthesize evaluative data from these various sources. Their suggestions, impressions, and overall assessment of their involvement in the orientation process may help in program modification as well as provide the foundation for future participation in the orientation effort.

WHEN AND HOW SHOULD EVALUATION OCCUR?

Many decisions face the evaluator in determining exactly when and how orientation evaluation data should be collected. Both unobtrusive and obtrusive measures are useful and should be incorporated into the evaluation design.

UNOBSTRUSIVE MEASURES

The number of orientees attending programs and activities and observations of their reactions to the experience are examples of unobtrusive measures. These methods are frequently used to provide immediate feedback regarding the effectiveness of program offerings. Student paraprofessionals and other staff members working with the program can also provide continuous feedback which can be used to modify the program during the orientation process.

Somewhat different unobtrusive measures can be used to gauge the long range impact of the orientation effort. Follow-up studies using data regularly collected by the institution can chart academic performance, retention, frequency of major change, housing patterns, and involvement in organized collegiate activities. Samples can be drawn from those attending orientation and non-attenders, and comparisons can be made across groups and within groups to determine if significant differences exist between them. Extensive instrumentation is not required and students are not asked to respond to lengthy questionnaires and other data collection devices. However, an extensive record-keeping system is necessary and the evaluator/planner should determine that all data that are to be examined are readily available and easily accessible early in the planning process.

Obtrusive Measures

These efforts are more characteristic of a formal evaluation process. The instrumentation need not be complex and should be designed to provide necessary data without producing an overload on the orientation staff. The type and complexity of evaluation instruments are not only determined by the evaluation questions but are dictated by local campus conditions and the number of individuals who will provide evaluative data. The options are infinite and range from a computerized system of data collection to simple hand-tallied frequency counts. Any evaluative instrument should be related to program goals and objectives, and provide information which assists in determining whether the stated goals and objectives have been met.

For example, a structured interview format often can provide the evaluator with rich insights into the responses to and usefulness of the orientation experience. Use of such an evaluative tool on a large campus with thousands of orientees each year, however, would not be practical or economically feasible unless it was applied to a random sample. It could be, however, a very appropriate evaluation device on a small campus with a very limited number of orientees. An elaborate computer based evaluation program providing cross tabulations across sub-groups could be very useful, justifiable, and economically feasible in the larger campus setting. The choice of the most appropriate evaluation procedures should be determined by program goals, number of orientees, available funding, availability of evaluation expertise and technical support, and the needs of the particular campus setting.

Whatever type of instrumentation is used, opportunities should be provided for orientees to write open-ended commentaries about their experience with the program. Although individual responses are difficult to quantify, valuable insight into the nature of the orientation process as well as immediate reinforcement for staff members justify this exercise.

Timing Of Evaluation Procedures

The evaluation process should not interfere with the primary program goal of providing service to new students. For years, individuals have debated whether evaluation data gathered at the conclusion of the orientation experience have enough validity to warrant collection of these data. Critics believe that a "halo" effect accompanies these efforts and that the data tend to favor the program because respondents are imbued with a generally positive feeling about the entire experience and therefore cannot make useful discriminations. The evaluator is also faced with potential cynicism on the part of the staff when presenting immediate post-experience data. If the results are skewed positively, it is difficult for staff members to put these results into perspective when they can easily recall negative experiences and interactions.

There is some evidence, however, which indicates that evaluation data obtained immediately after the orientation experience are as valid and reliable as measures taken some weeks after the orientation experience. Smith and Hurst (1974) found that evaluation data gathered at the conclusion of the orientation experience will yield the same results as evaluative data collected 10 days to two weeks after the experience. A follow-up study of a parent orientation program conducted by Celio (1973) found that parents continued to regard the program highly.

Further investigation regarding the validity and reliability of immediate post-experience evaluation data is necessary. If results prove to be consistent regardless of when data are collected, then considerable staff time and financial resources could be saved by eliminating expensive follow-up studies for the sole purpose of evaluation.

Use Of Evaluation Data

In order for evaluation data to be useful to staff they must be placed in perspective. Criteria for success must be established before any evaluative data can be effectively used to improve the orientation process. Multiple criteria for success are often appropriate but a clear delineation must be made of what those criteria are and what levels of performance are deemed satisfactory to satisfy the criteria. Programs and procedures related to the orientation process are often evaluated by the rate and level of participation by orientees, the perceived value or usefulness by the orientee of the activity, and/or the self report of the orientee regarding the degree of satisfaction with the procedure.

Direct services offered by staff members associated with the program should be evaluated against different criteria. Student paraprofessionals and other staff members associated with orientation need to receive feedback and evaluative data related to: accuracy of information provided, availability to new students, interpersonal skills, and sensitivity to the new student. Many of these criteria are more subjective and require greater caution in interpretation of data.

Presentation and interpretation of evaluation data require considerable attention. Translation of the raw data into concise, comprehensible reports is indeed an art that has been long neglected. The first step in such a process is to determine who needs to know what from the evaluation.

In broad terms, evaluation data are collected to meet any or all of five purposes:
1. To modify, eliminate or reorganize the orientation program effort;
2. To provide future funding support;
3. To set priorities for the future;
4. To assist in the staff development process;
5. To assess the validity of current policies.

Therefore, who is receiving the data, what they will do with it, and the overall purpose(s) of the evaluation report will dictate the format and emphasis of data presentation (Brown, 1978).

PROGRAM MODIFICATION

Summative data on the reaction to and impact of the orientation program are most useful to the orientation planner. Presentation of the data in a manner which highlights any differences between sub-populations will assist the orientation planner in future program design.

Since the orientation staff rely on other offices and agencies to present portions of the program, it is particularly helpful for them to receive data about these programs' presentations. Members of the orientation staff can use these data when consulting with other agencies concerning their presentation to new students.

Low satisfaction ratings, poor attendance, and evidence of dissatisfaction with particular aspects of the program indicated by open-ended comments are all indicators of problem areas which need to be carefully considered. Programs producing relatively stable positive reactions over time need not be evaluated completely after each presentation. Periodic sampling procedures can then provide sufficient data for use in program assessment.

FUNDING SUPPORT

A clearly written evaluation report can be of inestimable value in sustaining institutional support for orientation. Such a report should highlight evaluation results which illustrate the need for continuation of funding. When preparing such evaluation documents, staff members need to provide answers to those questions which will be most significant to decision makers.

If funding is not provided by the institution, evaluation data become even more important. In many institutions student fees administered by the student government support the orientation programs. In order to assure continued support, students must believe the program is of value to new students. Too often orientation planners assume continuation of funding at present levels from student committees and are surprised when it is withheld. Student groups should receive the same type of information to make decisions as is provided other institutional decision makers. Attention should be given to compiling a relevant and easily understood report to assist students in evaluating the efficiency of orientation.

Evaluative data can also be used to secure funding from outside resources. Evidence of a rigorous evaluation design can lend credibility to grant applications. Current data can also be used to point out needs for innovations which are likely to be supported by grant sources.

Staff Development

Staff members must understand the need and purpose for evaluation of their performance. Obtaining data from orientees may often be viewed by staff as threatening or inconvenient (see Chapter 1). It is not uncommon to encounter resistance to the evaluation process. In addition to clarifying why evaluation is necessary, careful attention must be given to the procedures used to provide evaluative feedback to student and professional staff. A clear explanation of what the data convey is essential. Many times in the pursuit of a perfect performance, staff will overreact to performance ratings which are not ideal. Because needless self-examination can result, supervisors must be sensitive to this potential problem by assisting with a realistic interpretation of the data. The timing of this feedback is crucial and should be delivered in such a way so as to not interfere with the staff member's ability to deliver services to new students.

SUMMARY

Evaluation of orientation programs and activities is necessary in order to plan adequately for the future. Any evaluation design should begin with the questions, "What should be evaluated?"; "Who should provide data?"; "Who should carry out the process?"; and "When and how should the procedure occur?". Of particular importance is determining how the evaluation data will be used. There are a number of practical problems surrounding the effective implementation of an evaluation process which need to be addressed. Orientation staff members must become cognizant of these problems and improve skills, and perhaps seek assistance from the campus community in order to eliminate potential pitfalls.

REFERENCES

Aiken, J., Barr, M., & Lopez, H. Orientation advisor effectiveness: A continuating search. *Journal of College Student Personnel,* 1976, *17,* (1), 16-21.

Ayres, J., & Wood, P. Changes in the perception of the college environment. *Improving College and University Teaching,* 1975, 165-167.

Barr, M. J. Goals. *National orientation directors handbook.* National Orientation Directors Association, Austin, Texas, 1972.

Bonner, D. Evaluating the effects of using upperclass advisors trained in group dynamics to lead small process oriented freshman orientation groups. Final report. *National Center for National Research and Development.* Washington, D.C. December, 1972.

Brown, R. D. Implications of new evaluation strategies for accountability in student affairs. *Journal of College Student Personnel,* 1978, *19,* 123-125.

Butts, T. New practices in student orientation. *Personnel Services Review,* ERIC, Counseling and Personnel Services Information Center, Ann Arbor, Michigan, 1971.

Celio, D. L. After innovation: Perspectives on a parent orientation program. *Journal of College Student Personnel,* 1973, *14,* 216-219.

Conrad, R. W. Parent attitudes change as a function of orientation program participation. *Journal of the National Association of Women Deans and Counselors,* 1976, *39,* 136-139.

Dannells, M., & Kuh, G. D. Orientation. In W. Packwood, (Ed.), *College student personnel services.* Springfield, IL: Thomas, 1977.

Keating, L. A., & Hurst, J. The evaluator as consultant. *New Directions for Student Services,* 1978, *1,* 77-87.

McCannen, R. *Effectiveness of an orientation and counseling program for adult evening students at Drake University.* Paper presented at the Adult Education Research Conference, St. Louis, April, 1975.

Mitchell, M. A. *A student-to-student guidance program for college freshmen.* Paper presented at the American Personnel and Guidance Association Convention, Dallas, 1967.

Smith, T. T., & Hurst, J. C. Immediate follow-up in orientation program evaluation. *Journal of College Student Personnel,* 1974, *15,* 46-48.

Terranova, C. The effectiveness of a summer freshman orientation conference. *Measurement and Evaluation in Guidance,* 1976, *9,* 70-74.

Van Eaton, E. N. National study of trends in orientation. *The National Orientation Bulletin.*Oklahoma State University, Stillwater. October, 1972.

6
RESIDENCE LIFE
Barbara A. Phillips and John H. Schuh

Evaluations in residence life examine educational, social, and recreational programs; managerial and administrative services; professional development of residence hall staff; and general benefits of residence halls for students. Thus, evaluations of the residence life area can have a very broad scope.

The first section of this chapter outlines a rationale for evaluation of residence life programs and services. The second section summarizes the current state of the art of evaluation in residence life. The third section presents major issues of importance to residence life evaluators. The final section describes one approach to evaluating residence life programs.

WHY EVALUATE

There are several important reasons for evaluating residence life programs, services, and personnel. The need for evaluation was recently reiterated by Riker (1977-78):

> A growing and more sensitive attention to students as consumers is indicated by a more active response to student needs, greater efforts to upgrade the quality of the living environment, and more studies of organizational structures as bases for changes that will produce improved services and programs for students (p. 7).

For the purposes of this discussion, the rationale for evaluating residence life have been divided into three categories: (a) need for more accurate information to improve current programs and services, (b) accountability demands made by several constituencies, and (c) professional development of staff.

THE NEED FOR MORE ACCURATE INFORMATION

Miller and Prince (1976) suggest that "the single most important purpose of evaluation is to provide accurate information that can be used for revising the program" (p. 143). During the last two decades, residence hall staff have attempted to provide an atmosphere which facilitates student growth. Nevertheless, numerous questions continue to be raised about the nature of student development in the residential setting. What are the benefits of recreational and social programming,

77

varied life styles, or leadership development programs in residence halls? What student learning and growth have taken place? What are the effects of residence hall programs on student residents? Why do students live in college and university residence halls?

Observations by residence life staff can provide some answers to these questions. However, more systematic data gathering is required to describe how student needs are being met by specific residence life programs. Information collected through evaluation activities can help identify which programs should be continued or terminated.

The changing characteristics of college students suggest the need for frequent revisions of residence life programs and services. Evaluative information is critical in assisting staff and students in recommending appropriate changes.

Systematic evaluation in residence life can assist staff in decision-making. When an evaluation process is a component of the residence life program, staff are better able to determine the value of current residence life objectives and can identify strengths and weaknesses of individual programs or services.

Accountability To Several Publics

"At all levels of the organizational structure, in every department, and in the use of each resource, accountability is being directly encouraged and demanded by others" (Stimpson & Simon, 1974, p. 235). Residence life programs are accountable to the following groups: resident students (the consumers), senior administrators, faculty, parents of resident students, members of the local community, the legislature or other funding body, trustees, and alumni. In short, accountability has become an important consideration for student affairs administrators as Trembley and Sharf (1975) have reported:

> It is ... clear that student affairs personnel ... food and housing experts ... should actively seek to insure that questions of 'worth' and the value judgments inherent in them are influenced as much as possible by accurate accountability data (p. 250).

Staff who work with residence life programs increasingly are being asked to justify the worth (value) of their program and to provide evidence which supports the need for new and improved programs and services.

The Professional Development Of Staff

The topic of staff evaluation is addressed more specifically in Chapter 12. When implemented correctly, yearly evaluation provides an opportunity for professional growth of staff; however, additional staff development benefits can result from an on-going evaluation program. For example, staff who participate in the planning and execution of evaluations have an opportunity to learn new skills or to improve those previously acquired. Staff who have evaluated programs and services may contribute to the profession by sharing their results with professionals in residence life. These contributions may take the form of presentations at state, regional, and national conferences or dissemination through publications.

Residence life staff conduct informal evaluations of programs and services on a daily basis. They make observations about the perceived successes and failures of a program and they solicit suggestions for improving the quality of programs. Formal evaluation projects, however, enable staff to describe more accurately the outcomes and efforts of residence life programs. Much evaluation information is quantifiable and in this form can identify the impact residence life programs have on students in measurable terms.

Residence hall programs should be planned to provide the time and money needed for evaluation. While lack of training or experience in the evaluation process can be a problem for staff or students, this concern can be overcome through reading, experimentation, and practice. As a result, the evaluation process as an integral component of the total residence life program will contribute to the development of involved staff.

CURRENT STATE OF THE ART

A review of the residence life literature discussing evaluation can be separated into three categories: (1) the need for evaluation (primarily due to increasing demands for accountability data); (2) reports of evaluations which have been conducted; and (3) descriptions of evaluation processes.

Need For Evaluation

Scott (1975) questioned the assumption that students benefit from university programs such as those related to residence life. He suggested that evaluations be conducted to determine the impact of programs and services on the development of students in residence halls. Evaluative information is probably needed to respond to accountability questions raised from within and outside the institution.

In a recent discussion of trends in college and university residence halls, Riker (1977-78) predicted that accountability to student residents (consumers) would be a growing concern of residence life staff. He suggested the evaluation of residence hall programs and services for use in responding to students' needs and improving the quality of life in residence halls.

Reports Of Evaluation

Several reports have indicated a variety of approaches to the residence life evaluation process. The purpose of Whittington's (1974) evaluation was to examine the renovation of an older residence hall before initiating further renovations on campus. Whittington focused on the renovation process with particular emphasis on students' perceptions of the living and academic atmosphere in the "new" residence hall. A random sample of students residing in the hall completed a questionnaire and several students were interviewed.

Magnarella (1975) conducted an evaluation of a living-learning center at the University of Vermont. He used informal conversations with residents, a content analysis of the Living-Learning Center documents, and a questionnaire to student residents to collect evaluative information. The evaluation was aimed at comparing the Living-Learning Center to other residence halls, especially the academic and intellectual experiences of the student residents.

The impact of residential academic unit programs on students was examined at Colorado State University by Madson, Kuder, Hartanov, and McKelfresh (1976). Their study was designed to determine whether the goals of the housing staff, the faculty, and the students in the program were being met. A questionnaire was used to measure satisfaction, agreement, awareness, and involvement in the program.

Harshman and Harshman (1974) were interested in evaluating the effectiveness of undergraduate residence hall staff and they described the development and validation of an evaluation instrument. A similar process was outlined by Rodgers and Goodman (1975) in developing an evaluation scale for paraprofessional residence hall counselors.

Residence life staff appear to be most aware of the need to evaluate programs and services for the purpose of meeting the needs of resident students and reporting accomplishments to others. As Kuh (Chapter 1) has suggested, residence life staff at most institutions are probably evaluating their programs and preparing accountability reports for their several constituencies. However, most have not had these reports describing their evaluation efforts published in professional journals.

MAJOR ISSUES FOR RESIDENCE LIFE STAFF

Major issues concerning evaluation in residence life programs may be divided into three categories: (1) topics for evaluation; (2) problems for residence life evaluators; and (3) evaluation strategies. Each of the categories is discussed.

Topics For Evaluation

The programs, services, and staff of a residence hall system create numerous opportunities for evaluation activities. The topics suggested seem to be appropriate for evaluation in residence life.

Resident Life Environment

Evaluations of the physical environment in which students reside should examine the availability of services to students, the appropriateness of such services, and the need for change. Special concern should be given to the accessibility of facilities and services to all students including the handicapped.

The variety of life styles available to residence hall students today merit evaluation. Single-sex housing units, coed units, apartment-type units, and visitation and meal plan options may be assessed to determine their value to students as well as their contribution to the residence life program.

Regulations concerning student behavior also greatly influence the residence life environment. These regulations should be evaluated periodically to determine their contribution to the residence life system and to examine suggested revisions designed to improve the residence life environment.

Learning And Enjoyment

The focus of many residence life evaluations may be to assess what students have learned from their experiences in the residence life setting. Staff may wish to examine what has been learned from a specific educational, cultural, social, or recreational activity or program in the hall. A more ambitious evaluation effort would emphasize the overall personal development of students associated with living in a residence hall.

The enjoyment students receive from residence life experiences is another topic worthy of assessment. Interest in programs and activities is one of the reasons students choose to live in residence halls, particularly at those institutions which do not require students to live on campus. These types of evaluations need to examine the interests of all student residents: men and women, healthy and disabled, minority and white.

Such assessments should request data in addition to reports of attendance. Evaluation criteria may include such variables as cost effectiveness, quality of presentation, contributions to the overall residence life program, and how closely the program meets the objectives stated for the event.

Students' Needs

When staff have assessed the needs of student residents, it is logical to expect they will evaluate how well those needs are met by the residence life program. Needs which are appropriate for assessment and evaluation closely parallel the general objectives for college student housing outlined by DeCoster and Mable (1974) and include the following: safety and security needs, comfort needs, social interaction needs, academic needs, and personal growth needs. Meeting students' needs should be a global challenge for most residence life programs because of the increasing consumer movement in higher education. Moreover, an accurate assessment of students' needs is extremely helpful in allocating limited resources. In many ways, a clearer understanding of students' needs will result in a program thrust that will closely parallel the expectations students have for the living environment.

PROBLEMS FOR RESIDENCE LIFE EVALUATORS

Four specific problems exist for residence life evaluators: (1) the transient nature of residence hall students, (2) the existence of intervening variables, (3) the lack of control groups, and (4) the lack of experience and training of some staff.

Transient Nature Of Students

In large residence hall programs student residents may (1) move from hall to hall; (2) leave the residence halls completely; or (3) remain a resident for only a semester or a year. This "transient" phenomenon results in two problems for the evaluator: (1) longitudinal studies may be nearly impossible to conduct; and (2) data collected from one year's evaluations may not be applicable another year. However, experienced evaluators will find that these problems can be overcome without great difficulty. Longitudinal studies which examine a different population each year often can be useful in determining how students needs and perceptions gradually change over the years. It is rare that student needs will change dramatically in the period of a year or two. Hence, the longitudinal study will help in making long-range predictions of trends of student needs.

Data collected from one year to the next can be helpful in beginning to develop plans for a comprehensive program before residents arrive on campus. A skeleton approach to the residence hall program can be outlined, and then as soon as is practical, student needs can be determined and appropriate adjustments can be made as the program unfolds.

Existence Of Intervening Variables

Student attitudes, behavior, performance, and growth in a residence hall are influenced by the total experience in residence halls. The evaluation of one program or service will be affected by the fact that students reside, eat, interact, and study in the halls. Hence, intervening variables such as campus activities, stress associated with classroom activity, and national or international events will influence student satisfaction with their residence hall environment. Therefore, it is imperative that the evaluator schedule the data gathering phase of the process at a time when the impact of intervening variables is perceived to be minimal.

Lack Of Control Groups

Some residence life programs provide little or no variety in the life styles of residents. Others offer little variety in the major programs and activites in residence halls. Staff often may want to know how the benefits of their programs compare with those of another residence hall. Residence life systems without a variety of programs cannot usually consider the use of a comparative evaluation because they lack a control group.

Lack Of Experience And Training

While most student affairs professionals have studied research design and statistics, many are uncomfortable undertaking projects which require considerable expertise in these areas. To compensate, residence life staff should seek out resources available on most campuses which can be helpful in the evaluation process. Faculty in education, sociology, and psychology as well as institutional research office staff are often familiar with techniques that can be applied to the evaluation process. These resources should be utilized in related tasks such as sampling, instrumentation, design, and data analysis.

EVALUATION STRATEGIES

A variety of evaluation strategies presently exist for use in residence life. In addition to those discussed in Chapter 3, the management by objectives (MBO) approach which assesses the degree to which objectives are accomplished also has utility for residence life (Saurman & Nash, 1975).

Evaluation Components Of MBO Systems

Advocates of management by objectives utilize a systematic process for management planning and decision-making, which are usually comprised of six steps. In a residence hall setting these steps include: (1) the identification and clarification of the needs of residents; (2) the preparation of objectives for residence hall programs which correspond to these needs; (3) the planning of specific programs, activities, and services designed to meet the objectives; (4) the development of strategies for evaluating the effectiveness of programs, activities, and services; (5) the evaluation of a program when implemented; and (6) the redefinition of objectives, and the re-assessment of needs of residents. MBO is a cyclical process designed to improve the planning and decision making processes.

The greatest value of MBO evaluations is that they force residence life staff to write specific objectives for their programs. Because the systematic approach is cyclical, staff continually must rethink the objectives. Rogers (1975) insisted that reassessment is imperative in a residence hall setting if programming efforts are to be improved and a growth facilitating environment is to be promoted.

A second value of the MBO evaluation is the measurement of objectives which identifies the effects and outcomes of a program. Ultimately, these quantifiable data will assist staff in making decisions. When successes and failures have been identified and benefits have been assessed, decisions can then be made concerning the continuation, revision, replacement, or deletion of programs (Dressel, 1976).

For many residence life staff a potential disadvantage of a MBO evaluation is related to the experience required to write measurable objectives. An additional problem is the tendency of staff to write objectives with expected outcomes in mind, rather than the needs of the program. This point of view will prejudice the results of the evaluation because of the possible omission of very important findings such as unintended effects.

Another difficulty of the MBO evaluation is the potential for considerable time involvement. When goals and objectives have been written and appear to be measurable, or can easily be converted to measurable objectives, time is not a problem. However, when outcomes are not easily quantified the inexperienced staff member may devote considerable time to developing objectives.

Although there are some problems associated with MBO evaluations, it is a viable technique for documenting the accomplishments of a residence life system. However, MBO evaluations may not be appropriate for programs where outcomes are difficult to quantify.

SUMMARY

This chapter has briefly considered the topic of evaluation of residence life. Rationale and strategies for evaluation of residence life programs and services have been suggested. The current level of knowledge about evaluation exhibited by residence life professionals has been summarized, and one approach has been discussed for those who wish to begin resident life evaluation. Evaluation requires skills which residence hall staff should develop and use regularly. When evaluation becomes a natural part of the residence life system, the decisions to delete, improve, and add new programs and services will be based on information which is relevant to the needs of an individual campus, rather than being based on incomplete information.

REFERENCES

DeCoster, D. A., & Mable, P. (Eds.), *Student development and education in college residence halls.* Washington, D.C.: American College Personnel Association, 1974.

Dressel, P. L. *Handbook of academic evaluation.* San Francisco: Jossey-Bass, 1976.

Harshman, C. L., & Harshman, E. F. The evaluation of undergraduate residence hall staff: A model and instrumentation. *Journal of College Student Personnel,* 1974, *15,* 125-132.

Madson, D. L., Kuder, J. M., Hartanov, T. F., & McKelfresh, D. A. Residential academic groupings — A program evaluation. *The Journal of College and University Student Housing,* 1976, *6,* 16-20.

Magnarella, P. J. The University of Vermont's Living-Learning Center: A first-year appraisal. *Journal of College Student Personnel,* 1975, *16,* 300-305.

Miller, T. K., & Prince, J. S. *The future of student affairs.* San Francisco: Jossey-Bass, 1976.

Riker, H. C. Trends. *The Journal of College and University Student Housing,* 1977-78, *7,* 5-7.

Rodgers, R. F., & Goodman, J. The development of a Residence Hall Counselor Evaluation Scale. *Journal of College Student Personnel,* 1975, *16,* 400-404.

Rogers, D. G. Management by objectives: A practical application for residence hall systems. *The Journal of College and University Student Housing,* 1975, *5,* 13-16.

Saurman, K. B., & Nash, R. J. M.B.O., student development and accountability: A critical look. *NASPA Journal,* 1975, *12,* 179-189.

Scott, S. H. Impact of residence hall living on college student development. *Journal of College Student Personnel,* 1975, *16,* 214-219.

Stimpson, R., & Simon, L. A. Accountability for the residence program. In D. A. DeCoster & P. Mable (Eds.), *Student development and education in college residence halls.* Washington, D.C.: American College Personnel Association, 1974.

Trembley, E. L., & Sharf, R. S. Accountability strategies for student affairs. *NASPA Journal,* 1975, *12,* 249-256.

Whittington, T. B. An evaluation of a renovated residence hall. *The Journal of College and University Student Housing.* 1974, *4,* 19-22.

7
COUNSELING CENTER
John G. Corazzini

Counseling centers are relatively recent additions to divisions of student affairs. They were established to respond to returning World War II veterans' needs and over time have evolved into a myriad of services for various groups of students. Like other student affairs functions, counseling centers are confronted with the dilemmas associated with restricted or diminishing resources.

Since their inception, counseling centers have experienced fortuitous and untold growth. That growth has resulted more from expediency than by design. Throughout the 1950s and 1960s counseling centers were able to add staff and develop new programs. At present, the competition for limited resources is keen. Given the current demand for accountability information, counseling center staff must respond with creativity and clarity by employing evaluation methods. This chapter will outline the evaluation issues and tools necessary for a counseling staff which is determined to provide quality and relevant service to their constituents. Pertinent evaluation behaviors will be illustrated and suggestions will be presented about implementation and application.

NEEDS ASSESSMENT

Of all the requisite evaluation skills, needs assessment is probably the most crucial (see Chapter 14). Without it, a staff cannot be certain that the programs and services it offers are needed by its constituents. Additionally, student characteristics constantly change, making the needs each particular student group exhibits potentially different. Student needs are not necessarily obvious. Consequently, programming designed for other populations may not be relevant for contemporary student subgroups on a given campus. For example, personal growth and communication workshops were popular offerings to students in the late 1960s while students today seek ways to cope with the pressures related to financial insecurity and the difficulties involved in making career choices. The increase in non-traditional students also has required some different behaviors on the part of counseling centers. These students are usually quite different from traditional age (17-20) undergraduates and, therefore, present new challenges to a counseling center. Ongoing needs assessments enable the staff to describe its constituents and identify current needs which can be met with effective program development.

If a counseling center staff bases its program on continuing needs assessments, one of the major characteristics it must exhibit is flexibility and openness to change. If budgetary restrictions continue, a needs assessment approach in concert with systematic program evaluation might be one mechanism that could produce information documenting effective use of resources. If a counseling center staff adopts this approach, an ongoing assessment team (Aulepp & Delworth, 1976) comprised of individuals from both the university community and the counseling center should be responsible for collecting the necessary data for programming decisions. Team members should be selected to include individuals with expertise in basic research skills with special emphasis on survey research, sampling techniques, questionnaire development, knowledge of unobtrusive measures, and computer use.

There are a number of methods through which an assessment team might gather the required data. The mail survey is common and useful especially when techniques that increase the percentage of respondents are utilized. Telephone surveys are also helpful when there is limited time to gather information about specific questions. The assessment team should also attempt to systematically compile data that are already available within a system (secondary analysis). Attrition rates and the number of students changing majors or seeking counseling are but a few examples of usually available data that only need to be collated. The worth of these data is further enhanced when comparisons within the university are made. For example, in a project at Colorado State University, the evaluation team in the Counseling Center worked closely with the staff responsible for meeting with students desiring to withdraw from the university. Since each student was required to use this office, the necessary forms were put on mark sense forms and analyzed periodically to assess withdrawal trends according to sex, age, major and college. These data already existed in the system, and with a simple intervention the assessment team was able to gather valuable information about possible student stress points which could be ultimately used to influence program development.

The identification of environmental referents (Aulepp & Delworth, 1976; Corazzini, Wilson & Huebner, 1977) has provided some counseling centers with assessment data which can be readily used for program development. In addition to Likert-type statements (e.g., My major is preparing me for a job. Strongly agree, agree, uncertain, etc.), some instruments include a section that asks respondents who express dissatisfaction with a particular part of their environment three questions: (1) What has caused you to feel this way (the referent)? (2) How have you coped? and (3) What would you do to change the environment? After content analysis of the responses, suggested programs can be designed to respond to constituents' verbalized problems.

In a recent evaluation project under the auspices of the Women's Educational Equity Act in the College of Agricultural Sciences at Colorado State University, the environmental referent procedure was utilized to better understand the needs and pressures of women students in that college. An analysis of Likert data showed mean differences between men and women on the item, "Finances are not a significant problem for me." A review of the referent data from those who disagreed with the item provided some enlightening information about the unique financial situation of women in this college. Some of the particular sources of financial stress for women included: (1) parents who would provide financial assistance for only a traditional course of study (e.g., education), and (b) single women incurring child care expenses. When coping mechanisms were reviewed it was learned that summer work was one alternative that could relieve some financial stress. Evaluation of this strategy, in light of actual earning power of women in part-time jobs, indicated that this alternative would likely be ineffective. A more helpful solution was drawn from the suggestions offered by the students. A number thought a special scholarship program or alternatives to the traditional approach to financial assistance would help. This example demonstrates the potential of this technique. It requires flexibility on the part of the evaluator, however, and receptivity to new technology.

PROGRAM EVALUATION

The worth of a program cannot be measured by counselors' satisfaction or numbers of clients. Effectiveness only can be measured when needs are identified, responses made, and evaluation data indicate decreased or satisfied needs. Evaluation is an essential step in any program development model (Moore & Delworth, 1976). All too often programs have been developed because of the particular interest or expertise of a staff member and continued, not because of demonstrated effectiveness, but because of an identification or territoriality issue. Staff members sometimes associate professional success or value with a particular program for which they are responsible. This identification often contributes to a reluctance to collect evidence which could support the efficacy of a particular program.

Program evaluation is an integral part of program development and performance. If evaluative data are gathered on an ongoing basis, they can be returned to program developers via a feedback loop so that the developer can (a) ascertain if the program is doing what it purports to do, (b) makes small adjustments in the program if there should be an area of ineffectiveness, or (c) discontinue the program. These careful and important decisions cannot be made without the data generated from ongoing evaluation.

In addition to general program evaluation skills, a unique skill for the evaluator in this context is sensitivity toward and an ability to use political processes. Program evaluation is used to make decisions. "The assumption is that by providing the facts, evaluation assists decision-makers to make wise choices among future courses of action. Careful and unbiased data on the consequences of programs should improve decision-making. But evaluation is a rational enterprise that takes place in a political context" (Weiss, 1973, p. 37). Because there are so many human factors involved, program evaluators must winnow these out and respond if they wish the data to make a difference. For example, whether the data are used may depend on who collects them and how they are reported. Other factors such as administrative structures and personality style of the evaluator definitely affect the receptiveness of the individual receiving the evaluation report.

This point cannot be over-emphasized. If a counseling center staff decides to collect information about stress points students encountered within a particular university, utilization of those data by administrators with the authority to make stress reducing changes depends in large part on the relationship between the assessment team and the administrator. In other words, the extent to which an administrator may be receptive to the data is related to the degree to which the administrator has been involved in the evaluation (see Chapter 2).

COUNSELING RESEARCH

In addition to the skills of needs assessment and program evaluation, the counseling center evaluator should be prepared to study various aspects of counseling and therapy in order to improve service delivery. All too often there has been a hiatus between research and practice, leaving practicing psychologists without the useful information they need to improve the quality of their work. While there has been no dearth of research publications, the consumers of research literature in large part have been other researchers. "The fact is that to date research has exerted little influence on clinical practice, and the clinical work of the therapist has generally not been informed, much less altered by empirical research results" (Bergin & Strupp, 1970, p. 22).

Although there is a temptation to dichotomize evaluation and research, that division is not always clear (see Chapter 1). Oetting (1974) distinguished scientific inquiry resulting in the advancement of knowledge from data that are used to make decisions about programs. An evaluation plan may include several research questions as part of its design. It should not automatically be assumed that scientific or applied research is always inconsistent with evaluation. At times, seeking answers to research questions may be a legitimate activity for an evaluation unit in a counseling center. In general, the evaluator has a responsibility to contribute to the growth of knowledge as long as doing so does not impede the evaluation process.

To meet the demands of this dual role the evaluator must be flexible and creative, in addition to having the necessary skills such as design, instrumentation, and data analysis. Research questions will probably be generated in the context of gathering evaluative data and problems may result if both types of questions are raised concurrently. Whether asking research questions or determining the efficacy of various therapy approaches, evaluators must communicate the results of their investigations in a clear, concise, and articulate manner (see Chapter 3). The information gathered by evaluators is useful only if it is accessible and easily understood by those who are affected by it.

ACCOUNTABILITY

The financial difficulties confronting many counseling centers today may serendipitously benefit the centers. With the increasing pressure to account for monies, some counseling centers have begun developing management information systems to respond to the "who does what to whom, for how long, and at what expense" questions (Coffman, Slaikeu & Iscoe, 1977; Warsaw, 1976). Although these data may not now be demanded by most administrators, counseling center personnel would be wise to collect and use them in concert with other evaluative information for decisions about service delivery and resource allocation.

With the careful acquisition of accountability data, counseling center staff may be able to justify the expenditure of funds and document areas for growth and expansion. Furthermore, they will probably be able to spend and allocate resources more judiciously. A management information system developed at Colorado State University provided weekly accountability data which included information about which programs were being used at what particular time during the semester. Once this information was made available it was learned that the use of some programs by clients was limited to specific weeks during a semester. The staff then had an opportunity to choose either to allocate the unused time to other programs or to investigate how the program in question could be better utilized.

Once a management information system is established and data are readily available about the utilization and cost of a specific service, this information can be used in decision making. When this information is coupled with evaluative data similar to those generated by the Counseling Services Assessment Blank (Hurst & Weigel, 1966), or Goal Attainment Scaling (Kiresuk & Sherman, 1968), staff or administrators can make an informed decision about the continuance of a program. For example, a counseling center staff decided to offer daily relaxation training sessions on a drop-in basis. It was thought that clients and non-clients would profit if this training was made available. Attendance at the sessions was poor and after a number of months the program was discontinued. After the management information system was operational and this program was reviewed, it was discovered that it received favorable evaluation while costing only twenty-five cents for each client session. If this information had been available earlier, perhaps the issue would have been one of marketing rather than termination.

Systematic review of accountability data has further implications. One of the tensions many counseling center staff feel is related to the dilemma between outreach versus direct service. In recent years there has been a movement toward a more remedial approach to service delivery. Although this choice seems to reflect a more conservative use of funds, perhaps the primary allocation of outreach monies would yield the greater return. When programs are offered on a large scale preventive basis in residence halls, or students are instructed in class settings about various ways to cope with life crises, the counseling center is able to increase student contacts, maximize resources, and perhaps reduce the cost of individual therapy. This approach has been discussed and in some cases implemented. In most instances the evaluative data have not been gathered in such a way that a decision could be reached as to the relative efficacy of a remedial or a proactive approach to mental health. The evaluator should attempt to reach closure on this issue.

OTHER SKILLS

Besides those general skills mentioned in this chapter, there are several other competencies that are important for efficacious evaluation in university counseling centers.

Counseling center evaluation interfaces with various components external to the counseling center. Evaluators should have an understanding of organization or systems theory. As mentioned earlier, evaluation data are used for decision making. Evaluation can also be used as a mechanism for change as in a feedback model of organizational change. If evaluators wish to maximize utilization of data gathered then it would be advantageous if they had a knowledge of organizational development or systems theory.

Evaluators should also have familiarity and experience with at least one model of consultation. Evaluation does not take place in a vacuum. Its success depends upon the relationship established between the evaluator and other individuals within the client system. Consultative experience is particularly important if the evaluator of the counseling center is to work outside the center in the university community. This is a very common occurrence. The evaluator is constantly asked to respond to research questions and share expertise or collaborate with others in various research projects. If evaluators wish to be effective change agents (one of their implicit functions), then it behooves them to be as knowledgeable about consultation theory as they are about evaluation methodologies.

Evaluators of counseling centers will be more effective if they have certain personal qualities (Broskowski & Schulberg, 1974; Oetting & Hawkes, 1974) that complement the other skills discussed here. First, tolerance of ambiguity is an absolute necessity. As evaluators attempt to work with various individuals and groups, they will constantly be confronted with ambiguously defined responsibilities and tasks. Secondly, evaluators should be mature with adequate communication and social skills to enable them to work constructively with people. All too often evaluators have functioned independently and in isolation. This has been a result of some stereotyping of evaluators as well as some "ivory tower" attitudes held by evaluators themselves. As Brown has indicated in Chapter 2, such barriers must be removed if evaluation results are to be used for decision making.

CONCLUSION

Counseling centers have made significant strides in their relatively short history. These advances, however, have been in large part haphazard and serendipitous. This growth clearly cannot be sustained if centers persist in allowing their fate to be determined for them by central administration. Evaluation can insure that future growth and development can be directed by the center itself. The use of evaluation data is one method which can allow the counseling center to be controlled by its staff as well as enhance the quality and quantity of service of its constituents.

In many respects the evaluator is a change agent who, like a conscience, challenges administrators or staff to document what it is they do. This role demands that evaluation becomes an integral component of the programs of the counseling center. The evaluator's success depends not only on the ability to report understandable data but also the degree of interpersonal skill which will result in appropriate use of these data.

REFERENCES

Aulepp, L., & Delworth, U. *Training manual for an ecosystem model.* Western Interstate Commission for Higher Education: Boulder, CO., 1976.
Bergin, A.E., & Strupp, H.H. New direction in psychotherapy research. *Journal of Abnormal Psychology,* 1970, 76, 13-26.
Broskowski, A., & Schulberg, H. A training program for clinical research and development. *Professional Psychology,* 1974, 5, (2) 133-139.

Coffman, D., Slaikeu, K., & Iscoe, I. *Cost effectiveness in the delivery of campus mental health services.* Paper presented at the American Psychological Association, San Francisco, August, 1977.

Corazzini, J., Wilson, S., & Huebner, L. The environmental satisfaction questionnaire: A guide to assessment and program development. *Journal of College Student Personnel,* 1977, *18,* 169-173.

Hurst, J., & Weigel, R. *Counseling services assessment blank.* Rocky Mountain Behavioral Sciences Institute, Fort Collins, CO, 1966.

Kiresuk, J., & Sherman, R. Goal attainment scaling: A general method for evaluating comprehensive community mental health programs. *Community Mental Health Journal,* 1968, *4,* 443-453.

Moore, M., & Delworth, U. *Training manual for student service program development.* Western Interstate Commission for Higher Education: Boulder, CO, 1976.

Oetting, E., & Hawkes, F. Training professionals for evaluative research. *The Personnel and Guidance Journal,* 1974, *52,* 434-438.

Warsaw, P. *Developing an MIS at the University of Utah Counseling Center.* Proceedings of the 25th Annual Conference at University and College Counseling Center Directors, 1976.

Weiss, C.H. Where politics and evaluation research meet. *Evaluation,* 1973, *1* (3), 37-45.

8
STUDENT ACTIVITIES
Richard N. McKaig and Sharon M. Policello

The organization of student activities on college and university campuses has taken many administrative forms. As a consequence, a consensually validated description of a student activities unit does not exist. In fact, student activities seems to be one of the most diverse of the functional areas of student affairs. As a result, it is necessary to establish some parameters within which evaluation in student activities can be discused.

Student activities typically includes: (1) administrative; (2) programming; (3) advising; and (4) some direct teaching functions. The student activities unit is usually responsible for administrative functions that relate to student organizations, such as the recognition or registration of student organizations, coordination of student organization events, and the supervision or control of student activity monies. Other common administrative functions are those of professional staffing, planning, budgeting, policy formation, and the reporting or recording of the year's activities.

Programming functions are also often assigned to student activities. In some institutions, programming includes events such as movies, dances, cultural activities, lectures, and the performing arts. In other institutions, however, it is more broadly defined to include recreational sports and the college union.

The student organizations which are advised by activities staff can be quite varied. They may include groups representing: student government; religious denominations; special interests such as environmentalists; minority students; academic and professional societies; and student publications. The type and the amount of services provided and the degree of accountability of the office for the activities of these organizations vary greatly.

Credit and non-credit courses or workshops in leadership development and organizational development are examples of the direct teaching function. With the recent emphasis on experimental education in student development programs, teaching through activities has become recognized as a necessary component of the operation. Efforts to demonstrate the educational impact of programs supported by activities fees or to measure the quality and quantity of services offered students by the activities office are examples of attempts to respond to demands for accountability. However, direct teaching by the activities staff is not as common across institutions as are other functions.

For purposes of this discussion, student activities will be considered to include all of the functions previously listed. Examples of evaluation issues are drawn from campus programming areas, college union settings, university recreational program offices, and college arts programming.

RATIONALE FOR EVALUATION IN STUDENT ACTIVITIES

An interaction of several factors has resulted in increased attention on evaluation of student activities. For the most part, these forces are similar to those influencing other functional areas of student personnel. These forces might be viewed on a continuum ranging from those clearly external to the unit (i.e. state legislature demands for accountability) to staff-initiated efforts at program improvement to the intrinsic need for personal and professionl growth.

Pressures originating within the institution have emphasized the need for evaluation. Students are seeking a clearer explanation of the benefits derived from activity fee dollars. Faculty and administrative staff are concerned with the allocation of limited institutional resources. Efforts to document the impact of programs financed by activity fees or to measure the quality and quantity of services provided by the activities office are examples of attempts to respond to demands for accountability.

Staff initiated evaluation efforts directed toward program improvement, revision, modification, rejection, or termination may be a reaction to external pressures. They may also result, however, because of an increased level of awareness of the need for evaluation on the part of the student activities professionals. Activities professionals who recognize that resources are limited have attempted to implement evaluation strategies to improve program administration decisions.

Some on-going evaluation efforts have been guided by a personal and professional commitment to the development of student activities as an integral part of the student's educational experience. Those who share this perspective consider knowledge of higher education and the application of behavioral science principles to be requisite to the efficacious administration of student life programs (Bloland, 1967). In this sense, evaluation becomes an integral step in decision making.

Some people question whether evaluation is motivated only by survival instincts. Others cynically suggest evaluation is undertaken to justify decisions that have already been made. The facts are that if program review and improvement are to proceed in a systematic manner, evaluation must be viewed as a logical step in activities administration. In reality, evaluation is a common phenomenon that is often based on personal assumptions and professional hunches. Activities staff regularly make judgments on the worth of proposed programmatic changes or policy alternatives. The standards used in making these decisions are seldom explicitly stated or available for review and discussion by others. Given the integral role evaluation can serve in decision making, there is a need to improve current techniques and develop new methods of evaluation so that the activities staff can determine with more certainty the worth of the programs and services offered.

DECIDING WHAT TO EVALUATE AND HOW

Specific activities requiring evaluation include: office goals or objectives; specific programming events; specific teaching programs; students' development through participation; general satisfaction of participants in or planners of a program, the organizations themselves (Do they really serve a need? Should they exist?); staff skills, performance, and staff development programs. When determining what to evaluate, program priorities, available staff, and technical resources must be considered. Equally important is determining when an evaluation of a specific program will be most helpful for the decision maker. In most cases, answers to when and what to evaluate should come from the staff directly involved in the activities program.

When it has been recognized that an evaluation of some component is warranted, the specific technique, format, or strategy must be outlined. After the evaluation questions have been formulated, and the sources of information have been determined, then the appropriate strategy should be selected.

Both macro and micro approaches to evaluation in student activities are possible. A macro evaluation could consider the total campus environment and attempt to monitor general attitudes on the effects of multiple programs. Efforts to evaluate the activities office using a discrepancy model (i.e., comparing office goals and objectives with measurable outcomes – see Chapter 3; also Worthen & Sanders, 1973) can also be considered macro in orientation. Similarly, efforts to assess extracurricular activities through surveys, expert analysis, or an inhouse review by constituent committees offer broad scale approaches to evaluation. On the other hand, micro evaluation focuses on a single activity program or service and seeks specific feedback from participants or attempts to assess the impact only on those students participating in a specific program. Micro evaluation efforts are easier to manage because the scope of the study is quite limited. Micro evaluations which produce empirical evidence also tend to be easier to interpret to decision makers.

Two of the most common evaluation strategies utilize the judgment of professionals or quasi expert individuals and simple measurements of participants interest or satisfaction (see Chapter 3). Because of the relative ease of implementation, use of outside experts or panels of quasi-experts selected from within the institution are frequently used to evaluate activities programs. Outside experts willing to serve as evaluators have often been identified from among the leadership of the several professional activities associations (e.g., Student Activity Commission of A.C.P.A., Commission IV). The experts' insights have often resulted in useful information to assist staff in program development and improvement. Some institutions have established student, faculty, and staff review committees representative of the campus community to function as an evaluation panel. However, use of the outside expert or the quasi-expert panel can be criticized as an evaluation strategy because it relies too heavily on subjective judgment and produces findings that are not often replicable.

Another popular approach utilizes surveys of participant interests in, attitudes toward, or satisfaction with a given program. The degree of sophistication of the instruments varies widely and generally the survey forms are not standardized and validated so as to preclude accurate comparisons of results across programs. Such surveys have been popular, however, because they provide quantitative data, are more objective than judgmental techniques, and facilitate student input into the planning process.

Evaluations based on the discrepancy between measurable standards of performance and predetermined objectives were implemented in many colleges and universities during the 1970's (Harvey, 1972). Problems common to this approach resulted due to the professional staff's inexperience in writing objectives and stating them in measurable terms. Further, measures were often overemphasized due to the relatively greater difficulty in determining and measuring quality. A positive result of the MBO movement has been the attention focused on the objectives of student activities and the importance of their use in program planning.

Cost effectiveness measures have also been used to determine the worth of a program. Attempts by programming boards to develop cost effective measures have been somewhat simplistic and often have not taken into consideration program variables other than costs and student attendance. A more thorough analysis would include factors such as audience satisfaction, quality of program as judged by professional staff, and educational experience realized by the student planners. The cost effectiveness and discrepancy models demand more skills in evaluation techniques than many student activities professionals currently have.

Although Scriven's goal-free model and the Stufflebeam's CIPP model have been used in some educational settings (Gardner, 1977), application of these strategies to student activities has not been substantiated in the literature (Brown, 1978). While both deserve consideration, the present level of evaluation expertise reflected by activities staff suggest that the leadership for such attempts must come from national organizations or faculty of graduate preparation programs (see Chapter 18).

THE STATE OF EVALUATION IN STUDENT ACTIVITIES

While it appears many activities professionals desire regular and reliable feedback on the programs and services they direct, the state of the art seems to be limited both in the quantity and the quality of evaluations conducted. For a number of reasons, evaluations have not been conducted extensively in the student activities area. The nature of the work itself is one such obstacle. Activities professionals tend to be action-oriented individuals whose days are filled with numerous consecutive meetings and programs. Evaluation is often viewed more as a luxury than as a necessity. As a result, evaluations are contemplated more frequently at a time when student traffic is reduced. Unfortunately, this may be the very time when individuals served by activities programs and services are less available for contact by the evaluator. In addition, few activities units have enough staff members to assign one to a full time evaluator role. Consequently, the program director is also often the program evaluator as well as the individual most directly affected by the results of the evaluation. Avoiding bias in the development of the evaluation plan and in interpretation of the results is impossible. Therein lies one of the major problems of internal evaluation mentioned in Chapter 2.

Consensus as to the objectives of student activities and measures of success of programs and activities remain elusive. The balance between quantative and qualitative measures is an issue of major concern. In addition, many argue that students learn from programming failures as well as from successful ventures. Weighing the value of the student planner's learning experience against the cost of an inadequate program is not easy to determine. Even the most sophisticated evaluator encounters difficulty when attempting to assess the quantitative and qualitative components of the educational process.

Determining what specific programs to evaluate and the value or utility of the evaluation itself are other issues of concern. Activities offices often support a variety of organizations or activities whose appeal may be somewhat limited. Attempting to measure the worth of some activities by surveys might yield results which — if accepted at face value — would undermine professional priorities related to the cultural and educational functions of the office.

The present level of knowledge about evaluation of actitivies staff suggest additional reasons for the relative dearth of evaluations in the area. Individuals performing activities functions come from a variety of educational backgrounds and often have limited classroom training in evaluation techniques. On the job, skill development tends to be focused on the immediate pressing concerns such as budgeting, contracts, legal liability, and the technical components of program planning. At many institutions, positions in activities areas are characterized by frequent turnover and often are viewed as a stepping stone to professional advancement. Given this situation, more emphasis is placed on program creation, maintenance, and improvement based on impressions rather than on formal evaluations.

EXAMPLES OF EVALUATION EFFORTS

Encouragement for professional development in evaluation of the activities area has been provided by several professional associations. The American College Personnel Association through Commission IV (Students, Their Activities and Their Community), the National Entertainment and Campus Activities Association, the Association of College Unions-International, the National Intramural-Recreational Sports Association, and the Association of College, University and Community Arts Administrators, Inc., have indicated an interest in evaluation and have provided forums for the sharing of both techniques and results. NECAA's bi-monthly publication, *Programming,* includes a regular feature of evaluation reports from member institutions. The standard format adopted has generated quantitative and qualitative information which can assist activities staffs in program decisions. In a more subjective format, the Association of College, University and Community Arts Administrators, Inc., regularly issues evaluative reports from member institutions regarding touring artists and their performances. In a recent report an audience profile was suggested as a complement to the annual surveys of audiences' attitudes, preferences, and satisfactions (Nevin, 1978). The sharing of these types of data can result in program decisions based on more reliable data and ultimately improve the specific activities programs.

Evaluations at individual institutions have also been conducted. At Pennsylvania State University, the Student Activities Office selects several programs each year for an evaluation. One member of the staff is responsible for the coordination of the evaluation. Several data collection instruments are typically used to evaluate a wide variety of program components including: satisfaction of the participants, demography and number of the participants, and the ability of the staff to effectively coordinate the program. In this setting, evaluation is directed toward program improvements. Since this is an on-going process, there are comparative data for subsequent evaluations.

Evaluations have also been conducted in the area of recreational sports programming. Hanniford and Watson (1978) published a report entitled *Purdue's Students Opinion of Policies Governing Their Participation in the Recreational Sports Program.* This study was an attempt to evaluate the current policies governing student participation in recreational sports through the use of student opinion questionnaires distributed to a random sample of participants. Findings were submitted to various administrative officers and representative student groups for their consideration and action as considered warranted. Similar efforts are underway at Indiana University to provide a standardized format for systematic evaluation in the recreational sports area. The plan is to provide for longitudinal assessment of student opinions regarding the organization and administration of recreational sports, the rules and regulations governing participation, the facilities and equipment, and the officiating.

A second project recently undertaken at Indiana University is a macro evaluation of the student activities milieu. Student affairs staff and the campus Student Life Committee designed an instrument to assess student perceptions of the campus environment and various campus groups (Utz, 1978). The questions focused on extra-curricular life. Is the University as a social community a positive place to live? Does the University provide adequate opportunities to satisfy recreational and leisure needs? Does the University provide adequate opportunities to satisfy intellectual needs? Data were also gathered from: the student organizations themselves (structure, financing, programs and perceived problems), a survey of information from student activities units at a sample of similar institutions across the country, and a historical review of student activities and related policy development. These data provided the basis for recommendations made for new policies which will govern campus organizations at the institution.

An evaluation effort conducted in 1976 at the State University of New York at Buffalo included an example of an evaluation based on the quasi professional judgment of a review committee. The evaluation was part of an overall assessment of the Division of Student Affairs and provided specific comments on the Norton Union. Included was an assessment of the Union's leadership direction, quality and quantity of staff, facilities, communication, student perceptions, intradivisional relations and intra-university relations. The review committee included undergraduate and graduate students, members of the faculty, representatives of the SUNY system office and an off-campus expert in student affairs. The committee studied statements of philosophy and goals, results of an intensive self-study, annual reports, budget data, and met with the directors and members of the staff within student affairs to discuss related issues. Results submitted to the University President were provided as information for institutional planning and decisions about the student affairs unit *(Reporter,* 1976).

The Bulletin of the Association of College Unions — International also provides other examples of student activities evaluation efforts. Cantonsville Community College described its efforts to improve the student activity programs for their adult students (Chambers, 1974).

An adult students' interest survey which included an extensive check list type questionnaire concerning programs and services of interest was administered to a random sample of students. The data were shared with various campuses and offices, and resulted in determining new program directions and reaffirming many existing efforts.

An evaluation at Old Dominion University was designed to assess the effectiveness of the services of the Student Affairs Division for commuter students. As part of that effort, a needs assessment instrument was designed and sent to all full-time students of the university (Lardy, Worley & Moore, 1978). Responses assisted in the reordering of priorities of the student affairs division.

RECOMMENDATIONS FOR IMPROVING EVALUATION IN STUDENT ACTIVITIES

Much more must be done in student activities if evaluation is to assume an integral role in program administration. Efforts to date have been few and techniques are in need of refinement. Leadership must come from professional associations, graduate preparation programs, and those institutions with established activities programs, and available staff and resources. The following recommendations are suggested for staff interested in conducting evaluations in student activities.

1. Complete course work in program evaluation within graduate preparation programs. Where possible attempt to gain practical experience in evaluation through course projects involving the assessment of student activities services and programs.
2. Through related national and regional associations, participate in courses, workshops and convention sessions designed to build skills in student activities evaluation.
3. Recognize that evaluation must be routinized as an office function and not as a reactionary defense mechanism. Consider evaluation to be a specific job responsibility assigned to a specific member of the staff.
4. Initiate evaluation efforts at the micro level. Unless staff resources and expertise are already available, avoid broad scope evaluation efforts. Reasonable scale evaluation efforts can result in direct program improvements and will build staff skills in evaluation.
5. When attempting to evaluate programs and activities, choose techniques appropriate to the information desired, and time and resources available. If measures of program effectiveness or efficiency are desired, be sure the factors identified reflect program objectives and do not distort activities to accomplish a positive rating.
6. Use the available expertise of other divisions in the institution. Offices of Institutional Research, Departments of Educational

Research, and Counseling Centers have qualified staff who often can assist with evaluation efforts.
7. Replicate evaluation efforts over a period of years so that comparisons can be made and growth, progress, or improvement documented. Regular data collection methods should be adopted which record activities information for use in evaluations.
8. Share evaluation efforts with other activities professionals. Short articles in appropriate journals, newsletters, or presentations at professional meetings are excellent ways to inform others of evaluation strategies which have application in student activities.

REFERENCES

Bloland, P. A. Emerging patterns in student activity programs. *Journal of College Student Personnel*, 1967, *8* 390-392.

Brown, R. D. Implications of new evaluation strategies for accountability in student affairs. *Journal of College Student Personnel*, 1978, *19* 123-126.

Chambers, G. Adult student interests surveyed. *The Bulletin of the Association of College Unions — International*, 1974, *41* (4), 1.

Gardner, D. E. Five evaluation frameworks: Implications for decision making in higher education. *Journal of Higher Education*, 1977, *48*, 571-593.

Hanniford, G. W., Watson, J. F. *Purdue students opinion of policies governing their participation in recreational sports programs.* West Lafayette, Indiana: Purdue University, 1978.

Harvey, J. Administration by objectives in student personnel programs. *Journal of College Student Personnel*, 1972, *13*, 293-296.

Lardy, B. A., Worley, C. W. Moore, P. *ODU student profile 1978.* Unpublished manuscript, Old Dominican University, 1978.

Nevin, J. R. Marketing research and the arts administrator. *ACUCAA Bulletin*, 1978, *67*, 1-4.

Report on division of student affairs. *Reporter,* State University of New York — Buffalo, 1976.

Utz, P. A. *Students' perceptions of the Indiana University environment: Student life questionnaire.* Unpublished manuscript. Indiana University, 1977.

Worthen, B., & Sanders, J. *Educational evaluation: Theory and practice.* Worthington, Ohio: Jones, 1973.

9
CAREER PLANNING AND PLACEMENT
Marvalene H. Styles and Sara Beth Hull

Student affairs programs have become especially vulnerable as the consumer and accountability movements have gained momentum. In order to respond proactively to the issues raised by Kuh (Chapter 1), career specialists must do more than alert students to job vacancies. The contemporary comprehensive mission of career planning and placement includes workshops, seminars, and credit courses designed to provide students with the skills necessary to make career decisions and to be successful in a competitive labor market. Additional relevant services include career information libraries, internship and field placement opportunities, and individual career counseling (Sovilla, 1972). A carefully conceptualized evaluation process is required to ensure that staff resources are optimally used in the provision of these services, and to maximize student participation by determining whether programs are available in the areas in which students indicate the greatest interest.

The questions that are related to evaluating career planning and placement are "who" and "what" questions. As noted in Chapter 2, the constituents of student services — faculty, students, alumni, and employers — evaluate services both formally and informally. Informal evaluation seldom provides useful feedback to program planners who could benefit from constituents' observations. Career centers should attempt to make use of this potentially valuable input by conceptualizing and conducting evaluations which systematically gather feedback from relevant constituents. In executing the process, there are some basic principles to which the evaluator must adhere:

1. Evaluation must be sensitive to all constituents, including students, faculty and administrators, career program staff, alumni, and employers;
2. The evaluation plan must be consistent with objectives of programs and activities. An objective is not meaningful unless it is capable of being evaluated;
3. The evaluation must be evaluated.

It is essential for evaluations to elicit information which yields meaningful data. For example, it is not adequate to note that women and minorities continue to prepare for non-technological areas such as liberal studies and education, or to report that female mathematical aptitude scores and interest test profiles in technologically related areas are below average. It *is* important to consider these sociocultural findings when determining office objectives and to make certain that program planning is based on these objectives.

The contemporary career specialist is expected to apply theories and behavioral principles related to life planning, and to incorporate research findings from other social science disciplines into the planning of career programs. It is possible to respond to socialized problems such as the non-technological orientation of many women and minorities by: (1) exposing the student/alumni to new alternatives, (2) planning and implementing alternative programs, and (3) desensitizing students to their socialized, dysfunctional behaviors such as phobic responses to academic areas. When carefully considered office objectives have been established, evaluation is necessary to identify those programs and activities which contribute to the achievement of the goals and those which should be modified or discontinued.

With the knowledge that women and minorities at a given institution are not proportionately represented in the technological disciplines, a career planning/placement office might include as one of its objectives: "To promote equal participation in all areas of employment, regardless of sex, race, age, or physical disability." Program planning for the office might lead to a Career Night. Career Night objectives might include:

(1) To host an equal number of male and female representatives from technological career areas;
(2) To host minority representatives from technological career areas.

Evaluation of the Career Night program would assess the degree to which the objectives were attained. If the evaluation determined that minorities and women were being actively pursued and offered positions in technological areas, then the office would have been successful in promoting equal participation in all areas of employment.

ESTABLISHING GOALS AND OBJECTIVES AND DESIGNING PROGRAMS

Needs assessment is the first step in determining office priorities (see Chapter 14). Before goals may be established and programs and activities planned, a career specialist must collect information from a sample of constituents to determine areas requiring the most attention. Needs assessments in larger institutions should include a stratified population sample to permit identification of individuals by demographic variables such as age, sex, physical disability, and ethnic identity. These variables are useful when analyzing the career development needs of various population subgroups. Of importance to the career specialist is the level of competence in areas such as decision-making, interpersonal effectiveness, and values clarification.

A stratified needs assessment enables the career specialist to identify career development needs specific to various subgroups and to design and promote programs which might attract members of these groups.

Collection of demographic information about constituents is also important in setting goals. Useful information includes the numbers of students enrolled in major areas and the numbers of graduates anticipated (Thomas, 1966).

Faculty and employer needs must also be considered in determining program emphasis in a career planning/placement office (Blaska & Schmidt, 1977). Assessments of personnel needs and employer preferences for students with various backgrounds should be used in developing career awareness programs. Faculty input relative to curriculum content and course availability is essential for the development of career advising materials. Faculty may also be able to offer considerable insight into the career development needs of individual students based on classroom contact (Edwards, 1968).

Input from alumni should be solicited prior to finalizing office goals. Graduates of an institution offer a unique, long-range perspective on career development needs. Based upon experiences after leaving the campus, an alumnus can share "real-world" insights concerning what students can expect in the near future. Alumni may suggest new services to ease the transition from campus to work.

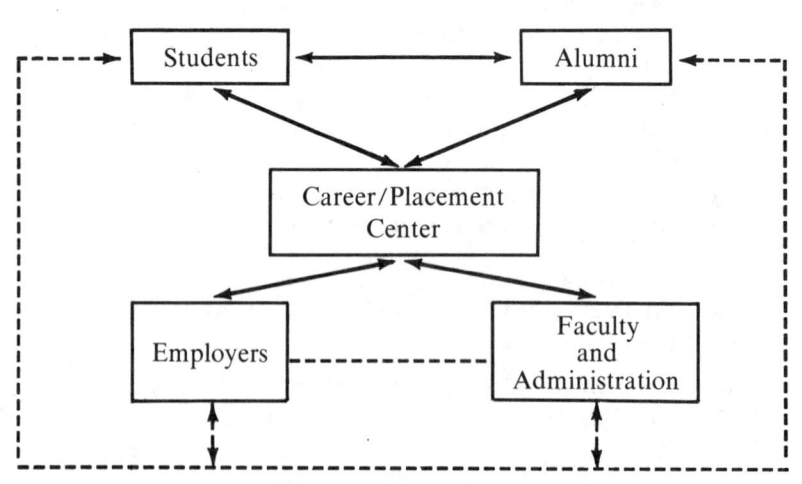

⟷ Represents DIRECT programming and evaluation responsibility.

◂--▸ Represents INDIRECT service delivery which is facilitated through College Career/Placement Centers.

Figure 1. Communication flow for career programming.

Figure 1 suggests the career specialist is in the central position of receiving and relaying information. The information flow must circulate through the Career Planning/Placement Center to ensure continuity of programming and accountability. It is the career specialist's responsibility to process information necessary to plan and implement programming and to inform constituents of available programs.

The career planning and placement staff may not be able to simultaneously attend to all program needs which are identified. Establishing goals based on priorities, time, and resource constraints may become an important staff task. When the goal-setting step has been completed, the various constituencies should be informed of the office goals and the programs and activities designed to meet the goals.

The career planning and placement office goals and objectives must be meaningful and measureable, and reflect the staff's planning activities and commitment. The manager of the office is responsible for matching staff skills and work assignments in order to achieve program goals. A format similar to the one in Figure 2 can be adopted to encourage staff to institutionalize the evaluation process.

Name of Staff: _____

Semester: _____

Program Title: _____

Goal: (Since the goals of the office should have already been stated, you should relate your program to one of these previously-stated goals) _____

Behavioral Objectives: (How will you approach the above goal?)

Activities: (State specifically what you plan to do)

Target Population: _____

Dates (When): _____

Location (Where): _____

Needs (Include budgetary, space staff, etc.): _____

Evaluation Plan (How will you measure the results of this activity?):

Figure 2. Program outline.

At the beginning of each semester, staff members should plan their various individual activities and collaborative efforts by completing one form per activity. The supervisor monitors the program balance using the determined priorities as a yardstick. It is important to insure flexibility so that program commitments can be renegotiated during the implementation stage. This enables inclusion of serendipitous insights and realistic appraisal of time commitments.

WHO EVALUATES WHAT AND HOW

The who, what, and how questions in evaluation of career planning and placement will vary by institution. The input and output flow of career center information presented in Figure 1 suggests the need to maximize the involvement of various constituencies in the evaluation process. Identifying what is to be evaluated requires a thorough understanding of program goals and activities.

An evaluation matrix such as the one presented in Figure 3 summarizes the who and what questions of career planning and placement evaluation. This matrix is intended as a diagrammatic indicator of who evaluates whom in any given career planning and placement center. There will be institutional variations, but the diagram emphasizes the fact that evaluation can be conducted by several populations, regardless of their actual relationship to particular programs. It is recommended that each institution complete the appropriate data for its unique matrix. Program goals are evaluated by everyone, formally and informally, regardless of the level of actual familiarity with the program. The fact that the identified populations may not be particularly well acquainted with various program goals may suggest that the office priorities should be clarified for the campus community.

A critical aspect of the evaluation matrix relates to the inter- and intra-components of staff evaluation. In addition to being evaluated by all other constituents, the staff should engage in a peer review process. A sensitive peer review process is especially important in creating an honest, non-threatening environment where a staff member can select an evaluation team, pursue a performance review, determine the need for growth and change, and propose a program for action (see Chapter 12).

HOW TO EVALUATE: SELECTING AND DESIGNING EVALUATION INSTRUMENTS

The selection of a particular evaluation design or methodology should be appropriate to the purposes of the evaluation (see Chapter 3). Therefore, consideration must be given to the conceptualization of an evaluation design at the time career planning goals and activities

Support Staff	Career Administrator	Staff Career Specialists	Administration	Faculty	Employers	Alumni	Students	
	+o	+o		+	+	*	o	Aptitudes
	+o	+o		+	+	*	o	Interests
	+o	+o		+	+	*	o	Personality
	+o	+o		+	+	*	o	Achievement
	+o	+o		+	+	*	o	Values
	+o	+o		+	+	*	o	Intelligence
	+o	+o		+	+	*	o	Self-Concept
	+o	+o			+	o	o	Interviewing Skills
	+o	+o			+	o	o	Job Search Strategy
+o	+o	+o	+o	+o	+o	o	o	Attitudes
+o	+o	+o	+	+	+	+	+	Staff Preparation
+o	+o	+o	+	+	+	+	+	Staff Efficiency
+	+	+	+	+	+o	+	+	Employer Efficiency
+o	+o	+o	+	+	+	+	+	Program Goals
+o	+o	+o	+	+	+	+	+	Job Placement
	+o	+o	o+	+o	+	+	+	Curriculum
+o	+o	+o	+	+		+	+	Centers' Publication
+	+o	+o	+	+		*	+o	Career Counseling
+o	+o	+o	+	+	+	+	+	Job Development
+o	+o	+o	+	+	+	+	+	Placement Folder
+o	+o	+o	+	+	+	+	+	Career Library
+o	+o	+o	+	+	+		o+	Student Employment
+o	+o	+o	+	+	+	+o*	o+	Resume Writing
+	+o	+	+	+	+	+	+	Physical Facility
	+	+	+	+	+	+o	+o	Student Experience, Leadership

Code:
 o = person evaluated
 + = Persons conducting the evaluation activity
 * = possible contracted services

Figure 3. Who evaluates, what matrix for career planning and placement services.

are determined. Of equal importance to design selection is the appropriate choice of instrumentation.

There are a number of information categories from which instruments may be designed. The most commonly applied technique in higher education is the teacher-made test designed to measure learning. There is definite applicability of this testing procedure to career centers if retention of content is considered important. Since job search strategy workshops have specific content information, the career specialist may consider regular classroom test construction to include objective (true/false, multiple choice) or essay items.

Evaluation methods range in scope from the most informal experience of inviting verbal feedback to more formal use of instruments which have been pretested on local populations. Regardless of the formality of the evaluation, there should be a provision for eliciting both positive and negative feedback about the service of program.

Most career center staff members have become acquainted with body count instruments such as the one in Figure 4. This type of instrument provides useful quantitative data and enables weekly assessments of work loads and traffic patterns in the center. Data may be collected continuously with such an instrument, or the staff may choose to take periodic samplings.

From the data collected with body count instruments, a *Fact Sheet* may be prepared, informing the campus community of who is using the career center for what. Such information is also typically included in annual reports and budget requests.

In addition to gathering quantitative information about clients, an evaluation should attempt to answer the question, "How do our constituents perceive the services provided?" Fischer (1976) has developed a comprehensive summary of areas for evaluation in a career planning and placement office. Figure 5 lists many of the possible areas for evaluation. Feedback may be collected using a simple checklist format or Likert-type scale. This questionnaire format can be used with walk-in, short term office contacts because it can be completed quickly and specifies the areas to be evaluated.

Using this type of evaluation form, employers can provide feedback about the organization of the center and professional behavior of the staff. Another form could be constructed with which employers could provide feedback to student interviewees following on-campus recruitment. Students could benefit from the employers' comments on their interview behavior and preparation for employment. Employers might also be encouraged to inform staff members of students experiencing particular difficulties in the interview. An employer's evaluation of student performance would greatly assist the counselor in working with unsuccessful job hunters.

In addition to the more general attempts at office evaluation,

Counselor _____ Date _____

CLIENT DATA (#)
___ Male   ___ Anglo   ___ Alumni
___ Female   ___ Am. Ind.   ___ Fac/Staff
                   ___ Black   ___ Employer
                   ___ Chicano   ___ Non SDSU
                   ___ Asian/Pan-Asian   Student
                                          ___ Reciprocal
                                          ___ SDSU Student

CONTACT PLACE
On Campus
___ HA-630
___ HA-858
___ Off Campus
___ Other

PURPOSE OF CONTACT

Administrative ( )   *Services (#)*   *Counseling (#)*
___ Gen. Admin.   ___ In-Service Training   ___ Acad. Planning
___ Committee   ___ Library   ___ Group
___ Records/Files   ___ Job Search Strategy   ___ Career/Life
___ Intra-Center   ___ Orientation   Planning
___ Media/PR   ___ Resumes   ___ Personal
___ Job Develop-   ___ Intern Superv.   ___ Placement
    ment (#)   Training   ___ Test Inter-
                           ___ Co-op Programs   pretation
                           ___ Interviewing
                           ___ Mid-Life
                           ___ Student Employment
                           ___ Organization
                               Development

TYPE OF CONTACT
___ Classroom   ___ Telephone   ___ Letter/Memo
___ Individual   ___ Workshop   ___ Group

MAJORS SEEN _____

REFERRALS TO _____

TOTAL: ___ PEOPLE SEEN   ___ CONTACTS MADE

*A body-count instrument designed collaboratively by the staff at San Diego State University.

Figure 4. Client contact information.

The following areas are suggested as possible items to include in an evaluation of career planning/placement *services:*
1. Assistance with preparing the job resume
2. Identifying prospective employers
3. Strategies for contacting prospective employers
4. Interviewing prospective employers
5. Interview preparation program
6. Internship information
7. Publications issued by career planning/placement service
8. Part-time employment information
9. Assistance in choosing a major
10. Assistance in choosing a career/occupation
11. Placement files
12. Information concerning graduate or professional schools
13. Job listings
14. Cooperative education program
15. Assistance in obtaining volunteer experiences
16. Assistance for special populations (women, minorities, mid-life career changers, etc.)
17. Classroom presentations
18. Interest/aptitude testing
19. Career information library

The following areas are suggested as possible items to include in an evaluation of career planning/placement *facilities:*
1. Location
2. Attractiveness
3. Room temperature
4. Room size
5. Furnishings
6. Lighting
7. Noise level
8. Privacy
9. Telephones
10. Ventilation
11. Accessibility
12. Display areas for employer literature
13. Parking

The following areas are suggested as possible items to include in an evaluation of career planning/placement *programs:*
1. Length
2. Timing in relation to other campus events
3. Promotion
4. Nature of students in attendance
5. Success in meeting stated objectives

6. Volume of material presented
7. Handouts provided
8. Audiovisual presentations
9. Guest speakers
10. Relative amounts of time spent on various content areas
11. Organization and pacing of program
12. Preparedness of staff member in charge

Figure 5. Suggested areas for evaluation.

career specialists must engage in individual program evaluations. Assuming that a program has been designed to meet assessed needs and objectives have been written in measurable terms, the evaluation should be relatively straightforward. The evaluator's task is simply to determine whether the program has accomplished what was intended.

The following example may illustrate the evaluation of a program based upon stated objectives. A course in job seeking skills was developed in the College of Arts and Sciences at Indiana University to prepare seniors for entry into the job market. The objectives of this course were derived from a study by Stevens (1960) in which the behavioral characteristics of successful and unsuccessful job hunters were identified. Course activities were designed to increase students' job placement readiness by providing instruction and practice in ten vital areas identified in Stevens' study. The instrument in Figure 6 was developed to measure the level of achievement in each of these ten areas. The primary course objective was to ensure that students exhibited a high placement readiness quotient (a total score of at least 40 on the evaluation instrument). Success at meeting the course objective could be determined by administering the evaluation tool at the end of the course and deriving a placement readiness quotient for each student.

For year-end reporting on the success of the course, concrete data were available in the form of actual numbers of students attaining the level of placement readiness which indicated that they were ready to compete successfully in the job market. Program modifications were made based upon the areas in which several students fell short of a high score.

It should be noted that the evaluation instrument in Figure 6 was designed for use with course participants. A similar form could be used by career specialists in determining areas for attention with individual students or for rating students' job placement readiness during intake interviews in the career center. In this way, the instrument can be used to assess needs of students rather than determining whether a course had accomplished its objectives.

The career planning and placement office should have as one of its primary goals the teaching of skills useful for job seeking and self-assessment over the course of one's vocational life. Unfortunately, there is no easy way to evaluate the success of the staff in achieving this goal. The effects of career planning programs may not be evident until students have left the campus. Some effects may not be evident until an individual is confronted with a career change and draws upon the career specialist's advice or instruction provided years earlier. Follow-up studies of alumni may suggest the relative merits of career development programs. Unfortunately, alumni studies in career planning and placement are difficult to conduct, but they are a potential source of invaluable input into program planning and student advising.

NAME_____ I.D._____

ADDRESS _____ PHONE_____

MAJOR __ CLASS (circle one)   FR.   SOPH.   JR.   SR.   GRAD

AGE __ SEX (circle one)   M   F

DIRECTIONS:

READ EACH OF THE FOLLOWING QUESTIONS CAREFULLY. FOR EACH QUESTION, CIRCLE THE LETTER OF THE *ONE* RESPONSE WHICH BEST DESCRIBES YOUR JOB PLACEMENT READINESS TODAY. PLEASE ANSWER ALL TEN ITEMS.

1. Do you know what job you would like to have?
    A. I don't want to make that decision on my own.
    B. I have some vague ideas, but I have not identified my primary job interests.
    C. I have done preliminary thinking about jobs but need additional information about job trends and opportunities.
    D. I know the duties I'd like to perform, but I can't define a specific job title.
    E. I know definitely what job I desire.

2. Can you identify the occupational field in which you want to find a job?
    A. I would like someone to assess my qualifications and match me with the appropriate fields.
    B. I'm vaguely interested in several fields but don't really know if I am qualified for the opportunities which exist in these fields.
    C. I am looking for a job directly related to my major, but I am interested in learning about placement opportunities in other fields.

D. I have looked into the opportunities within one or more fields and am attempting to make a decision based on job opportunities and my own qualifications.
E. I am certain of the field in which I am seeking employment.

3. Will you have met all of the requirements (education, experience, etc.) for entry into your desired job by the time you wish to be considered for employment?
   A. I am not aware of any specific entry requirements for employment.
   B. I know entry requirements exist for employment, but I don't know what these are or how to meet them.
   C. I have begun to look into entry requirements for employment and am looking into how to meet these requirements.
   D. I know what the entry requirements are for employment and I am in the process of meeting these requirements.
   E. I will have met all of the necessary requirements by the time I wish to be considered for employment.

4. Can you identify a specific geographic region in which you will be seeking employment?
   A. I would prefer to have someome else tell me where I should seek employment.
   B. I have some ideas about where I'll be seeking employment, but I can't be specific.
   C. I am interested in finding out about job opportunities in various geographic areas before stating a preference.
   D. I have narrowed my geographic preference to a few options which I am currently considering.
   E. I have definitely decided on the geographic area or areas in which I will be seeking employment.

5. Have you developed a resume which you are certain is effective with employers?
   A. I am not aware of the need for a resume.
   B. I know I should have a resume, but I have not yet developed one.
   C. I am currently seeking out information about how to construct a resume.
   D. I have a rough draft of a resume but would like help in assessing its effectiveness.
   E. I have developed a resume which I am certain is effective with employers.

6. Do you think you are able to interview effectively with employers?
   A. I have not considered the possibility of being interviewed for jobs.
   B. I don't know what is involved in effective interviewing.
   C. I am looking into what I can expect in a job interview and am interested in improving my interviewing skills.

D. I have some knowledge of effective interviewing techniques, but would like to have someone evaluate my skills.
E. I know that I have developed interviewing skills which are effective with employers.

7. Do you have a definite strategy or plan for finding the job you want?
   A. I have not thought about how I will find the job I want.
   B. I have thought about how I might find the job I want, but I have not taken any action toward formalizing my plan.
   C. I am seeking more information about how I might find the job I want.
   D. I have a tentative plan for finding the job I want, but I would like to talk with someone about how effective my plan is likely to be.
   E. I have a definite strategy for finding the job I want and I am confident that my plan will be successful.

8. Have you decided upon the salary you are seeking in a job?
   A. I will accept whatever salary an employer thinks is fair for someone with my qualifications.
   B. I don't know what salary is appropriate for someone with my qualifications.
   C. I am looking into what salary is appropriate for someone with my qualifications.
   D. I am attempting to establish a broad salary range which would be acceptable to me.
   E. I know definitely the salary I am seeking and I am certain that this salary is appropriate for someone with my qualifications.

9. Can you identify which qualifications from your background would support your application for a job?
   A. I am not able to identify any of my qualifications for employment.
   B. I am not certain how my skills and past experiences relate to what I would like to do on a job.
   C. I am exploring ways of identifying how my skills and past experiences relate to future jobs.
   D. I know how my skills and past experiences relate to future jobs, but I would like help in conveying my qualifications to employers.
   E. I am able to clearly state my qualifications for employment.

10. Have you contacted appropriate persons to serve as references in support of your application for employment?
    A. I did not know that I would be expected to ask people for recommendations.
    B. I don't know which people would be appropriate to ask for references.

    C. I am looking into which people would be appropriate to ask for references.
    D. I am trying to decide among several people whom I might ask for references.
    E. I have already selected people whom I would like to write my letters of recommendations.

Figure 6. Hull job placement readiness inventory*

Copyright 1979 by Sara Hull. Reprinted by permission.

PROBLEMS AND ISSUES IN CAREER PLANNING/PLACEMENT EVALUATION

Career specialists encounter many of the same problems as other student services practitioners in evaluating programs and activities. Earlier chapters have dealt with common problems such as defining goals and objectives with enough specificity to allow for evaluation, selecting the appropriate design, and constructing adequate evaluation instruments. Another problem in conducting evaluations of career planning and placement is the actual collection of data. Students, faculty, administrators, alumni, and employers may not place a high priority on responding to solicitations for input into improving the office functions. Those who do cooperate are likely to be biased toward the service as inferred by their willingness to give the time to provide feedback. In spite of these common, persistent problems, evaluators must continue in their efforts.

    Career planning and placement offices are constantly develping new programs to respond to student needs associated with the changing employment market. As a result of the pressure to develop more and better services, often less time is devoted to systematic evaluation of existing programs. It is conceivable that a service which has existed for many years may be overlooked in the evaluation process which focuses on planning and modifying new offerings. For example, an outdated system for registering seniors with the placement service may go unnoticed if the evaluation focuses on more recent program additions.

    Evaluation must be perceived as a positive component in office procedures rather than as a bothersome additional step. Evaluations can offer insights into efficiency of delivering services as well as into the effectiveness of the office as a whole. For example, if evaluations of a workshop for 50 people indicated that the same objectives were reached to the same degree as in a seminar for 10 students, then future program revisions could streamline service delivery by addressing students in large groups rather than in several small seminars.

SUMMARY

Carreer planning and placement services must continue to clarify their mission in higher education. To the extent that this mission can be articulated to student consumers and other constituents (faculty, employers, alumni, and administrators), a greater infusion into the educational mainstream could be expected.

The need to identify specific, measurable goals is the central issue in career programming. Goal-specified feedback is essential to insure that program planning is systematic and responsive. The primary foci should be on: (1) assessing needs, (2) developing and implementing programs, (3) evaluating, (4) report writing, (5) eliciting and disseminating feedback, (6) incorporating feedback and (7) re-examining the entire process.

There are many options available to the evaluator of career services. It is important to review evaluation methodologies (Chapters 2 and 3) in order to appropriately select a design which is compatible with the purposes of the evaluation.

Career planning and placement services may be considered to be effective if graduates: (1) have acquired skills necessary for job searches, job acquisition, and job maintainance, (2) are prepared for life transitions, (3) can apply the academic skills acquired in college to the job, (4) are able to experience intrinsic and extrinsic satisfactions on the job, (5) value the balance of work, continuing education, and leisure, and (6) maintain a healthy, active alumni identity with their institutions.

Program organization and implementation, execution of the evaluation design, data analysis, report writing, and dissemination become routinized once the procedures outlined in this chapter have been established. The entire undertaking could, however, be less influential if the career center staff fails to use the evaluation data to improve services. Program changes should lead to program re-evaluation, advancing the entire process into a new, improved cycle.

REFERENCES

Anderson, B., Ball, S., Murphy, R. T., & Associates. *Encyclopedia of educational evaluation.* San Francisco: Jossey-Bass, 1975.

Blaska, B., & Schmidt, M. R. Placement. In W. T. Packwood (Ed.), *College student personnel services.* Springfield, IL: Thomas, 1977.

Edwards, R. M. Faculty members need placement participation. *Journal of College Placement,* 1968, *28* (4), 46-49.

Fischer, G., Jr. *Assessment of job placement services in colleges with pre-dominantly black students.* Irvine, California: Ultra Systems, 1976.

Hull, S. B. *A comparative assessment of the job placement readiness of college seniors.* Unpublished doctoral dissertation, University of Iowa, 1979.

Sovilla, E. S. A new functional balance for career planning activities in the 1970's. *Journal of College Placement,* 1972, *33* (1), 62-66.

Stevens, N. D. The relationship of placement readiness to placement success. (Doctoral dissertation, New York University, 1960). *Dissertation Abstracts,* 1960, *21,* 1251. (University Microfilm No. 60-3761)

Thomas, W. G. Placement's role in the university. *Journal of College Placement,* 1966, *26* (4), 87-92.

10
THE CHIEF STUDENT AFFAIRS ADMINISTRATOR
Robert H. Shaffer

During the last two decades, the evaluation of administrators in higher education has been given increasingly more attention. Various applications of management science such as Management by Objectives, programmed budgeting, and job classification principles particularly embodied accountability procedures. Usually these were instituted by the top administrators and applied to lower echelon administrators and to the faculty. As early as the 1950s, the National Student Association identified faculty evaluation as a major national program emphasis. Only recently, however, has evaluation of top administrators been included in the general movement. A number of universities now regularly review the administrative performance of the president and other chief administrative officers. Given the current emphasis on accountability in higher education in an era of diminishing resources, governing boards and top administrators can be considered negligent if they do not insist upon formal programs of administrative review.

WHO SHOULD EVALUATE THE CHIEF STUDENT AFFAIRS ADMINISTRATOR?

The performance of the chief administrator of student affairs is inevitably subject to continuous scrutiny by a wide variety of constituencies. The president and governing board come immediately to mind when issues such as continuation of contract, promotion and salary are considered. However, this formal evaluation is often influenced by formal and informal judgments and comments from a wide range of other individuals; e.g., spouses, colleagues, neighbors, etc. The evaluative criteria used by these "other" individuals are often vague, nonverbalized, limited in perspective, and distorted by personal interests and concerns. To say that the situation should be different, however, is unrealistic.

Therefore, it is important and in the best interests of chief student affairs administrators to support implementation of formal systems of evaluation in their institutions. Formal evaluations can not replace the continual, informal process but they do broaden perspective, encourage fairness, and require verbalized and, preferably, consensually validated evaluation criteria.

Since in most situations the institution's president is the key superior and nominal employer, it would appear that a conference regarding job review and performance should be held not less than once a year. Many individuals, particularly in their early years of employment, might feel the need for two or three conferences a year. The specific number would have to be determined by the preferences and administrative style of the president and other key administrators. However, it is important to recognize the importance of such conferences and to develop an expectation within the institution that they will take place periodically. In this way the tendency for such meetings to be used to discuss crises and transient developments can be minimized and evaluative inputs from diverse sources can be interpreted relatively objectively.

Formal performance reviews in which all relevant publics and constituencies may participate should be held as a regular component of the institution-wide review of administrative performance. An ongoing program of periodic reviews reduces the danger that the initiation of evaluation is seen as a vote of "no confidence" or a reflection of an administrative crisis. Where only the student affairs administrator is to be reviewed under an *ad hoc* procedure, the appearance of doubt regarding performance or even antagonism in the process is often present. As emphasized in this chapter, the dominant purpose of evaluation is increased personal and professional effectiveness and growth, not merely to pass judgment upon satisfactory or unsatisfactory job performance (see Chapter 12). Consequently an established administrative reveiw visible to all publics in the campus community is essential for institutional effectiveness as well as for the personal and professional effectiveness and growth of all administrators.

THE PROBLEM OF CHANGING CRITERIA

It is difficult (and unfair!) to play a game while the rules of the game are being changed while one is playing it. Yet that is almost precisely the situation involving the administration of student affairs on many campuses. The 1960s and 1970s resulted in new expectations for divisions of student affairs and new criteria for judging their value and effectiveness. The student affairs administrator should have written consensually validated job performance criteria. Otherwise, the evaluations which occur inevitably will be based upon unknown or vague criteria and domination by the most visable or outspoken groups and individuals participating in the evaluative process.

Perhaps no other aspect of academe has changed as markedly within the last 15 years as has student life. There have been changes in student life styles, designation of students as adults, acceptance by society of vastly different standards of behavior, and more heterogeneous student bodies. These and similar factors often require novel and non-traditional responses. Yet many student affairs administrators are being judged by criteria and perspectives typical of earlier decades. Consequently, many of the criticisms of student affairs programs are based on the use of obsolete criteria or on the continuation of obsolete practices demanded by one or more publics to whom chief student affairs administrators and their operations are accountable.

Another reason student affairs administrators are often under pressure is that the variety of interest groups which have a legitimate concern for the administration of student affairs is wider than for almost any other field in academe. It is a generally accepted principle that all constituencies with whom the chief student affairs administrator interacts and who have a legitimate concern for the quality of campus life in a particular institution should be involved in the review and evaluation of that individual's work. Obviously, this principle would suggest that not only the governing board, other general administrators, faculty and students be involved, but also that representatives of the sponsoring constituency, alumni, parents, subordinate staff and perhaps civic leaders should be included in the process.

The appropriateness of involving representatives of such a wide variety of constituencies must be determined in the light of each specific institutional situation. However, failure to include a particular interested constituency may result in subsequent challenges to the legitimacy of the evaluation, visible disagreement with summative judgments, and the gnawing, carping criticism which can undermine even the most efficient organization.

An example of shifting criteria or at least different criteria being used for a specific activity occured on a campus of a large complex state university. The chief student affairs administrator with the support and cooperation of several leading faculty members and some administrative officials overcame vigorous opposition to create a "Hyde Park" on the campus where any point of view – regardless of its political taint, social acceptability or method of delivery – could be expressed. The process took almost two years and finally was approved by the top governing board only to have the action questioned because of its potential to limit freedom of speech to a particular area of the campus. Therefore, the recommendation was challenged as an unconstitutional limitation on assembly and expression. Some of the specific faculty members who lobbied for the creation of an area for demonstrations and expression of free speech supported the subsequent challenge and criticisms. The fact that social mores and standards are reviewed and refined through such a process is little solace to harried administrators who perhaps think they are performing adequately only to be judged and challenged by a particular constituency as ineffectual or incompetent.

Not only are the bases of criteria for evaluating the work of the chief student affairs administrator ephemeral and the relevant and interested constituent groups varied, but the reference points for evaluating the administration of student affairs are vague. It is difficult to compare the chief student affairs administrator with predecessors because of changing times and conditions. There is usually no other individual in a similar or comparable position with the institutional setting to which an incumbent can be compared. Performance expectations vary widely from one constituency to another, often within the same campus, and certainly within the regional and national context. It would appear that the most logical grounds for evaluation would be an incumbent's own performance goals established in conference with significant others such as the president, coordinate administrative officers, and perhaps other individuals designated by them. Only with such reference points can any discrepancy between actual and expected or desired performance be identified, assessed, and judged.

CRITERIA TO BE USED IN EVALUATING THE ADMINISTRATOR OF STUDENT AFFAIRS

In a discussion of the evaluation of college and university administrators, Fisher (1977) emphasized personnel evaluation as a process of assessing individual performance and making a value judgment concerning this assessment for the benefit of both the individual and the organization. The assessment of individual performance serves to identify areas of needed or desired individual improvement. The value judgment component compares performance with consensually validated criteria and parallels the assessment component in identifying areas of personal and professional improvement.

As stated previously, evaluation of individual performance is continuous, usually informal, and often haphazard. A structured, planned process, however, can provide a concrete foundation, greater breadth and fairness, and increased effectiveness. There will be differences in expectancies and judgment even with the most meticulous effort to establish clear criteria and an orderly process. However, the establishment of criteria is an essential element of an evaluative program. With such a program at work, discrepencies between the goals of chief student affairs administrators and performance expectations of the president, board members, faculty, students, alumni, parents and subordinates can at least be placed in perspective. Rarely will differences in the expectancies of these constituencies be completely resolved due to the ambiguous nature of the chief student affairs administrator's position as it is perceived by the campus community (Rickard, 1972). It fact, one of the evaluative criteria which may be used is the manner in which the chief student affairs administrator deals with differences in performance expectations!

Agreements regarding expectations and goal performance obviously should be verbalized specifically and placed in writing. Often it is difficult to draft precise job descriptions for administrators in colleges and universities. Therefore, the document may consist more of role definitions and expectations than specific job descriptions in a technical sense.

Difficult as it is to describe clearly the criteria to be used, it is most important to make every effort to do so to keep disagreement to a minimum. In student affairs, new challenges or issues often surface for which there are few precedents. The slow and cumbersome nature of the collegial process on some campuses often makes it extremely difficult to involve all relevant parties in the process as traditional academic expectations would demand. For example, the chief student affairs administrator is frequently in the position of having to make policy decisions in the late spring and summer for the following fall. Yet on many campuses it is difficult if not impossible to consult with relevant student and even faculty representatives before decisions must be made. Procedural ambiguity and conflicting demands become significant issues although they may be unstated evaluative criteria (Cohen & March, 1974).

AREAS TO BE COVERED IN EVALUATIONS

In an effort to identify salient evaluation concerns, a letter was sent to approximately 20 chief student affairs administrators in large institutions and 20 in relatively small institutions. The letter simply requested that the respondents list three or four aspects of their work which should be included in any formal evaluation of their effectiveness at the end of the 1978-79 academic year.

An unstated hypothesis was that there would be differences between the responses of the chief student affairs administrators in large and small institutions. This hypothesis was not confirmed as there was remarkable unanimity in the responses from officers at both large and small institutions. In only one or two responses could a reader discern whether the respondent was fom a large or small institution. Therefore, evaluative procedures discussed here apparently would be applicable to administration of both large and small institutions. The responses are presented in four sections: (1) staff development and leadership, (2) administrative competencies, (3) institutional contributions, and (4) student concerns and relationships. Obviously, these headings are arbitrary. However, they provide a framework for evaluating the work of the chief student affairs administrator.

STAFF DEVELOPMENT AND LEADERSHIP

Almost every respondent included a comment about staff development and productivity as one of the criteria to be used in evaluating the work of the chief student affairs administrator. Suggestions included: the extent to which administrators inspired their staffs to high levels of performance; initiative and assumption of professional responsibilities; and the ability to supervise and promote professional development within the division. Several mentioned that the visible existence and implementation of staff development programs directed to the professional and personal development of the staff would be an important criterion. Most implied that the continued growth and development of the chief student affairs administrator was also an important element as it was perceived to be related to the growth and stimulation of staff members. Another respondent listed as a possible criterion the professional accomplishments and productivity of the student affairs staff. Related to these concerns were the criteria involving the chief administrator's skills and abilities to motivate and reinforce staff members to exercise initiative and assume responsibility.

Encouraging staff growth and development is not new to the administration of student affairs. Truitt and Gross (1966) emphasized the importance of staff development as an essential aspect to the total student affairs program. Shaffer (1972) and Stamatakos and Oliaro (1972) among others have written specifically to this point. In spite of its importance, many administrators still perceive staff development programs as little more than occasional staff meetings, periodic memoranda, or informal visits with staff.

Another group of responses related to staff development might be classified under the general heading of leadership. An example of a criterion under this heading was stated as "the degree to which I as chief student affairs officer provide conceptual leadership in the student affairs area to my divisional staff as well as to the total institution." Another respondent listed visibility on the campus and the degree to which the chief student affairs administrator attempted to interpret the student development philosophy throughout the institution and all of its activities. Still another reply related professional leadership to the inspiration and motivation of staff members. An elaboration of this criterion was suggested by another who desired to be evaluated on the basis of the effectiveness of his leadership to the various publics of student affairs.

The existence of a systematic and effectively implemented staff development program seemed to be an essential and almost unanimously recognized criterion for the evaluation of chief student affairs administrators.

ADMINISTRATIVE COMPETENCIES

Administrative competencies were listed by most of the respondents as bases for judging the effectiveness of their work. Items included under this heading were: (1) goal setting, (2) budget and resource management, (3) fiscal responsibility and accountability, (4) manpower management, (5) problem solving and issue resolution, (6) personnel management, and (7) planning and coordinating divisional activities. These items, of course, are included on most lists of administrative skills required for effective administration (see Gulick, Urwick, 1937). Procedures required by due process and sound administrative practice require supervisors to carefully document their activities with personnel. The administrative competency involved required the careful development and implementation of personnel evaluative procedures within the division and at the same time careful, consciously planned steps to prevent such procedures from contributing to deterioration of effective and productive staff relationships.

Objectivity and aggressiveness in representing the student affairs area to the total institution is a related competency. As the executive vice president of a complex urban university commented in another context, "I want a chief student affairs officer who will present the needs of the student area as thoroughly, objectively, and aggressively as the representatives of other areas of the university do. Without that type of representation, it is impossible for me at least to make valid judgments."

Another respondent suggested that he be evaluated according to the degree to which department and program heads had successfully implemented and executed an effective student affairs program. The emphasis upon effective work through and with staff members obviously follows logically with the respondents' emphasis upon staff development as a major responsibility. Utilizing professional and paraprofessional staff effectively appears to be a major challenge to many administrators.

Still another respondent suggested the area of communication as an important aspect of any set of evaluative criteria. This comment emphasized the importance of the chief student affairs administrator's ability to communicate institutional policies to various staff members, students, and various other publics to which they are responsible.

Contribution To The Total Institution

As with the two preceding components, the contribution of the chief student affairs administrator to the institution was attended to by most respondents. Obviously such a global aspect of an administrator's work is difficult to assess. Several respondents focused upon the degree to which the work and effort of the student affairs division was integrated with institutional objectives and needs.

Another respondent suggested that any evaluation of chief student affairs administrators should include the division's contribution to the achievement of institutional goals. Related aspects included the level of institution-wide awareness, involvement of the student affairs staff in total institutional concerns, the direction and coordination the chief student affairs administrator gave to division-sponsored programs and activities, and their relationship to the academic programs of the institution. Several indicated that they would want to be evaluated on the basis of their relationship to others in the institutional community. In this respect, they paralleled the responses to the study by Dutton, Appleton and Birch (1970) in which presidents listed relationships with faculty as an essential element in their judging the effectiveness of their chief student affairs officer.

Interpreting the nature and characteristics of students and their needs to the business, academic, and development areas of the institution was suggested by several respondents. A related suggestion involved the degree to which programs and activities were responsive to the changing characteristics of the student clientele of the institution.

The specific criteria used to evaluate a chief student affairs administrator may vary from one setting to another. However, it is clear that their contributions to the total effort of their institutions are viewed as being significant and important aspects of their evaluation.

STUDENT RELATIONS

Another major category for which a large number of respondents suggested criteria was that of student relationships. A number of responses were concerned with the ability to understand, communicate, and respond to the needs of students. One administrator specifically stipulated that he would want to be judged in part upon the degree to which student needs at his institution were recognized and that the student affairs division responded to them. A number referred to the task of establishing procedures to assess and respond to the needs of nontraditonal students. For example, the reorientation of existing services to needs of non-traditonal and specialized clientele was listed as an important aspect of maintaining effective student relationships and service. One respondent commented that the non-negotiable demands of some militant protests of the 1960s' really meant "listen to us." He hoped that his organization currently had an openness and receptivity which would make it unnecessary for new needs and concerns to be recognized only through protest activity.

Some observers have commented that student leaders — militants particularly — feel that the only way they can maintain student support and credibility is to attack the administration, usually the office of student affairs. Entering into dialogue with such students would seem to be essential in view of the greater diversity of students and the increasing range of needs and interests.

Student relationships are the very essence of effective student affairs work in most colleges and universities. The evaluative criteria related to the administrator's effectiveness in this area should, therefore, be based upon the effectiveness of the administrator in establishing policies and procedures for continuous assessment of student needs, successful outreach to various types of students, involving students in institutional activities, and concerned, responsive communication with students.

SELF EVALUATION AS THE INITIAL STEP IN THE EVALUATIVE PROCESS

The first step in the evaluation process is self assessment by an individual administrator. The following are examples of evaluative questions which might be used in an annual self evaluation of the chief student affairs administrator. These and similar questions and topics could then provide a basis for an evaluative conference with the president, other relevant administrative officers within the institution, or even representative members of the divisional staff.

STAFF DEVELOPMENT AND LEADERSHIP

A. Is there a visible and systematically planned and implemented staff development program on my campus?

B. Have I continued my own professional development not only as a model for my staff but also to enable me to lead the various members of my staff in their continued development?

C. Do I encourage the members of my staff to exercise initiative and assume responsibility?

D. Do I recognize, stimulate, and facilitate professional accomplishments and contributions by members of my staff?

E. In what ways have I provided opportunities and encouragement for members of my staff to have professional interaction and development?

F. Are the staff development efforts of my organization based on clearly verbalized objectives, known and accepted by all staff members?

G. Are my staff members involved in the organization and operation of the staff development program?

H. Do my organization and administrative styles function effectively under ambiguous and changing conditions or do I have rigid, planned procedures for responding to all situations?

I. What specific steps or methods can I cite as evidence that I have provided professional and conceptual leadership to my staff and institution this past year?

J. In what specific ways is my leadership of student affairs visible to my staff and to other segments of the institution?

K. Have I taken any specific, consciously planned steps this past year to inspire and motivate my staff?

ADMINISTRATIVE COMPETENCIES

A. Does my division have written objectives known and available to all staff members?

B. Did the various staff members participate in establishing division objectives?

C. Did the staff members of the division participate in establishing evaluative criteria to be used in judging the degree to which the division achieved its objectives?

D. Have I periodically discussed my budget management record and methods with the appropriate individuals within the institution?

E. In what specific planning activities have I and my staff engaged this past year?

F. Have I established a clear and visible evaluative procedure for all staff members?

G. In what ways have I specifically presented to the institutional community new needs, characteristics, points of view, and expectations of current students?

H. In what ways have I involved staff department and program heads in total divisional and institutional efforts?

CONTRIBUTION TO THE TOTAL INSTITUTION

A. What policies, procedures, and activities can I cite as evidence of contribution to the institution's mission by the student affairs division?

B. In what ways have I and my staff taken specific steps to integrate our programs and activities with those of the total institution?

C. What specific steps have I and the staff taken to integrate our efforts more closely with those of the faculty and academic administrators?

D. During the past year, have I and my staff members discussed our work with faculty and other administrators regarding the integration and coordination of student affairs with other aspects of the institution?

E. In what specific ways have I presented the views of my staff to other administrative officers and faculty members during the past year, and in what ways have I presented their views to my staff members?

STUDENT RELATIONS

A. What evaluative procedures have I and the members of my

staff followed this past year to assess the nature and quality of our student relationships?

B. What do I know about the needs, aspirations, and other characteristics of students on the campus this past year?

C. What specific policies and procedures do we follow to ascertain and respond to new needs, changing desires, and different characteristics of students which might be different from past years?

D. What specific outreach activities and procedures can I cite as being representative of the division's desire to be responsive to all types of students?

E. With what new or different student groups have I worked this past year?

The preceding list of evaluative questions may require modification to be applicable to individual situations and specific institutional settings. It is important, however, to use a wide range of probing questions in order to broaden perceptions and contribute most effectively to personal and professional growth. Chief student affairs administrators who are continuing to grow are in the best position to contribute to the continued growth of their staff. Evaluation perceived as the basis for growth and increased professional achievement thus becomes challenging, exciting, and supportive as opposed to the all-too-common perception of evaluation as antagonistic, threatening, and purely judgmental.

REFERENCES

Cohen, M.D., & March, J.G. *Leadership and ambiguity: The American college president.* New York: McGraw-Hill, 1974.

Dutton, T., Appleton, J.R., & Birch, E.E. *Assumptions and beliefs of selected members of the academic community.* (Monograph #3), Portland, Oregon: National Association of Student Personnel Administrators, 1970.

Fisher, C.F. *The evaluation and development of college and university administrators* (ERIC/Higher Education Research Currents). Washington, D.C.: American Association for Higher Education, 1977.

Gulick, L., & Urwick, L. *Papers on the science of administration.* New York: Institute of Public Administration, 1937.

Rickard, S.T. The role of the chief student personnel administrator revisited. *NASPA Journal,* 1972, *9,* 219-226.

Shaffer, R.H. Staff development — key to survival. *NASPA Journal,* 1972, *9,* 261-262.

Stamatakos, L.C., & Oliaro, P.M. In-service development: A function of student personnel. *NASPA Journal,* 1972, *9,* 269-273.

Truitt, J.W., & Gross, R.F. *Professional development in student personnel work through in-service education.* (NASPA Bulletin #1), Portland, Oregon: The National Association of Student Personnel Administrators, 1966.

11
EVALUATING EXPERIMENTAL STUDENT AFFAIRS PROGRAMS

Carl L. Harshman

A chapter designated specifically for the evaluation of experimental programs can be misleading if it is expected that the *design* or *approach* to evaluation differs from those used in established programs. In reality, evaluations of experimental programs are designed and implemented in a manner similar to that for established programs. However, it is important to note that the *content* of the evaluations may differ. The questions asked, the values on which the program is based, and the kinds of evidence sought will probably (but not necessarily) be a function of the program under study. The similarities and differences in evaluation of experimental and established programs are the primary foci of this chapter.

The goals of this chapter are: (1) To present a systems approach to evaluation and the particular issues related to each systems stage or component; (2) To outline the basic activities of evaluation which apply to the various system components; (3) To stimulate new thinking about questions and values, sources of evidence, and judgments in evaluation.

The chapter is divided into two sections. The first addresses the design of evaluation; the second presents specific applications to experimental student affairs programs.

THE ACTIVITIES OF EVALUATION

A model for evaluation is developed by combining the activities of evaluation with the decisions or program components toward which these activities are directed.

The conceptual basis of this chapter resulted from a project funded by the Ford Foundation and directed by Rev. Paul C. Reinert, S.J. The project was conceived to develop a model for assessing the quality of nontraditional programs in higher education. Copies of the project report are available from the author on request.

Evaluation has been described in a variety of ways ranging from measurement to a judgment about the quality (relative goodness or effectiveness) of an effort. Some evaluation models emphasize the congruence between stated purposes and actual outcomes while one is reported to be goal-free and responsive to issues relevant to various program participants (see Chapter 3).

There are, however, three kinds of activities common to all evaluations: (1) stating the questions or articulating values; (2) identifying and collecting relevant evidence; and (3) judging and recommending; i.e., looking at the questions and values in light of the evidence and deciding how the judgments affect the program.

ASKING QUESTIONS/ARTICULATING VALUES

Determining what issues are at stake is the first step in designing the evaluation. Why is it being done? How will the evaluation data be used? The evaluation may simply test the extent to which stated goals and objectives have been accomplished. A more complex approach might have decision-makers, program administrators, and/or other relevant publics identify questions that are important. Suppose, for example, a new computerized career information system was installed and an evaluation was requested. If concise objectives had been stated (e.g., "The system will be utilized by 100 students per month," "Four out of five students who use the system will become aware of a new career cluster as a result"), and the primary issue or question was whether these criteria were met, then the objectives might become the cornerstone of the evaluation. If, on the other hand, the question-approach had been taken, the following questions might result:

(1) Is the machine more cost-effective than people? (2) Do students prefer people to the machine or vice versa? (3) Does it appear that the system will positively impact the career development of students?

Related to stating relevant questions is the articulation of values. Evaluation questions (whether stated as objectives or in interrogative form) imply or express values. Consider question number one above. The key word for determining pertinent values is "effectiveness." If effectiveness means simply a high volume of student use (many administrators take pride in large numbers) without concern for other qualities such as satisfaction or impact on careers, then one set of values exists. If, however, satisfaction with the experience is the main measure of effectiveness, another set of values exists. The ability to ask clear, relevant questions and to make explicit the values behind a program are essential to the further design and ultimately to the successful conduct of evaluations.

EVIDENCE

The term in this context is broader than data. The term "data" tends to suggest statistics, numbers, and paper-and-pencil instrumentation. Here the use of the word *evidence* is intended to convey a concept more encompassing than the notion of data.

In the past many evaluations were based almost entirely on data generated by standardized instruments. Even when evaluative information came from other sources, the options selected were neither creative nor extensive (e.g., dropout rates, GPA, admission to graduate school). The concept of evidence yields many more possibilities. Evidence may also come from observation (e.g., a speaker's effectiveness or length of presentation can be estimated by watching the audience's body movements), interviews (the opportunity to talk out a response instead of circling "1-5" often makes a difference in interpretation), and perceptions of participants, administrators, observers, and others are often critical evidence in various aspects of the evaluation (see Kunkel & Tucker, 1976).

There is one additional point about evidence. As often as possible more than one measure of a phenomenon (multiple sources of data) should be used in order to accumulate sufficient evidence. Many settings require at least two measures of a given construct or phenomenon. In other settings, more than two may be desirable. The profession may be haunted for the rest of this century by the heavy reliance in the 50s and 60s on grade point average (GPA) as the measure of success. More than one successful program was terminated because of its failure to yield a significantly higher GPA at $p.05$. The use of creative and relevant evidence in evaluations should increase the utility of those evaluations.

JUDGMENTS AND RECOMMENDATIONS

The activities of judging and recommending are the points at which the evaluation is linked to future program operation. Once questions are asked and evidence is gathered, the final phase of the evaluation begins. This phase involves three steps:

Step 1. The questions are considered in light of the evidence and conclusions that are drawn. The conclusions normally fall within one of three categories: positive, negative, or unable to be determined.

For example, assume the question, "What is the dropout rate in XYZ program?" has been asked. The issue is whether the rate is consistent with other programs of that type and whether the program is functioning well (a high dropout rate is negative evidence; a low rate is positive evidence). In this case assume the evidence is merely the percent of dropouts each academic term.

Further, assume the evaluation revealed that the average dropout rate per academic term was 32%. A conclusion in this case is difficult to make until further information is available. If the data are for undergraduate enrollments in a primarily residential undergraduate school, then the conclusion might be negative since the dropout rate is above average. On the other hand, if we are looking at day undergraduates on a commuting campus or at an evening program for working adults, the conclusions might be different. For the sake of discussion, assume this program is for working adults, for which the average dropout rate per term is between 35-45%. If this were the case, it appears that this program is functioning well (assuming an average or below average dropout rate is of value).

Step 2. Causal analysis occurs; i.e., inferences are made about the relationship between variables (determined primarily by the category of evaluation taking place) and the questions/evidence under study.

If in the example above (Step 1) the dropout rate was of prime concern, then it is important to ascertain why it is below average. Are there particular aspects of the program which encourage persistence? Are the participants better matched to the experience than in other cases? Is the goal or reward structure more appropriate than in other cases?

Rarely will this analysis identify a direct relationship between the cause and the observed effect. The process is, however, invaluable to future planning and decisions (Note: The fact that the evidence for the dropout phenomenon was represented by a single variable made drawing a conclusion and causal analysis more difficult. A second measure such as participants' perceptions of the program might help in both cases).

Step 3. The conclusions and cause/effect analysis are used to develop recommendations for the future of the program. The final step ties the evaluation directly into the operation of the program.

Presume that the conclusion in the above example was that the program had a better than expected dropout rate. Further, the analysis of cause-and-effect resulted in a feeling that having prospective participants do a personal goals analysis resulted in a better self-selection process. That is, people who were more likely to drop out if they enrolled had more often than not simply chosen not to participate. In this case, there could have been two recommendations: (1) to reinforce the goals analysis activity in the program in order to determine if the causal hypothesis is correct, and (2) to add a second measure to the evidence on dropouts in the future; e.g., interviews.

THE OPERATION OF PROGRAMS

An open systems perspective of organizations and programs describes how programs operate and is, therefore, helpful in conceptualizing an evaluation design. The systems perspective can be visualized as follows:

1. ENVIRONMENTS

2. INPUTS -------> 3. THE PROGRAM <---- 4. OUTCOMES

The terms used to label some components of an open system are in some cases the same as or similar to the terms used in constructing the CIPP model for evaluation (Stufflebeam, Foley, Gephart, Guba, Hammond, Merriman & Provus, 1971). The similarity arises out of the fact that the CIPP model is based on the program planning cycle which is not unlike the flow in an open system. There are four major components in the systems view: environments, inputs, the program, and outcomes. In the following paragraphs each is defined and its relationship to program evaluation is explaned.

ENVIRONMENTS

Environments is the label used to represent the multiple contexts within which a program operates or to identify the constituents to which it must respond. Depending upon the definition of "program" there can be many contexts/constituencies and levels of complexity within them. If, for example, a counseling center is considered a program, then there are at a minimum the following environments and constituencies (in increasing order of complexity): (1) student affairs division; (2) the student body; (3) the institution; (4) the community (surrounding area, i.e., neighborhood, town, or city); (5) the state; (6) higher education; and (7) the federal government.

Each of these directly or indirectly influences to varying degrees the structure and operation of the program. Continuous evaluation of contexts is important because (a) awareness of context is essential for successful programs, and (b) the accuracy of that awareness should be positively correlated to the rate and duration of success.

In this model, it is generally assumed that the nearer the particular environment to the program, the more influence the environment will exert. In the case of the aforementioned counseling center, the student affairs division (through budget, staffing, reward structures, etc.) and student body (through use, student government pressure, protest or the like) will probably exert the greatest influence, while the federal government and trends in higher education will have the least.

It is possible to envision contexts or constituents in layers or levels and thus get a perspective on their relationship to each other and to a program. An awareness of the influences exerted by each context and the relationship of that influence to the structure and conduct of a program are the keys to environmental evaluation.

INPUTS

In this model, inputs are defined as those people (or institutions) who (which) are served by a program and who are expected to be changed in some way by it. If we were evaluating a faculty or an institution for its community service activities, the entire community (or various parts of it) might be defined as input. For the entire community, input would include business, organizations, and economy as well as people. In student affairs, however, we are likely to deal primarily with people. Some systems schemes and evaluation models also treat materials, staff, etc., as inputs. In this model these items are a part of the program category, thus eliminating some potential confusion.

The need to evaluate students' characteristics (needs, aspirations, abilities, etc.) as inputs is considered essential to the design of a successful program. It seems, for example, that traditionally organized student activities on a commuter campus are less well attended than those on a predominantly residential campus. The reasons vary for less participation but may include: (a) many commuter students hold part-time jobs and they have little time for activities; (b) commuting students maintain friendships with pre-college acquaintances and are less in need of the social referent group provided by student activities; and (c) activities are often structured and scheduled in a manner which is inconvenient to commuting students who may have transportation problems. If a program is already operational (rather than merely in the design phase), evaluation of inputs is used to make modifications in the program. For example, assume a faculty member has been teaching a course which requires a significant amount of writing by students. If the writing skills of students are declining each year, the professor may have to make adjustments to accommodate changes. Adjustments might include: (a) structuring the course to require less writing; (b) adding a supplementary writing skills component; or (c) screening students the first day of class and, if a minimum skill level is not exhibited, recommend that students improve skills prior to enrolling. In this systems component the evaluation focuses on the target population's needs, characteristics, and expectations and the extent to which these data are linked to program structure and operation.

The Program

This category includes all the elements involved in the operation of a program and is concerned with their arrangement (structure), as well as with the ways in which the components interact with themselves and with their target groups (functioning).

The structure of a program consists of a large number of components. Some are listed here:

Goals (clearly stated, related to needs);
Organization (efficient, effective);
Staff (competent, trained, enthusiastic);
Literature/Materials (appropriate, interesting);
Budget (sufficient, appropriately allocated);

Program Activity (related to goals, interesting).

In parentheses following the program components are sample qualities or characteristics which might be applied to them. For example, if goals were being evaluated, qualities such as *clarity* and logical *relationship to need* might be sought. Examples of staff values which might be applied are competence, prior training, and morale. Of course, not all components exist in all programs nor do all that exist have to be evaluated.

Structure is defined as the components of and manner in which the program is organized. Functioning is the interaction of program components during operation. In this care, structure is a static concept; function is a dynamic one. In a course, functioning might include the delivery of a lecture or the interaction between instructor and students, while structure could be the syllabus, text, and content of examinations.

The evaluation of the functioning of a program is important because it is often assumed that if certain structural characteristics exist, then the program will function well. However, what happens if an Ivy League, research-oriented professor is placed in a community college classroom in downtown Los Angeles? There is a possibility that the professor is mismatched with the clientele and it should not be assumed that everything will go well just because the professor was well-qualified according to some standards. The evaluation of program functioning is an essential element not only for judging the quality of the program but also for doing the cause-effect analysis in the evaluation of outcomes.

OUTCOMES

The work of the National Center for Higher Education Management Systems (NCHEMS) has been helpful in conceptualizing outcomes. Outcomes can be divided into two categories – outputs and impacts. In this definition, outputs are viewed as the intended products of a program (e.g., graduates of a college, well-adjusted counselees). Impacts are unintended or indirect effects of a program. If a federal grant to add a new program to a small college resulted in additional staff and hence improved the economy of the small community in which the college is located, the economic benefits to the community would be considered an impact.

Evaluations which look beyond the program tend to concentrate on outputs more often than on impacts. The potential pitfalls are: (a) a tendency to avoid evaluating outcomes; and (b) choosing limited or inappropriate outputs of a program. The most universal example of evaluating everything but outcomes is the typical college classroom experience. For years evaluations of instruction were based on faculty credentials, course syllabi, student evaluations and teaching methods. The amount of learning resulting from the course (output) was almost never assessed.

The second problem, limited or inappropriate outcomes, is equally pervasive. For years the universal measure of success was GPA. Many programs did not increase participant's GPA and were terminated because of this shortcoming. The fact is many of those programs may not have influenced GPA under any circumstances, but they may have a positive impact on other variables such as career maturity, sense of community, values, etc. There were numerous programs in the late 1960s designed to reduce attrition. Many advising programs, for example, may well have had a *negative* influence on retention if they resulted in students with more accurately defined personal goals or who had clearly identified a more appropriate educational program. In the former instance, a student may have determined that college was not compatible with the newly clarified goals; in the latter, transfer to another institution may have resulted.

Two final points about the evaluation of outcomes are warranted. First, outputs and impacts may be positive, negative, or neutral. It may be, for example, that for married students additional education results in some psychological distance between student and spouse (who is not getting further education) that is subsequently detrimental to the relationship. The consequences of negative outcomes should be used for future decisions and not necessarily to condemn a program. Second, the cause-effect analysis in the evaluation of outcomes in highly dependent upon evaluations of environment, inputs, and program. Without the other evaluations, outcomes evaluation may be isolated to the point of being useless.

CONCEPTUALIZING THE EVALUATION

Evaluation of experimental programs is conceptualized from a matrix consisting of the activities of evaluation and the four system components (Figure 1). The three activities of evaluation are applied to each system category.

The time at which the evaluation occurs in relation to an experimental program will determine the purpose of the particular evaluation activity. For example, environment and input evaluations can be used to design the program. After a program is operating, evaluation activities provide information for other judgment phases (program or outcomes), for establishing baseline data for other evaluations, and/or for making program modification decisions.

The evaluation of the program itself should occur at pre-specified times in the program cycle and prior to the ending point. Consider a sixteen-week, three-semester-hour class to be a "program." Various kinds of evaluation activities aimed at the program's components might

	System Components			
	Environment	Inputs	Program	Outcomes
THE ACTIVITIES OF EVALUATION				
Asking Questions/ Articulating Values				
Identifying and Gathering Evidence				
Making Judgments & Recommendations				

Figure 1. Conceptualizing the evaluation of experimental programs.

take place from the first through the twelfth weeks. Thereafter, evaluation activities might focus on gathering outcomes data.

Outcomes evaluation by its very nature occurs near the conclusion of or after programs have ended. The notion of "ended" does not have to be taken literally. Program administrators and evaluators can create artificial termination points. For example, the evaluation of a two-year experimental program to reduce freshmen dropouts might monitor dropouts on a term-by-term basis. The scope of evaluation within a system category will depend upon the state of program development and operation and upon the scope of decisions to be made.

It also is important to relate various evaluative categories. For example, as the judgment phase occurs, the analysis should include not only the specific questions and evidence under consideration, but also the questions and evidence from the other categories. In this instance, if outputs are not judged to be satisfactory, a review of the environments, input, and program evaluations may be helpful in determining why.

THE EVALUATION OF EXPERIMENTAL STUDENT AFFAIRS PROGRAMS

This section considers some specific issues related to the evaluation of experimental student affairs programs. The discussion is organized around the four system components presented in the preceding section.

Issues In Evaluation Of Environments

One of the more important forms of evaluation is that which attempts to assess environments. Of all the different contexts, the respective college or university environment is the one most important for most student affairs programs. The reason is fairly obvious. In socio-political terms the academic departments of the institution tend to wield the majority of power and to represent the priority area for the allocation of resources.

Evaluation of context is also important because many experimental programs are *post hoc* additions to established student affairs programs rather than reformulations of them. This phenomenon is a result of several factors. First, it is easier to control the creation, operation, and destiny of experimental programs if they are added to existing programs. Other factors are an organization's need to maintain stability, the ever-present desire to minimize risk, and the availability of external funding; e.g., federal aid, foundation grants, etc. Some major additions to student affairs programs in the past are special advising/counseling programs to reduce attrition, special services programs for culturally different students, and, more recently, career development programs in counseling and placement centers.

In environmental evaluation, it is important to accurately assess the relative importance of a given program to various individuals and constituencies and to translate these assessments into program decisions. The best way to assess environments is to talk directly (interview) with the people who represent various perspectives. If the environment evaluation is being done during planning stages, then a program administrator and external evaluator might conduct interviews. If the evaluation is done while the program is in process, the external interviewer is preferred.

What kinds of questions should be asked? The first might be, "Why do you need this program?" The responses from various persons can be compared and the overall picture compared with needs assessment data. Another question could address the goals of the program. "What are goals or what should they be?" Another might ask how the proposed program is related to the division's or institution's missions and goals.

If during the course of a context evaluation major discrepancies between the program goals and external data are discovered, they must be dealt with as soon as possible. More than a few programs have been terminated prematurely because people thought the program was not meeting certain needs when in reality it was or because major decision-makers held different values about the program than those who operated it.

Issues In Input Evaluation

There is no substitute for accurate, relevant data about potential target populations. A frequent error in program development is that professionals design programs to solve problems which are not appropriately defined.

Probably the most frequent error is identifying a need which is different than the real one (see Chapter 14). A second kind of error is the attribution of "false cause." In this case, the cause of a state or condition is attributed incorrectly and programs are designed to address the perceived (false) cause. The resources expended for retention programs is a classic example. Many administrators and program planners assumed that (a) students wanted to be in college in the first place and (b) if they were properly counseled and advised they would be more likely to stay. While focusing on the lack of adequate counseling/advising as the cause, it probably did not occur to many people that if students were properly counseled, even more might drop out.

The key is to consider the people involved: their characteristics, needs, and/or goals. The less evidence available, the more likely there is to be an error in judgment. For example, a midwestern university

created a three-week summer program in a mountain resort area. It was a failure the first year. An evaluation of potential target groups yielded the following:
1. Of the undergraduate full-time student population (the perceived market), a majority (70%) needed to work full-time during the summer to earn money for the following year.
2. The older, part-time student rarely had a three week period available. (A two week period was the longest period for most; however, many were limited to one week).

In the following year the program was structured into two weeks and more effort was devoted to recruiting older students. Enrollments exceeded goals halfway through registration. The final enrollment was almost twice the goal. When the right questions are asked and sufficient evidence is accumulated, a program can be structured to meet real needs.

The importance of input evaluation in the overall program planning process cannot be overemphasized. Without sufficient and accurate evidence, the probability of program success is decreased.

ISSUES IN EVALUATION OF THE PROGRAM

It is assumed that most of what is currently called evaluation is directed at the program. Included in these efforts are staff evaluations, cost analyses, and surveys of participants. As such, evaluation of this nature is somewhat more common than are the other kinds.

Data about structure and functioning are essential to the final analysis of the program and to the attribution of cause in outcome evaluation. The problem usually encountered in the evaluation of the program is that it is not sufficiently comprehensive. For example, if only two or three dimensions out of a possible 20 are evaluated, there is a high probability that an important aspect of the program will be overlooked. The solution is to broaden the focus of the evaluation thereby reducing the probability of error through oversight.

Suppose that a lecture series in the residence halls resulted in low attendance, a general lack of awareness, and mediocre to poor ratings by those who actually attended. The program was not successful. Why? There are myriad possibilities:
(a) The topics selected were of little interest to students;
(b) Students would prefer to keep academic-like programs out of their living space;
(c) The speakers were not good;
(d) There were competing activities at the same time.

This list is not by any means exhaustive. The extent to which any of these statements or others can be verified or rejected will determine whether the program is repeated. With only the data outlined in the first paragraph there is little hope that the program will survive.

In program evaluation there is an opportunity to be creative in the kinds of evidence considered. The suggestion to build sidewalks over worn paths on the campus green is a classic example of such data. Student dining areas can be places to observe relationships among various subgroups of students. Because how people feel about an experience may be as important as any kind of evidence, students' perceptions are important.

Perhaps the best way to conclude the examination of relevant issues is with an example of some evaluative questions, the values or qualities sought, and one or two kinds of evidence appropriate to answering the questions. Figure 2 portrays three of the elements necessary for evaluating one portion of structure and function. Each question stems from a major concern about the program. The values listed are benchmarks from which the evidence is chosen, gathered, and analyzed. For example, a major criterion for goal statements is clarity. To test the clarity of program goals, evaluators could use third party analysis, interviews with pertinent people, etc.

Evaluation Questions	Values/Qualities	Sources of Evidence
1. How well developed are the program's goals?	The goals should be: —clear —appropriate —agreed upon	a) Review of goal statements b) Interviews with staff c) Compare to context/input data.
2. Is the staff well-qualified?	—trained and oriented —experienced	a) Review of staff development plan b) Review of staff evaluations.
3. How do the students respond to the program?	—program is liked —generated enthusiasm —is visible on campus	a) Attendance b) Students' perceptions c) Extent to which non-participating students are aware of the program.

Figure 2. Examples of structure & function (program) questions, values, and sources of evidence

Issues In Outcomes Evaluation

Of the four kinds of evaluation, this may be the most difficult to implement. There are at least three reasons for this:
   (1) In the past, the failure to reach stated outcome goals was often viewed as failure rather than as feedback to the program. Program administrators, therefore, tended to shy away from outcomes evaluations;

(2) Often there were insufficient outcomes explored (only one or two variables) or the wrong ones were chosen (recall the earlier discussion about grade point average);

(3) Program termination or continuation decisions were often made for reasons other than the outcomes (e.g., the grant expired or the crisis disappeared).

Given the above, it is easy to see why evaluations tend to focus on the way a program functions rather than on its outcomes, and why outcomes evaluation when done is approached with some anxiety.

The student personnel profession has failed to capitalize on current thinking about outcomes. Chickering's (1969) vectors, for example, provided a conceptual framework within which to design output evaluations as well as some measures to use for it. A recent NCHEMS publication (Lenning, Lee, Micek & Service, 1977) provides an even more extensive framework.

Evaluators should not overlook the opportunity to study impacts; i.e., the indirect or unintended results of the program. Recently there was an evaluation of a program involving faculty, students, and student affairs staff. The purpose of the program was to foster students' development of students' values through regular contact with older adult role models. During the evaluation it was learned that one impact of the program was a better understanding of the respective roles and pressures of being a faculty member or student affairs staff member. Even if the program had not affected students' values, the impact on faculty and staff involved might have justified the expenditure of resources. Another important result was the program's positive effect on the reputation of the student affairs division. If a program is visible and works well, then the division's reputation will probably be enhanced as a result of the effort.

Since there is little experience with outcomes evaluation and there are few tested conceptual frameworks for determining outcomes, there will be a slow, evolutionary period to full implementation. It is hoped that the airing of prior limitations as well as a clearer perspective on the place of outcomes evaluation in the entire spectrum of evaluation will encourage more and better outcomes evaluation.

CONCLUSION

This chapter presented a systematic view of evaluation and its importance to experimental programs. Experience has indicated that experimental programs are typically under more pressure to suceed (or continue to exist) than established programs. An inadequate evaluation design may actually hinder program continuation if, indeed, the program ought to be continued. In order to increase the probability that experimental programs become institutionalized, such programs deserve the highest quality evaluation that can be delivered.

REFERENCES

Chickering, A. W. *Education and identity.* San Francisco: Jossey-Bass, 1969.

Kunkel, R., & Tucker, S. *Overview of program evaluation literature and introduction to the perception-based theory of program evaluation.* A paper produced as a part of Project Values in the Department of Education at Saint Louis University, 1976.

Lenning, O., Lee, Y., Micek, S., & Service, A. *A structure for the outcomes of postsecondary education.* Boulder, Co: WICHE/NCHEMS, 1977.

Stufflebeam, D., Foley, W. J., Gephart, W. J., Guba, E. G., Hammond, R., Merriman, H. O., & Provus, M. M. *Educational evaluation and decision-making in education.* Itasca, Ill.: Peacock Publishing, 1971.

12
STAFF EVALUATION
J. Roger Penn

People comprise the most important component of complex organizations including institutions of post-secondary education. The effectiveness of an educational enterprise is measured in human terms; for example, the extent to which educational programs and services make a positive contribution to society. Within the overall structure of a college or university, there is a complex network of interdependent activities related to the administration of the institution. These activities generally fall into two related categories: (1) development processes such as planning, organizing, coordinating; and (2) maintenance processes such as the daily tasks of financial management and personnel management.

Personnel management consists of activities associated with the coordination of the goal-related work efforts of staff. Managers or administrators control the personnel function and are responsible for decisions which directly and indirectly influence the behavior of people within organizations. Since organizations are created and maintained for various reasons, the behavior resulting from an administrator's decision should contribute to the accomplishment of organizational goals. Therefore, it is expected that managers devote a great deal of attention to evaluating the effectiveness of staff in accomplishing tasks and moving the organization toward defined objectives. Although considerable discussion has centered around the issue of assessing staff performance, the fact is that the evaluation of personnel typically occurs in a haphazard fashion. Further, because of the amount of literature and number of theories on this subject, many administrators who wish to implement staff evaluation procedures are confused and bewildered.

If an organization is really in the "people business," its entire operation should reflect an orientation which is responsive to people considerations. Organizational effectiveness depends upon the ability of people to accomplish organizational goals. Therein lies the rationale for effective personnel management. Of course, personnel management is directly concerned with a number of activities associated with the recruitment, selection, utilization, and development of human resources within the organization. Also, central to any plan for the effective utilization of resources within an organization is the reality of division of labor. Through the division of labor, an organization divides various functions into manageable sub-units which are then associated with specific tasks. This process of specialization permits departments and individuals within them to focus on specific work functions which can be performed efficiently and yet are directly related to the mission of the organization.

Within higher education is a sub-division or specialization known as student affairs in which student affairs staff perform specific tasks related to the well-being of an institution and its students. Student affairs as a helping profession has as its major goals the development and maintenance of sound educational environments on college campuses and the provision of quality programs and services for college students. These goals are realized through the effective administration of programs. Unfortunately, the professional preparation of student affairs administrators seldom emphasizes the management of programs and personnel. However, the evaluation of professional staff and their efforts is a critical part of the management and assessment of programs and services that are provided students. Athough the evaluation of staff performance may be unpleasant and difficult, in the final analysis personnel must be accounted for (Robinson, 1962).

This chapter reviews the issues, procedures, and problems associated with evaluating the performance of student affairs staff. For a vice president of student affairs, a dean of students, or a program director concerned with getting things accomplished, the ability to observe and analyze various work processes can be of inestimable value. Therefore, this presentation has been organized into three major sections. The first introduces the use of the staff evaluation process as a management tool. The second explores various reasons for evaluating staff and the resulting benefits. The last section provides an overview of different approaches, procedures, and techniques available for use by administrators.

EVALUATION AS A MANAGEMENT TOOL

A successful administrator must be cognizant of organizational realities in a collective way as well as understand the general state of affairs from moment to moment within an administrative unit. To a considerable extent, the daily tasks of the chief student affairs officer at many colleges and universities revolve around management functions such as organizing, planning, controlling, and communicating. The issues, problems, and principles concerning working with staff in a division of student affairs are similar regardless of the type of institution. Whether at a community college or a university, successful programs have staff which carry out their responsibilities in an efficient and effective way. The chief student affairs officer is responsible for controlling and directing staff activities and determining whether division or department goals are actually accomplished.

Unfortunately, many of the issues confronted by vice presidents, deans of students, and program directors are of such an immediate nature that it is possible to lose sight of the broad picture or to ignore concerns of equal importance in the effective delivery of programs and services. Thus, most student affairs administrators must constantly remind themselves that fundamental administrative problems such as poor communication, competition and conflict between staff members, and dysfunctional behaviors are often associated with the more pervasive problems of complex organizations. Also, it is easy to lose sight of the fact that administrators are very much a part of the overall work environment in which their own perceptions and decisions are shaped. The decisions they make and the way in which policy is implemented directly influence staff. In turn, staff responses and reactions influence the administrator's attitudes and behavior. Consequently, it is important for those who supervise staff to realize that, while they can be the architect of solutions to problems, they may also be a part of many problems. Given the complexity of this situation, personnel issues often seem insurmountable and impossible to resolve. Fortunately, various management tools are available to assist administrators to carry out their responsibilities in working with their staff members.

The evaluation of staff through a systematic performance appraisal procedure is one such tool. As noted in some of the earlier chapters, evaluation involves the process of obtaining useful information for the purpose of making decisions. Therefore, evaluation of personnel should be action oriented in that it provides the administrator with an estimation of the value of staff activity as it is related to program goals. As Harpel (1978) explained, "professional staff members must be concerned not only about whether results are achieved but how they are achieved and at what cost" (p. 20). Evaluating staff effectiveness can help the student affairs administrator to assess overall program outcomes in order to make decisions about differential treatment of staff in such areas as in-service training, salary, promotion, demotion, and so forth.

Evaluating the performance of staff members is, in most cases, a difficult undertaking. It is hard to pass judgment on people, especially if these judgments become a part of the staff member's permanent performance record. Yet the attainment of an organization's goals requires that the performance of staff members be measured and compared. Another benefit is employee growth. For an employee to overcome weaknesses, build on strengths, and grow within a job, performance must be evaluated. However, if the evaluation process is handled poorly or occurs in a haphazard manner, these personal benefits may not accrue, and morale will be low, confusion will exist, and the organization may be weakened. On the other hand, if the evaluation process is well thought out and occurs in a systematic and objective manner, then harmony should exist between employee behavior and organizational goals.

Since the evaluation process as a management tool is a critical element in any administrative endeavor, the choice is not whether to undertake the evaluation of staff, but whether to select an approach that is not adequately planned or a system that is valid and contributes to organizational goals as well as employee growth. A division or department of student affairs with sound staff evaluation procedures recognizes the value of people, helps staff feel they are being treated fairly, and demonstrates a commitment of the effective delivery of services and programs as well as the utilization of human resources.

WHY EVALUATE STAFF?

Central to the evaluation process are a number of questions to which the administrator must find answers. Can the individual do the job? How long does it take? How accurately is the job being done? Is the individual effectively contributing to the organization's goals? What changes are needed to enhance further growth of the individual? How can each staff member be stimulated to put forth a better effort? Does the employee measure up to the organization's standards? What improvement is required? What are an individual's strengths that will benefit the organization? Likewise, employees within all organizations have a need to know the answers to similar questions. How am I doing? Am I making significant contributions to the overall operation? Should I be doing things differently? Are my efforts noticed and appreciated? Do I have potential for promotion?

Through an employee evaluation plan it is possible to collect objective data with which to answer these questions. The relative value of an individual to the organization including personal qualifications, attitudes, behavior, and performance is assessed in order to determine overall contribution to accomplishing the organization's goals. There are many benefits to be derived from a systematic, valid employee evaluation system. Such a system can serve as a work plan and stimulus for employee self-improvement; determine who should be rewarded through promotions and salary adjustments; assure equitable assignment of work loads in light of an employee's abilities; aid in negotiating disputes and grievances; provide a check on the adequacy of selection and employment procedures; improve the thoroughness of management techniques; record the bases for demotion or termination of an employee; identify an employee's weaknesses and strengths as well as professional development needs; serve as a basis for adjustments in the quality and quantity of work; and improve employee morale and confidence in management's procedures.

Although many people have a negative view of the staff evaluation process, the merits of a systematic evaluation procedure are clearly evident. Not only can formal evaluation techniques insure fair treatment for all employees, but they can also contribute to employee morale by identifying an individual's contributions. In most cases, the advantages of a systematic staff evaluation plan outweigh the disadvantages. Once administrators agree that formal evaluations should be conducted, the question of how the evaluation process should be implemented can be addressed.

PROCEDURES FOR EVALUATING STAFF

Evaluation is a means to an end, not an end in itself. As Rock and Lewis (1970) note, "performance appraisal, formal or informal, lies at the heart of the art of managing. Good managers do it well; poor managers do it less satisfactorily; only bad managers do it not at all" (p. 4, 80). Consequently, a staff evaluation plan is an intricate part of the management process and should be characterized by practicality and utility. A the same time, the process should not be overly complex or time consuming. Several basic tenets govern the evaluation process.

OBJECTIVITY

Methods for evaluating staff often fail because confusion surrounds the entire process. Often, it is unclear to staff what the evaluation process entails, for what purpose it is being used, and what employee traits or behaviors are being evaluated. The issue is whether clear communication exists within the organization. As previously mentioned, the purpose of staff evaluation is to generate information necessary for moving the organization toward defined goals. This fundamental purpose must be communicated to and understood by all individuals involved.

Therefore, the formulation of evaluation procedures should involve all staff to the greatest possible extent. The criteria used to evaluate staff must be clearly defined. Above all, a staff member should be observed and judged on the basis of the criteria that were consensually validated. And, it is of critical importance that these criteria relate to the requirements of the respective position rather than to general traits of the employee.

In other words, the staff evaluation process should be characterized by objectivity and should be as valid as possible. Those in a position to evaluate the performance of subordinates should be aware of and sensitive to the weaknesses inherent in most systems. For instance, Beach (1970) noted several problems common to any evaluation process including the influence of the "halo effect," the tendency of supervisors to be overly lenient or strict, the role interpersonal biases play in the entire process, and abdication of the responsibility for staff evaluation.

Evaluator

A number of options exist — supervisors, peers and colleagues, subordinates, clients and consumers, or groups and committees — when deciding who should evaluate staff. The most common practice is for people to be evaluated by their supervisors, and there is some evidence in the literature that indicates employees prefer this approach (Beach, 1970). One common problem, however, is that some supervisors are unaware of a staff member's performance simply because of the size of the department or because of the lack of proximity to the work being accomplished. As unlikely as this may sound, it is frequently the case.

A person's colleagues or subordinates, on the other hand, may have a more accurate perception of the effectiveness of an individual's performance. A major weakness with this type of evaluation, however, is that peers or subordinates often make judgments on the basis of performance which benefits them in their own positions. In contrast, a supervisor usually focuses on performance related to the overall goals of the department or division. Also, the problem of competition and conflict between peers should not be overlooked. In addition, major philosophical questions must be addressed before peer or subordinate ratings can be used in salary or promotion decisions. Evaluations by clients or consumers pose many of the same problems.

Of course, the unique characteristics of the work situation often dictate which approach should be used. All have advantages and disadvantages. According to Rowland (1958), a system that is used frequently involves group or committee evaluations. In this method, the chief administrator usually makes final decisions based on the input from several other sources. The rationale for this procedure is that several people can provide a more accurate assessment of performance than any one individual.

Whatever the procedure, the evaluation should be conducted by the person or group of people most familiar with the responsibilities and performance of the individual being evaluated. Whoever conducts the evaluation should also have a thorough understanding of the organization's goals and how each person's work relates to these goals. In other words, in order to accurately conduct an evaluation, the evaluator must be well informed, adequately prepared, and competent. Usually, evaluation data from several sources are more reliable.

Timing

Unfortunately, most evaluations are limited in that they call for infrequent periodic assessments which are considered time consuming and of little value. Thus, the issue of when and how often to evaluate must be resolved. Whatever the interval at which evaluations are conducted (annually, semi-annually, quarterly, etc.) a time frame should be established and honored. The time sequence selected should be practical. An excessive number of formal evaluations during any one period of time unduly burdens the person being evaluated as well as the evaluator. For the administrator with a large number of staff members, the evaluation process should be staggered throughout the year. Also, a single incident either of a negative or positive nature should not be allowed to outweigh a full year's work or to distort the perceptions of an individual's overall performance. Equal weight should be given all work undertaken within a work period. In addition, thorough assessment should occur during critical times of employment such as probationary periods.

Another important issue concerns the relationship between performance appraisals and salary reviews or adjustments. In general, it is appropriate to separate the two. Beach (1970) notes that the focus of staff evaluations should be on employee performance, growth, and development. Performance evaluations deal with the administrator's assessment of a staff member's productivity in relationship to department or division goals. In contrast, salary reviews require the administrator to make judgments on the basis of evaluation data as related to a specific amount of dollars which can be allocated. Concerns about salary levels should not distract from the evaluation of performance or the development of professional growth plans.

INFORMAL FEEDBACK

Ideally, it is best to discuss a staff member's work during the time the work is performed. For example, when an employee does an outstanding job, the person should be commended. This can occur through verbal praise, informal notes, or formal letters. If need be, such instances also provide an opportunity to discuss other aspects of work, including those needing improvement. If problems have been identified, it is important that when the problem has been corrected, immediate feedback be given to the employee. To merely criticize without discussing alternatives, identifying attainable goals, or recognizing improved performance may, in fact, lead to additional problems. Thus, informal sessions can be extremely effective in assisting individuals to grow and to associate their efforts with the success of the organization. However, the evaluation process also should include formal evaluation sessions and the careful documentation of plans and progress.

FORMAL EVALUATION

A number of methods are available for use in a formal and systematic plan for staff evaluation. Most approaches tend to compare selected traits such as employee dependability with some other criteria. Of critical importance to the evaluation process is the identification of the relevant criteria. Employees may be compared with an ideal of "100 percent" effectiveness, reviewed in contrast to other employees, or rated against consensually validated performance standards.

Rock and Lewis (1970) have identified a variety of methods available for use in formal evaluation procedures. For example, a "rating-scale" permits the evaluator to compare employees on the basis of the quality and quantity of productivity. A number of traits such as "thoroughness in accomplishing work" or characteristics such as "interpersonal skills" may be judged on a scale from high to low. In the "order of merit" approach, employees are ranked on the merit or worth of the quality of their contributions. In the "paired comparison" method, each person is paired with all other employees in a work group. Through a process of elimination, the administrator then decides which of the pair is more valuable. In the "forced-distribution" method, the evaluator ranks staff members on the basis of certain criteria and then arbitrarily groups them into several percentage divisions. Using the normal distribution curve, those in the top 20 percent are classified as excellent performers and those in the bottom 20 percent are considered poor performers.

All approaches have various advantages and disadvantages depending on the particular situation or setting in which they might be used. It is important to realize that a wide range of methods exist and that alternative approaches are available. When considering a particular method, it is essential that unnecessary paperwork be avoided and that the method have validity for its intended use in the organization.

Performance Standards

Probably the most valuable approach for evaluating staff in the field of student affairs involves the development and use of performance standards. The major advantage of the performance-standard method is that it recognizes the complexity of jobs held by those in professions such as education (Rock & Lewis, 1970). In this procedure, standards are agreed upon which have definite meaning in terms of the organization's goals. Therefore, people are rewarded primarily for their contributions to goal attainment. Work habits and personal characteristics are relevant only to the extent that they influence or are related to organizational goals.

For example, the vice president, dean of students, or program director and the individual staff member being evaluated, first identify and agree on department or division goals and then determine how and when these goals will be accomplished. All parties should be cognizant of the criteria for measuring performance. The supervisor's task is to insure that the needs of the organization will be met. Such a procedure tends to minimize defensive behavior which is often associated with staff evaluations. In its place, work objectives are established in line with job requirements, and performance standards are emphasized.

According to Rock and Lewis (1970), there are two critical factors which will determine whether this procedure is a success. First, the department's or division's goals must be consensually validated and clearly articulated to staff. Second, job descriptions should be written for every employee and should emphasize results.

Therefore, the starting point in developing performance standards is to analyze the nature of the job. In simple terms, a job analysis seeks to delineate the duties, requirements, and desired outcomes of work. According to Killen (1977), several basic approaches to the process of job analysis are frequently used: 1) rank order; 2) job classification; and 3) point system. The rank-order method is probably used most frequently and simply requires that each job be ranked in relationship to other jobs in the organization according to the relative value of each. The job classification procedure groups similar jobs together and then ranks one against the other. In the point system, factors such as "level of education," "analytical ability," or "mental effort" are assigned points. Each job is then ranked in importance according to the total number of points. In other words, determining how the job serves to accomplish organizational goals is the primary focus of the job analysis.

From the job analysis, a job description is developed. Jobs can be precisely defined or expressed in somewhat more general terms. But the elements of a job should be clearly stated and directly related to the individual's responsibilities and authority. For example, if the job description of an assistant dean of students indicates the person is responsible for the academic advising of students but the authority for academic advising rests with instructors who report to department heads in academic departments, a discrepancy will likely exist between program outcomes and the assistant dean's performance. Therefore, it is important that the goals and standards be realistic and attainable.

Of course, the factors included in a job description and the standards applied will vary across jobs, departments, and institutions. In an attempt to include factors other than those related to productivity, many systems also include an assessment of general knowledge, dependability, cooperation, and initiative. The list could be limitless including such things as enthusiasm, appearance, self-control, loyalty, intelligence, dependability, and so forth. However, it is important to remember that the standards used should have a demonstrable relationship to desired outcomes, and they should be measurable. A thorough job analysis, the development of a job description, and consensual validation of department goals and performance standards are necessary elements in an effective employee evaluation system.

Data Collection

In general, forms of various kinds (rating scale, checklist, essay) are used to collect information about an individual's performance. For example, the student affairs division at one university uses an evaluation form to assess staff performance on a scale ranging from unsatisfactory to superior. Performance is evaluated in the areas of job knowledge, interpersonal relations, professional judgment, leadership, composure under pressure, communication skills, commitment to the job, and job skills. A form used on another campus requires department heads to develop evaluative essay statements regarding the performance of subordinates based on standards associated with contributions to program objectives, ability in interpersonal relations, and needs for professional development. On the basis of these essay statements and in consultation with the staff member, it is determined whether the individual's performance is unacceptable, acceptable but needs improvement, acceptable, or above average. Combinations of the checklist form and essay form are also frequently used.

The kind of form used should not be a major issue provided that supervisors and their subordinates have a common understanding of the meaning of the factors included. The practice of sharing the evaluation results with the employee often insures fairness. During these feedback sessions, additional pertinent information may be obtained from the employee. Many systems have forms that require the supervisor to record the topics discussed with the employee and provide the opportunity for the employee to acknowledge or respond to the evaluation process and results. It is also common to note any plans and goals for future employee growth.

Communication

A major component in any staff evaluation system is effective communication between the supervisor and the employee. An evaluation procedure is of little value unless each employee understands the purposes and outcomes of evaluation procedures. For a variety of reasons, however, supervisors are often reluctant to communicate the results of evaluations to staff members. The personnel management literature indicates that many post-evaluation interviews are often emotionally charged experiences which are unpleasant for both the supervisor and subordinate. Without evaluative feedback, however, employees often feel isolated in their jobs and fail to identify with the organization's goals. Failure to effectively communicate the results of an evaluation to an employee undermines the basic intent of a sound evaluation system.

Several things can be done to ameliorate this problem. First, the individual conference approach is of critical importance. While the outcome of the evaluation should be recorded in a written document, each employee is entitled to a personal discussion of the matter with the administrator responsible for the evaluation. Prior to the interview, it is helpful to encourage the employee to conduct a self-assessment of performance compared with the agreed upon standards. This strategy tends to focus attention on the matter at hand and is helpful for determining future goals and standards.

The climate in which the evaluation meeting occurs is also important. There should be adequate time for discussion without any interruptions. An atmosphere of trust and confidence should exist. The employee must understand that the supervisor's remarks are intended to assist rather than impede progress toward goals. The discussion should focus on facts related to job performance. Criticism of personality traits such as "sense of humor" or personal idiosyncracies is usually not productive. Limitations should be discussed in light of performance standards, related to plans for improvement, and stated in understandable terms. A person's strengths should also be discussed. The primary goal of the session should be to encourage improved performance, not to discourage or alienate the employee. Also, as noted earlier, the evaluation interview is not the time to discuss issues concerning salary adjustments or employee benefits.

Occasionally, administrators have to confront the issue of inadequate performance by an employee. Because of the circumstances, this type of meeting may or may not be scheduled during the usual time for appraisal interviews. The outcome may involve modification of job responsibilities, transfer to another department, or dismissal from the organization. These sessions are uncomfortable for everyone. Of course, it is imperative that the decision to confront an issue of this nature be based upon fact which is documented over time and related to job requirements as well as performance standards. The matter should be handled in a professional, confidential manner and as rationally as possible.

CONCLUSION

The appraisal of staff performance is by no means an exact science (Taft, 1955). Further, a rich mix of professionals from a variety of disciplines comprise the work force in higher education. Therefore, staff performance and effectiveness within any particular department is as much a product of the administrator's ability to provide leadership, to motivate people, and to encourage and bring about cooperative work efforts as it is a product of professional competence. Unfortunately, the process of evaluating performance has a negative connotation. There is a common belief that defensive behavior is a natural by-product. Further, few successful student affairs administrators are themselves evaluated on or rewarded for successfully appraising employee performance or encouraging staff development (Beeler &

Penn, 1978). Yet it is known that the evaluation of people within an organization assists the organization and its employees to achieve defined goals.

As with any human enterprise, the evaluation process is subject to error. By definition, the end product of evaluation is not an exact measure, but rather is an estimate. Some administrators have a tendency to be more lenient, while some are consistently too demanding. Interpersonal relations and biases play a tremendous role and certainly influence objectivity in the evaluation process. Organizational influences also impact the nature of evaluations, for administrators often tend to consider how evaluative data may ultimately be used. When conducting staff evaluations, these factors must be considered. Failure to recognize limitations in a system and to expect a reasonable amount of ambiguity can result in misleading interpretations of employee performance.

The process of staff evaluation requires that goals be agreed upon and stated in understandable and measureable terms, that data relevant to the goals be collected in a systematic way and on a regular basis, and that goal attainment be evaluated fairly and objectively. Obviously, a systematic and objective procedure for evaluating staff is by no means a panacea that will create an environment in which everyone is satisfied. However, the dividends of an evaluation process conducted properly are well worth the time and commitment of resources.

REFERENCES

Beach, D. *Personnel: The management of people at work.* New York: Macmillan, 1970.

Beeler, K., & Penn, R. *A handbook on staff development in student affairs.* Corvallis, Oregon: Oregon State University Bookstores, 1978.

Harpel, R. Evaluation from a management perspective. In G. R. Hanson (Ed.), *Evaluating program effectiveness.* San Francisco: Jossey-Bass, 1978.

Killen, K. *Management: A middle-management approach.* Boston: Houghton Mifflin, 1977.

Robinson, D. Evaluation as a function of student personnel administration. *Journal of College Student Personnel,* 1962, *4,* 20-22, 40.

Rock, M., & Lewis, L. Appraising managerial performance. In H. B. Maynard (Ed.), *Handbook of business administration.* New York: McGraw-Hill, 1970.

Rowland, L. The mechanics of group appraisal. *Personnel,* 1958, *34,* 36-43.

Taft, R. The ability to judge people. *Psychological Bulletin,* 1955, January, 42-49.

13
EVALUATING STUDENT DEVELOPMENT PROGRAMS
Gary R. Hanson and Oscar T. Lenning

In the past, academicians have tended to emphasize students' cognitive development (increasing knowledge and acquisition of intellectual skills) as the primary goal of higher education. Ebel (1965) has articulated this traditional perspective:
> If we look at what actually goes on in our school and college classrooms and laboratories, libraries and lecture halls, it seems reasonable to conclude that the major goal of education is to develop in the scholars a *command of substantive knowledge.* Achievement of this kind of cognitive mastery is clearly not the only concern of teachers and scholars engaged in the process of education. But the command of substantive knowledge is, and ought to be, the central concern of education. (p. 64)

Academicians such as Ebel usually equate cognitive mastery programs with the rubric of "student development." However, student development programs in higher education can legitimately focus on much more than cognitive development. Numerous surveys of college students' expressed needs have found other areas of development to be important also.

Increasingly in recent years some faculty have recognized that morals and attitude development, developmental skills education, field work and off-campus experiences, and clarification of interests and values are a legitimate part of the formal college curriculum. Divisions of student affairs have usually assumed responsibility for these types of programs. However, both faculty and student affairs staff are now encouraging collaborative efforts to facilitate student development regardless of whether the activities or experiences are designed to occur inside or outside of the classroom, and on or off the campus.

The general principles for evaluating curricular or extra-curricular student development programs are similar. The characteristic to be developed must be clarified in terms of observable, concrete performance or behavior. This clarification will determine what data should be collected, and how. Once the appropriate data have been gathered, they must be analyzed and summarized, transformed into meaningful information (such as comparisons with absolute standards or normative reference groups), compared with predetermined goals and objectives, interpreted in terms of alternatives, and reported in meaningful and appropriate formats to the decision makers responsible for the program (see Chapter 2). Finally, judgments about the worth of the program and/or how it can be improved should be made (evaluation).

This chapter introduces the complexities of student development program evaluation by providing an overview of four major issues. First, the different purposes and contexts of evaluation (e.g., the competing value commitments in higher education) are considered; next, various definitions and approaches to understanding the concept of student development will be discussed; third, the measurement and data collection problems and issues inherent in the assessment of student growth and development will be presented; finally, problems and issues will be summarized that are related to analysis, interpretation, and application of the results to judgments and decisions.

PURPOSE AND CONTEXT ISSUES

Many student affairs professionals are dedicated to educating and developing the "whole" student (Brown, 1972; Miller & Prince, 1977; Sanford, 1962). The idea is not new, however. Fenske (in press) observed that the concept of educating the total student has endured with unusual consistency over the years:

> ... it (educating the total student) was elaborated on both a philosophical and psychological basis in the 1920s and the early 1930s. Successive statements of the "student personnel point of view" sponsored by the American Council on Education in 1937, 1949, and 1958 carried forward the concept of the post-World War II era. Influential books by the profession's leaders also espoused the philosophy through this period, including those by Wrenn and Bell (1952), Williamson (1949), and Mueller (1961).

Others claim, however, that development of the "whole" student is not realistic. For example, The Carnegie Commission (1973) maintained that " 'totalism' in the campus approach to students is ... neither wise nor possible" (p. 17). The rationale for this position was reflected in the following statement:

> The campus cannot and should not try to take direct responsiblity for the "total" development of the student. That responsibility belongs primarily to the individual student by the time he goes to college. The primary direct responsibility of the college is to assist with intellectual and skill development ... (p. 16)

The reason student affairs professionals have subscribed to the goals of student development are exemplified by Perry (1970):

> The word "growth" suggests that it is *better* to grow than to arrest growth or to regress. Where the development is laid out as a kind of scale on which a person's position and rate or progress can be measured, then a value becomes assigned to a person in an advanced position relative to others of his age. A similar

value is assigned to a person with a relatively high rate of growth. Where progress in the development can be assumed to involve not only "natural" endowments but such "personal" attributes as will, effort, and courage, growth becomes a moral issue. An advanced person showing a high rate of growth becomes somehow a "better" person. (p. 44)

In the student affairs literature, a high value is placed on the *process* of student development. To grow, to change, and to develop is considered good, and thus the profession strongly encourages that the process be emphasized. Nevertheless, all too infrequently this emphasis is not questioned. For example, postsecondary education also serves other "essential" purposes. Indeed, most institutions pursue multiple goals — at least in the abstract — and various constraints (money, staff, and other resources); have resulted in a system of priorities for goals and practices.

What are these competing goals and purposes of higher education? Two brief examples reflect the diversity and breadth of the universe of student development goals:

Few people would quarrel with the notion that, among other objectives, students should demonstrate a greater knowledge of subject matter, more skill in use of language, and increased reading ability — to read with comprehension, to apply their readings to new situations and to recognize writer's styles and biases. Further they should be able to analyze and solve programs, to make inferences, and to think critically. (Lenning, Munday & Maxey, 1969, p. 145)

Each of these major goals recognized to some degree the importance of an affective domain among educational objectives. Thus students are expected to develop a code of behavior based on ethical *principles.* They are to *participate* as responsible citizens. They should recognize *personal responsibility* for fostering international understanding. In addition to learning facts about their physical environment, they should *appreciate* the implications of scientific discovery for human welfare. They should attain a *satisfactory emotional* and *social adjustment.* They are to enjoy literature, art, and music and should acquire *attitudes* basic to a satisfying family life. (Dressel & Mayhew 1954, p. 209)

There are other goals of higher education that do not emphasize the process of student development. In fact, many goals do not even focus on students at all but rather emphasize service to the broader community and a commitment to research and scholarship as a vehicle for solving societal problems.

Student affairs professionals must learn to measure effectively and communicate to those outside the profession the worth of student development programs relative to the worth of other programs that compete for the same financial resources. Therefore, a central issue in the evaluation of student development programs is the evaluation of the goals of the programs within the context of higher education. All too frequently, the admonition of Scriven (1971) is forgotten: not only must the amount of achievment of particular program goals be evaluated, but also the appropriateness of the program goals should be determined and communicated to others.

In an era of accountability, it is necessary to evaluate the worth of student development program goals relative to other institutional goals. It is in this context that the evaluator of student development programs must question the worth of a particular program's goals and processes. For example, is it more important that students gain a greater sense of autonomy and independence than it is: (1) for the library to buy 2,000 additional books or (2) for a noted research chemist to be granted additional research funds to complete what seems to be an important study? The evaluator may not be responsible for such a decision, but the person who must interpret the findings of an evaluation report may very well have this charge. An understanding of and appreciation for the competing educational purposes and processes can result in more appropriate evaluation questions.

In a summative evaluation (see Chapter 2; also Scriven, 1967) of the worth of a program, the values prevailing within the institution, higher education, and society concerning the purposes of higher education constitute only some of the contextual factors that should be considered in planning and designing an evaluation of student development programs. The same is true of what Scriven has called formative evaluation — evaluation aimed at providing judgments about the ways in which the program can be improved. Other contextual factors that must be considered when planning an evaluation of student development program include: governmental policies, political and other social attitudes and climate external to as well as within the institution, and organizational factors within the institution or program such as traditions, mind sets, policies and procedures, governance structure, availability of resources, and so forth. For example, if a majority of program staff members have an emotional bias against using empirical data, a different evaluation strategy will be necessary than if such a bias is not present.

WHAT IS STUDENT DEVELOPMENT?

A second major issue related to the evaluation of student development programs concerns definition. A critical concern in the measurement, assessment and evaluation of student development programs is the lack of definitional clarity as to *what it is* that student affairs professionals have been trying to develop. Lenning (1977) has reviewed and summarized over 80 different classifications of student development that have been published over the years. Some focus specifically on different kinds of intellectual development; a second set of classifications focuses on various kinds of emotional, cultural and social development; a third set of classifications focuses on various kinds of physical and psychomotor development; and a large group consists of much broader classifications.

Apart from the work of Erikson, prior to 1970 the profession had little or no theory to adequately predict the behavior of college students and to provide a coherent explication of individual development (Keniston, 1968). Since that time models and theories of student development have been more numerous. During the past decade, each of the following writers has presented at least one major theoretical contribution regarding student development: Chickering (1969), Heath, D. (1968), Heath, R. (1964, 1973), Holland (1966, 1973), Hunt (1966, 1970), Kohlberg (1969, 1972, 1975), Levinson and others (1978), Stern (1970), and Vaillant (1977). Knefelkamp, Widick and Parker (in press) suggest, however, that while models of college student development are no longer lacking, other related problems have accrued such as the need to understand the differences and similarities between the various student development models and to translate the models into useful practice.

In order to systematically evaluate student development programs, the student affairs professional must be familiar with the program's theoretical orientation. To determine whether a program has enhanced the development of students, one must know what was being developed. Theories and models of student development provide the necessary clarity. Hence, an awareness of the issues related to the definition and meaning of student development is important. The purpose of this section is to reiterate some of the basic questions about student development and to discuss some of the general categories of theory.

IMPORTANT QUESTIONS ABOUT STUDENT DEVELOPMENT

If student affairs professionals expect to program for student development, staff must know what student development is — what changes can, do, and should take place (Kuh, Dannells, Doherty & Ganshaw, 1977). The following kinds of questions should not only stimulate thinking about the nature of student development but also assist in the conceptualization of evaluation strategies (see Chapter 3).

How can we describe students in developmental terms? What aspect or characteristics of students "develop," "change" or "grow"? It has been noted that students grow taller, gain or lose weight, and mature physically. Also students seem to learn to reason, judge, and analyze as part of their intellectual development and that they are better able to live independently, establish close friendships, and manage their emotions. But what other dimensions are further developed during the college years? What aspects of the individual resist change? Which characteristics of people have been developed prior to attending college and which characteristics develop after college? Where are college students developmentally, initially, and at any point in time?

How does the process of development occur? What are the signs, symptoms or qualities of development? What is the direction of development and at what rate does it take place? Do all students develop along the same dimensions? Is there a logical sequence of steps by which the developmental process takes place or are there abrupt changes and shifts from one stage or level to another?

What factors influence development? What psychological and sociological processes facilitate or restrict growth and development? What elements in the environment influence development? What conditions are necessary to stimulate development? What factors seem to retard growth? How critical is the timing of developmental program interventions? Can student affairs staff and programs influence student development? Does the program influence student development at all, or is development more appropriately attributed to maturation.

Toward what ends should students develop? Why should students develop and grow? What should students look like at the end of their college careers? Can students be taught how to continue their own developmental growth after they leave college? Is there an end to the developmental process?

Most of these questions do not yet have definitive answers. Consideration of these issues has resulted in theoretical speculation about the nature, process, and outcomes of student development. While a detailed presentation of the various theories is beyond the scope of this chapter, a general overview of the different theoretical approaches to student development should help structure the manner in which evaluation questions are framed.

Theoretical Approaches To Student Development

Knefelkamp, Widick, and Parker (in press) identified four clusters of student development theories: psychosocial, cognitive developmental, maturity models, and typology models. These authors suggested that each cluster provides a slightly different but equally useful vantage point from which to view college students and also outlines the parameters that must be addressed in practice. The following summaries draw heavily from the Knefelkamp et al. presentation.

Psychosocial theories. These theorists postulate that individuals develop through a sequence of stages which define the life cycle. Each developmental stage evolves from the interaction of a particular physical or biological growth stage and the mastery of certain tasks (e.g., learning specific skills, attitudes, formation of a given self-view, etc.). While development generally follows a chronological sequence, the rate and direction of development is influenced by particular personality components that have emerged at a given point in time as well as societal and cultural influences. From this perspective, the central questions for student affairs professionals are: At what developmental stage is the individual? What decisions, needs, or concerns are of greatest interest? What types of skills must the student acquire to accomplish the important developmental tasks associated with each stage? The key theorists that subscribe to this general approach are Erikson (1959, 1968), Chickering (1969), Katz (1968), Keniston (1968), Marcia (1966), and Sanford (1962).

Cognitive developmental theories. Development is viewed from a somewhat different perspective by the cognitive developmental theorists as most have adapted a structuralist approach (Piaget, 1964). Development is considered to be a sequence of irreversible stages, each reflecting a major shift in the way in which people think and reason about their immediate world. Most cognitive developmentalists have tried to identify the common pattern of stages that individuals experience and have reasoned that people at different ages have particular modes of thinking. The process of change is seen as an interaction between the typical or usual modes of thinking and specific environmental problems, dilemmas or crises that an individual confronts. If previous ways of thinking and reasoning do not solve the dilemma, then the individuals ways of thinking are forced to change to a form that is more appropriate or adequate. From this perspective, the concern with helping students grow and develop emphasizes *how* students think about particular issues and examines the relationship between the environment and changes in students' critical modes of thought. The cognitive developmental theorists include Piaget (1964), Kohlberg (1972), Perry (1970), Harvey, Hunt and Schroder (1961), Hunt (1970), and Loevinger (1966, 1976).

Maturity models. This approach, exemplified by the work of D. Heath (1965, 1968, 1977), provides a holistic picture of the "developed" person rather than emphasizing certain individual characteristics as do the psychosocial and cognitive developmental models. The maturity model describes the components of the maturational process in terms of self systems (e.g., intellect, values, interpersonal relationships, etc.) and growth dimensions (becoming other-centered, becoming integrated, becoming autonomous, etc.). Maturation and development involves movement along the major growth dimensions in each of the self-system areas. Hence, a person may be developing simultaneously in the different "self" areas along each of several growth dimensions. The model is not only dynamic but multi-dimensional. Based on empirical data, it appears that development in the various self-system areas proceeds in an ordered sequence; first occurring in the intellective-cognitive skills, next in same-sex and then opposite-sex personal relationships, followed by the development of an individual's values. The development or maturing of self-concept takes longer and proceeds through more transitional stages but eventually evolves to a stable integration of the individual's values. Student affairs professionals using this type of model may ask: How does development in one dimension interact with or influence development in another dimension? Through how many stages of development does an individual progress? What constitutes a mature, integrated individual?

Typology models. The typology models emphasize those factors which create stable consistent modes of coping with change. The focus is on those persistent individual differences, such as cognitive style, temperament, ethnic background, and sex which interact with the developmental process. The typological theorists seek to identify how different individuals may manage, delay, or cope with various developmental tasks. Because individual differences exist among people, these differences influence the direction, rate, and nature of the developmental process. Thus, different "types" of people tend to develop at different rates in different ways. Different theorists have tried to categorize or "type" individuals according to various criteria such as cognitive style (Witkins et al., 1962), personality functioning (Myers-Briggs, 1962), temperamental differences (R. Heath, 1964), or sociological differences (Cross, 1971, 1976). The typology generates several important questions: What are the critical developmental tasks for each type of individual? What skills does each type have to cope with in order to master the various tasks? How do the individual characteristics of the different types of individuals influence or interact with the developmental process?

IMPLICATIONS FOR EVALUATION

"What is student development?" The answer is important because evaluators must not only know *what* is intended to be developed and what is being developed, but must also know *how* the development process should or ought to proceed as well as the characteristics of the final product (the "developed student"). If student development programs are to influence the growth of students they must be designed in light of environmental factors that "make a difference." The four categories of critical questions should help shape the strategies used for program evaluation. The four categories of theories and models also provide structure for asking necessary evaluation questions. Both the complexity of the unanswered questions and the complexity of the various theoretical approaches accentuate the difficulties in evaluating student development programs. The evaluator should, in consultation with program designers, determine *what* is being evaluated. Are changes in the stage or level of student development of prime importance? Is it the rate of development that is being influenced by a particular program? Is it the manner in which students think or reason about problems that is the focus?

Evaluators who are familiar with the general theoretical approaches to student development will be able to assist program designers in determining goals and outcomes. Few programming efforts are specifically related to a particular theoretical orientation (Kuh et al., 1977). By inserting key constructs and ideas from theoretical positions, program designers should be able to define what is to be accomplished, how it is to be accomplished, and how long it might take to be accomplished. In addition, the use of theory provides the necessary perspective from which to evaluate whether *any* change or growth *can be expected.* If, according to a particular theory, certain developmental changes are not likely to occur until late in (or even after) the college experience, a program's efforts to influence development along the respective dimension would be ill-conceived. Theory may help provide the necessary perspective to know what, when, how, and to what extent student development might occur.

For example, if a residence hall director wished to evaluate the impact of various living arrangement patterns on the development of interpersonal relationships with members of the opposite sex, a particular theory could structure the evaluation plan by pointing out (a) the typical developmental level of heterosexual relationships among students of a given age, (b) the sequence of developmental activities that leads to the formation of such relationships, and (c) the likelihood that such relationships can, in fact, be influenced by external factors such as residence hall programming. Familiarity with student development theory could influence the evaluator to discourage the implementation of the program because of the low probability that any programming efforts could influence these particular aspects of college student development.

Evaluators cannot effectively evaluate student development programs without asking appropriate theory-based questions. Since there is no single theory of college student development, evaluators must be familiar with many different approaches and the various questions that are logical extentions of their particular sets of assumptions and constructs.

PROBLEMS AND ISSUES ASSOCIATED WITH MEASUREMENT AND THE COLLECTION OF DATA

The major purpose of designing and implementing student development programs is to facilitate the growth of students. Implicit in that purpose is the recognition of a change in the status of important student characteristics. If a program has been "successful," students somehow should be different as a result of the effects of the program. Two critical measurement issues are related to this assumption. The first issue concerns the reliability and validity of the measures and indicators used to identify the presence and amount of the particular student characteristic in question. The reliability and validity of various data collection instruments (whether standardized or locally developed) and methods can be suspect, especially if certain precautions are not taken. The second related issue centers on the measurement of "change," "growth," or "development." The psychometric and statistical problems of measuring change are complex and few "correct" procedures have been agreed upon (Cronbach & Furby, 1970; Harris, 1963; Nunally, 1975). If the change in the status of student characteristics cannot be assessed, how can a program designed to impact those same characteristics be evaluated?

RELIABILITY AND VALIDITY ISSUES AND PROBLEMS

Commonly used terms such as personal happiness, success on the job, personality development, social development, values clarification, competence in critical thinking, and good study habits are relatively vague and abstract constructs. Thus, two people may interpret the same construct quite differently when it is expressed in specific, concrete, observable terms. Therefore, some of the most widely used personality inventories and other psychometric instruments have questionable validity because of the vague nature of the constructs they attempt to measure.

Standarized instruments have an advantage in that they are more often carefully designed and have higher reliability estimates than instruments designed locally. On the other hand, a major limitation is that they may not measure exactly the dimensions along which change is desired, whereas instruments developed or revised locally can be designed with the specific developmental question in mind. Similarly, most standardized instruments used with college students have been normed on traditional-aged students from middle- and upper-class socio-economic levels, whereas many college student populations have been changing greatly and becoming quite diverse. As a result, many instruments may be inappropriate for use with special groups of students (e.g., adult learners and students from disadvantaged backgrounds). Other potential problems concern costs, ease of administration, and ease of scoring. Lenning (in press) gives some concrete examples of the problems related to validity, reliability, and ease of use. If standardized instruments are being considered, the instrument and supporting manuals must be studied carefully, the reviews of the instrument in Buros (1972) should be examined, and the instrument should be pretested with some students considered representative of the target audience before deciding to use it. For locally developed instruments, careful review and critique, field-testing, and refinement are required.

Another consideration is that most standardized instruments are designed for use with individual students, which means that they are designed to be stable over time; and not for being responsive to change processes. Instruments should be chosen which can indicate impacts on students in terms of changes in scores.

Cost and inconvenience to students is another potential problem area. Using random samples of students instead of the whole group (e.g., matrix sampling − part of the population completes one instrument, another part completes a second instrument, and so forth) is a judicious use of resources and student time and also enables cost effective examination of a greater number of variables.

Program evaluators have relied almost exclusively on traditional measures and methods of data collection; i.e., paper and pencil tests, questionnaires, and interviews. Almost 50 alternatives to such traditional methods exist (Lenning, 1978). Whenever resource and time considerations permit, multiple measures and data collection methods should be used for the same student development variable. Where one has limitations, the other may have strengths, and vice versa (see Chapter 14). Furthermore, the overall reliability of measurement can be increased without negatively influencing the ability to observe growth or other changes. For example, self-report data can supplement more objective measures, and can provide a detailed and accurate view if questions are presented in a specific and concrete way. Data that have been used for other purposes should not be overlooked, although they must be carefully interpreted with the knowledge of how and why they were collected.

ISSUES AND PROBLEMS RELATED TO MEASURING CHANGE

If a student development program is effective, the individuals who have participated in the program should have changed in some systematic way as a result. For example, if an intramural sports program has as one of its goals the development of physical coordination, the evaluator should expect higher levels of coordination at the end of a teaching/training program than at the beginning. While the concepts of growth and development appear simple and straightforward, the measurement of change in student development characteristics is a complex and difficult task.

Because student development programs are primarily concerned with pre- and post-program changes, it might be assumed that the basic unit for evaluating change along any given important student development dimension is the individual's change score: $X_2 - X_1$, where X_1 represents the status before the program was started. However, a number of experts (Cronbach & Furby, 1970; Harris, 1963; Nunally, 1975) caution against the use of individual and group average change scores without taking into account the related problems of *floor, ceiling,* and *regression effects* (see Feldman, 1972 for a succinct discussion of these phenomena).

A more acceptable approach to analyzing change has been the use of residual change scores which are simple deviations of the scores obtained at the second administration of an assessment instrument from those predicted by regression analysis from a knowledge of scores on the first administration (Lord, 1963). While the residual change scores effectively ameliorate the problems associated with the regression effect, they are not without other limitations. A major concern is that residual change scores fail to take into account the measurement error inherent in both sets of measurement, error which is additive in terms of observed or residual change. For example, if the time interval between assessments was only one day, the scores would not be identical but would differ because of errors in the measurement process and not because of systematic change in the dimension being measured. The same problem occurs when the time interval is longer, and is also complicated by the fact that development may have occurred along the dimension under study. In this situation, it is impossible to determine how much of the change is due to measurement error and how much can be attributed to a change along the particular dimension. Numerous suggestions have been made about how to correct for the measurement error but little agreement has been reached (see Lord, 1963; Tucker, Damarin & Messick, 1966).

Nunnally (1975) suggested avoiding change scores completely because they are: (1) based on questionable statistical assumptions; (2) derived by mathematical models which are controversial; (3) difficult to understand and subject to misinterpretation; and (4) computationally quite complex. This applies to both change scores for individuals and mean change for groups. Another problem, as inferred earlier, is that change scores are notoriously unreliable because error is introduced by the unreliability of both the pretest and the posttest.

Cronbach and Furby (1970) support Nunnally's position. They suggest that the critical questions about change be rephrased. For example, how do persons compare on posttest who scored the same on the pretest? Chapter 14 provides some alternatives for structuring the data to respond more appropriately to such a question.

It should be noted that individual change scores may be of some help to the evaluator interested in differences in individuals' *tendency to change*. For example, a goal of the evaluation project might be to identify individuals who change more and those who change less, and then try to identify the correlates of the change. Nunnally (1975) provided an example of an appropriate design for determining the correlates of individual differences in the direction and nature of change along some dimension. Basically, the design involves randomly assigning students to two groups and conducting a pre-program assessment of the dimension of interest. One of the groups participates in the program and afterwards both groups are retested with the same measure. The effects of the program are analyzed in terms of the differences in the distance between the scores of the program participants and the regression line predicted by the control group (those students who did not participate in the program). If a program participant's score is above the control group regression line, the program had a positive effect; if the score was below the mean the student actually lost ground on the particular dimension of interest.

Except for the above mentioned use, the best advice seems to be to avoid the use of change scores when attempting to assess the growth and development of college students or reword the questions about change in the manner suggested by Cronbach and Furby (1970).

PROBLEMS AND ISSUES ASSOCIATED WITH INTERPRETING AND USING THE RESULTS

A major analytical issue in the evaluation of student development programs is the attribution of the development or growth of students to various program components. In other words, which aspects of the program influenced which aspects of the student participants in which direction, by how much, and by what rate of change? This issue is directly related to evaluation design. Therefore, it is important to briefly review the characteristics of a good student development evaluation design.

Nunnally (1975) suggested that an ideal experiment has three essential features. They are: (1) the experimental manipulations should concern only the program or treatment variables and not some other confounding variable(s); (2) the dependent variables should be measured by reliable, valid, well-standardized, and practical instruments; and (3) there should be an explicit plan for applying the treatments (independent variables) to program participants and measuring their effect on student development.

In order to accurately assess the impact of student development programs, Oetting and Cole (1978) identified six design factors which facilitate the determination of developmental program effects. A brief review of these factors can serve as guidelines for a good design.

Sampling. Students chosen to participate in a program should genuinely need the service and not consist of "available" students. Also, students chosen should represent the target population of people the program was designed to serve so that results can be generalized.

Blocking. If program participants have characteristics (such as age, sex, ethnicity, attitudes) that will potentially interact with the treatment, then it may be necessary to match participants and randomly assign them to participation and nonparticipation groups. Later, the differential effects of the program on participants with various characteristics can be identified.

Randomization. This technique is probably the single best way to protect against spurious results influencing the interpretation of the effects of a program. Assigning people randomly to program groups breaks up any correlations between naturally existing factors and treatment effects and protects the evaluator from most sources of invalidity.

Pretesting. This technique results in mixed blessings. On the one hand, pretesting helps determine how similar or different groups were at the beginning of a program and how much they may have changes over the course of the program. On the other hand, pretesting may influence the performance of a student during the program and hence, confound the results.

Establishing Comparison Groups. The best way to determine the relative impact of a student development program is to provide contrasting treatments to different subgroups of the total population. By establishing one or more comparison groups it is possible to come to more definite conclusions about the effect of the program. There are four types of comparison groups that are routinely used: (1) a pseudo-treatment (placebo) group in which students are given a program with high face validity but of little impact on the desired dimension based on prior experience, (2) an alternative treatment group which allows judgment of the relative impact of two or more possible groups, (3) the wait-list control group allows the evaluator to judge the impact of the program relative to the effects of no treatment and still provides an ethical way of providing program services to those who desire them, and (4) the no-treatment control group which provides no program of services nor the expectation of any services.

Follow-up. This technique involves retesting to make sure that the program effects are durable and lasting.

These factors can be combined into an effective evaluation plan, but the particular combination will be dependent on the available time, energy, and financial resources. The greater the number that can be incorporated into the evaluation plan, the better the plan will be able to account for the impact of the program on student development. Regardless of the manner in which the elements are combined, Oetting and Cole (1978) have outlined a five step research strategy that gives the practicing evaluator a method of establishing the best possible evaluation design given the current, practical limitations:

    Step 1: Construct alternative treatment groups;
    Step 2: Determine the number of program participants;
    Step 3: Make random assignment to groups;
    Step 4: Plan the comparison group treatment program;

Step 5: Select the most powerful research design.

The last step is critical and requires additional comment. Several authors (Campbell & Stanley, 1968; Nunnally, 1975; Oetting & Cole, 1978) have differentiated between true experimental designs and quasi-experimental designs and determined the relative power of the various approaches. As the designs deviate from the true experimental approach, it becomes increasingly more difficult to attribute changes in students to a particular program. With each type of design additional alternative explanations are required and the accuracy of allocating the effects of the program to specific program elements becomes less clear. A detailed description of a wide variety of approaches is provided by Campbell and Stanley (1968).

A brief review of nine different types of program designs follows in the order of their relative power to detect and to correctly assign the impact of a given program to the appropriate treatment effects. Each evaluation plan incorporates varying combinations of the critical design factors identified by Oetting & Cole (1978).

Plan One: TWO GROUPS – BLOCKING – RANDOM ASSIGNMENT – PRETEST – PROGRAM – POSTTEST. This plan makes maximum use of the major design variables and is the most powerful of the plans presented in terms of attributing the effects of the program to the appropriate sources. The power of this design is derived from the consideration of individual differences in the key characteristics of participants through blocking, the elimination of most confounding sources of error through random assignment of participants to treatment and control group as well as the magnitude of change from before to after the program as a result of the pre- and posttesting. With this combination of design elements most, if not all, the major confounding sources of alternative program effect interpretations can be ruled out and the actual program effects, if any, can be identified. The only caution is to monitor whether the pretest influences in any way the reaction to or performance of program participants.

Plan Two: TWO GROUPS – RANDOM ASSIGNMENT – PRETEST – PROGRAM – POSTTEST. This plan offers most of the major advantages of plan one but fails to account for possible differences among the individual characteristics (e.g., age, sex, ethnicity, social class, etc.) of program participants that may interact in some way with the intended effects of the program. For example, if a program designed to improve the math skills of freshmen were evaluated using two groups where one of the groups had a disproportionate number of returning adult students who had not taken math courses since high school, it would be more difficult to attribute posttest differences in math skills to the effects of the program because it could not be determined whether the lack of recent experience in mathematics limited the manner in which the one group of students was able to utilize the math training program. Blocking by levels of age would have controlled for possible individual differences in age as an alternative explanation of any observed differences between the two groups.

Plan Three: TWO GROUPS – RANDOM ASSIGNMENT – PROGRAM – POSTTEST. This plan is somewhat weaker than the previous two plans because initial differences between the two comparison groups cannot be detected. Consequently, changes in students could not be attributed to program effects without determining whether the observed posttest differences were merely functions of existing differences between groups before the program started. Also it is impossible to detect whether the groups had changed by differing amounts (magnitude) and in fact, whether the changes had been in opposite directions. This plan is still a viable plan, particularly when the pretest may sensitize the participants to or in some way interact with the program effects.

Plan Four: TWO GROUPS (PRE-FORMED) – PRETEST – PROGRAM – POSTTEST. This plan, frequently classified as a quasi-experimental design, is considerably weaker than the previous design because it fails to account for the numerous potential differences that frequently exist between groups chosen on the basis of convenience. Differences *not* controlled in this type of design include, but are not restricted to: self-selection, level of motivation, acquiescence, mutual interests, demographic bias, and other factors. The pretest factor does allow for the determination of some of the potential ways that the groups could differ provided the evaluator includes such factors as part of the pretest.

Plan Five: TWO GROUPS (PREFORMED) – PROGRAM – POSTTEST. This evaluation strategy has the same limitations as the previous plan and also fails to detect initial differences between the members of the two comparison groups. It is difficult, if not impossible, to detect either the magnitude or nature of the change in participants. Conclusions can only be drawn about how the groups differed after the program was completed.

Plan Six: ONE GROUP – PRETEST – WAIT – PRETEST – PROGRAM – POSTTEST. While this plan is weakened by lack of a control group or alternative treatment comparison group, it does offer a strong design in terms of assessing the change over time of a given group of program participants. The two pretest options provide the development of a baseline of information about the participants which can subsequently be used to assess the magnitude and direction of change due to the effects of the program.

Plan Seven: ONE GROUP – PRETEST – PROGRAM – POSTTEST. This plan allows the evaluation of change over time for a single group of program participants and may provide an indication of the amount and nature of the change. It fails to indicate the relative impact of the program or to what extent other factors contribute to the observed differences.

Plan Eight: TWO GROUPS – NATURALISTIC OBSERVATION. Naturalistic observation allows a qualitative description of possible differences between two groups and the evaluator can speculate about the possible cause of the differences. Little or no control of alternative influencing factors is provided by this design, however.

Plan Nine: ONE GROUP – NATURALISTIC OBSERVATION. The weakest of all possible designs, this plan allows a qualitative description of what happened during the program but cannot attribute any valuable differences in the participants to any identifiable program factors.

All of these evaluation designs could be enhanced by careful follow-up testing to determine whether any changes attributed to the program were lasting. These basic designs can also be modified for use with more sophisticated programs by including additional comparison groups and by utilizing multiple outcome measures. In addition, combinations of the above plans can be used. The design and analysis of such programs probably dictate the services of a good consultant, however (see Chapter 18).

Evaluators and consumers of the evaluation results should recognize that moving from plan one to plan nine is associated with an increase in the types of errors and sources of multiple interpretation of effects. Obviously, the best possible plan that time, expertise, and resources allow should be used. At some point, the evaluator must make a judgment that the data obtained will still sufficiently justify the compromises that were made in order to obtain it.

There are other major concerns in this area that should be mentioned. The satisfactory integration of various types of data (e.g., "hard" and "soft" data), sometimes poses problems. Profile analysis is one good way of doing this. Another concern is how to best report and package the results of the analysis to make it most useful to various decisionmakers, and to the publics interested in the results (e.g., legislators). The key here is to tailor short reports for the respective person(s) or group(s) rather than rely entirely on a lengthy general report of the findings distributed to everyone involved (Brown, 1978).

CONCLUSION

When planning an evaluation of student development programs, it is necessary to determine the worth of the program's goals and to describe the internal and external contexts in which the evaluation will be conducted. In other words, what a program hopes to accomplish should be questioned, and the contextual factors present that can either facilitate or impede the achievement of the program's goals and the evaluation should be identified and analyzed.

Another area of particular importance is the need for evaluators to understand the various definitions of the concepts and underlying assumptions related to student development. Understanding the developmental process and the factors related to it are critical for designing and implementing effective programs. To evaluate student development programming, expectations must be delineated. Understanding of student development theory would help frame efficacious evaluation questions.

The third and fourth areas of concern in the evaluation of student development programs are: (3) the measurement of change and of the presence and number of factors on which change is desired; (4) the assessment of the impact of specific program components on the development of students and how the results of the assessment are integrated and used. The care with which evaluation plans are designed contributes greatly to evaluating the magnitude, direction, and quality of growth among students, and to using evaluation for decision-making.

REFERENCES

Brown, R.D. *Student development in tomorrow's higher education — A return to the academy.* Washington: American Personnel and Guidance Association, 1972.
Brown, R.D. How evaluation can make a difference. In G.R. Hanson, (Ed.), *Evaluating program effectiveness: New directions for student services.* San Francisco: Jossey-Bass, 1978.
Buros, O.K. *The seventh mental measurements yearbook.* Highland Park, N.J.: Gryphon, 1972.
Campbell, D.T., & Stanley, J.C. *Experimental and quasi-experimental design for research.* Chicago: Rand-McNally, 1968.
Carnegie Commission on Higher Education. *The purposes and performance of higher education in the United States.* New York: McGraw-Hill, 1973.
Chikering, A.W. Education and identity. San Francisco: Jossey-Bass, 1969.
Cronbach, L.J., & Furby, L. How we should measure "change" — or should we? *Psychological Bulletin,* 1970, *74,* 68-80.
Cross, K.P. *Beyond the open door.* San Francisco: Jossey-Bass, 1971.
Cross, K.P. *Accent on learning.* San Francisco: Jossey-Bass, 1976.
Dressel, P.L., & Mayhew, L.B. *General education: Explorations in evaluation.* Washington, D.C.: American Council on Education, 1954.
Ebel, R.L. *Measuring educational achievement.* Englewood Cliffs, N.J.: Prentice-Hall, 1965.
Erickson, E. *Identity and the life cycle: Psychological issues.* New York: International Universities Press, 1959.
Erikson, E. *Identity: Youth and crisis.* New York: Norton, 1968.
Feldman, K.A. Difficulties in measuring and interpreting change and stability during college. In Author (Ed.), *College and student.* New York: Pergamon, 1972.

Fenske, R.H. Some trends and issues in higher education which influence the student services profession. In U. Delworth and G.R. Hanson (Eds.), *Handbook for student services.* San Francisco, Jossey-Bass, in press.

Harris, C.W. (Ed.) *Problems in measuring change.* Madison: University of Wisconsin Press, 1963.

Harvey, O.J., Hunt, D.E., & Schroder, H.M. *Conceptual systems and personality organization.* New York: Wiley, 1961.

Heath, D. *Explorations of maturity.* New York: Appelton-Century-Crofts, 1965.

Heath, D. *Growing up in college.* San Francisco: Jossey-Bass, 1968.

Heath, D. *Maturity and competence.* New York: Gardner, 1977.

Heath, R. *The reasonable adventurer.* Pittsburg: University of Pittsburg Press, 1964.

Heath, R. Form, flow, and full-being – response to White's paper. *The Counseling Psychologist,* 1973, *4,* 56-63.

Holland, J.L. *The psychology of vocational choice: A theory of personality types and model environments.* Waltham, Mass.: Blaisdell, 1966.

Holland, J.L. *Making vocational choices: A theory of careers.* Englewood Cliffs, New Jersey: Prentice-Hall, 1973.

Hunt, D.E. A conceptual systems change model and its applications to education. In O.J. Harvey (Ed.), *Experience, structure, and adaptability.* New York: Springer, 1966.

Hunt, D.E. A conceptual level matching model for coordinating learner characteristics with educational approach. *Interchange,* 1970, *1,* 68-72.

Katz, J., & Associates. *No time for youth: Growth and constraint in college students.* San Francisco: Jossey-Bass, 1968.

Keniston, K. Social change and youth in America. In K. Yamamoto (Ed.), *The college student and his culture.* Boston: Houghton Mifflin, 1968.

Knefelkamp, L., Widick, C., & Parker, C.A. Theories of college student development. In U. Delworth and G.R. Hanson (Eds.), *Handbook for student services.* San Francisco: Jossey-Bass, in press.

Kohlberg, L. Stage and sequence: The cognitive developmental approach to socialization. In D. Goslin (Ed.), *Handbook of socialization theory and research.* Chicago: Rand McNally, 1969.

Kohlberg, L. A cognitive-developmental approach to moral education. *Humanist,* 1972, *6,* 13-16.

Kohlberg, L. The cognitive-developmental approach to moral education. *Phi Delta Kappan,* 1975, *10,* 670-677.

Kuh, G.D., Dannells, M., Doherty, P., & Ganshaw, T.F. Student development theory in practice. *NASPA Journal,* 1977, *16* (2), 48-52.

Lenning, O.T. *Previous attempts to "structure" educational outcomes and outcome-related concepts: A compilation and review of the literature.* Boulder, Colo.: National Center for Higher Education Management Systems, 1977.

Lenning, O.T. Assessing student education progress. *ERIC/Higher Education Research Currents,* April 1978. In *AAHE College and University Bulletin,* 1978, *30,* 3-6.

Lenning, O.T. Assessment and evaluation related to student services. In U.M. Delworth and G.R. Hanson (Eds.), *Handbook for student services.* San Francisco: Jossey-Bass, in press.

Lenning, O.T. Munday, L.A., & Maxey, E.J. Student educational growth during the first two years of college. *College and University,* 1969, *44,* 145-153.

Levinson, D., Darrow, C.N., Klein, E.B., Levinson, M.H., & McKee, B. *The season's of a man's life.* New York: Knopf, 1978.

Loevinger, J. The meaning and measurement of ego-development. *The*

American Psychologist, 1966, *21,* 195-206.
Loevinger, J. *Ego-development.* San Francisco: Jossey-Bass, 1976.
Lord, F.M. Elementary models for measuring change. In C.W. Harris (Ed.), *Problems in measuring change.* Madison: University of Wisconsin Press, 1963.
Marcia, J. Development and validation of ego-identity status. *Journal of Personality and Social Psychology,* 1966, *35,* 551-558.
Miller, T.K., & Prince, J.S. *The future of student affairs.* San Francisco: Jossey-Bass, 1977.
Myers-Briggs type indicator. Princeton, N.J.: Educational Testing Service, 1962.
Nunnally, J.C. The study of change in evaluation research. In E. Struening and M. Guttentag (Eds.), *Handbook of evaluation research.* Beverly Hills, CA: Sage, 1975.
Oetting, E.R., & Cole, C.W. Method, design, and implementation in evaluation. In G.R. Hanson (Ed.), *Evaluating program effectiveness: New directions for student services.* San Francisco: Jossey-Bass, 1978.
Perry, W.G., Jr. *Forms of intellectual and ethical development in the college years.* New York: Holt, Rinehart & Winston, 1970.
Piaget, J. Cognitive development in children. In R. Ripple and V. Rockcastle (Eds.), *Piaget rediscovered: A report on cognitive studies in curriculum development.* Ithaca: Cornell University School of Education, 1964.
Sanford, N. *The American College.* New York: Wiley, 1962.
Scriven, M. The method of evaluation. In R. Tyler, R. Gagne, and M. Scriven (Eds.), *Perspectives on curriculum evaluation.* Chicago: Rand McNally, 1967.
Scriven, M. *Evaluation skills.* Audio cassette tape. Washington, D.C.: American Educational Research Association, 1971.
Stern, G.G. *People in context: Measuring person-environment congruence in education and industry.* New York: Wiley, 1970
Tucker, L.R., Damarin, S., & Messick, S. A base-free measure of change. *Psychometrika,* 1966, *31,* 457-473.
Vaillant, G. *Adaptation to life.* Boston: Little-Brown, 1977.
Witkins, H.A., Dyle, R.B., Paterson, H.F., Goodenough, D.R., & Karp, S.A. *Psychological differentiation.* New York: Wiley, 1962.

14
NEEDS ASSESSMENT IN STUDENT AFFAIRS
Oscar T. Lenning and Andrea C. McAleenan

All social institutions presumably exist to meet individual and group needs. This basic value is reflected in student affairs which came into being during the early 1900s to meet student needs. By the 1960s there were large numbers of college staff members primarily engaged in specialized services to students such as admissions, records, financial aids, counseling, advising, orientation, housing, learning skills assistance, living-learning centers, career education, and athletics.

During the 1970s, field work and other off-campus experience became an integral part of the formal curriculum in many institutions. Other innovations such as internships, cooperative education, and external degree programs emerged from the emphasis on career education. Many faculty acknowledged the importance of teaching approaches that attempted to integrate the affective and cognitive domains. In addition, increasing numbers of non-traditional (older, low ability, disadvantaged, etc.) students with unique characteristics and educational needs were enrolling in postsecondary institutions. The collaboration concept (student development specialists and other members of the faculty working together to promote student learning) was recommended as the preferred approach to facilitating student development (Miller & Prince, 1976).

In concert with efforts to increase its status within the college community, the student affairs profession has underscored the importance of determining whether student needs are being met by the institution. Thus, during the last decade the profession has perceived the need for more objective, systematic, and effective evaluation procedures.

The evaluation literature generally acknowledges the importance of assessing needs as a prelude to or a part of a systematic evaluation process. The procedures for such assessment, however, are rarely explicated. For example, despite 603 entries in the *Evaluation Bibliography* (Bunda, 1976), perhaps the most comprehensive bibliography of evaluation references ever compiled, no mention of needs assessment is made. It is almost as if needs assessment is a self explanatory and, perhaps, elementary process. Yet, needs assessment is a complex, difficult set of procedures that are largely unresearched (Witkin, 1975).

The same conclusion can be drawn about needs assessment in student affairs. Student affairs staff are generally quite knowledgeable and proficient in identifying and assessing important needs of individual clients. When designing programs for groups, however, the identification and assessment of group needs tends to be subjective, unsystematic, overly simplistic, and as a result, often ineffective. Even when the student affairs literature discusses needs assessment as a prerequisite to or part of evaluation, it is dealt with in an introductory fashion (e.g., Burck and Peterson's [1975] discussion of five recommended steps for good program development and evaluation). Of course, in student affairs there is an additional problem in that reports of systematic evaluation appear only sporadically in the literature (see Chapter 1).

In this chapter, the concept of "need" will be clarified, and the importance of "which needs for whom" will be discussed, along with relevant classifications of needs that can be useful in planning student affairs needs assessment. Alternative approaches, strategies, techniques, and procedures relevant for needs assessment will also be examined.

WHOSE NEEDS?

Before needs can be assessed, it is essential to ask the following question: Which specific group's needs is it important to identify and understand for planning and evaluating a particular student affairs program? All students may have some needs in common that the program could help meet (e.g., the need for organized group recreational activities). However, various subgroups of students are likely to have different types and patterns of needs. For example, the following special groups of students have been found to have special counseling and/or other student service needs: commuting students versus resident students (Chickering 1974); environmentally handicapped students (Kapel, 1971); married students (Flores, 1973); minority students (Moore, 1970); students such as homemakers, military veterans, retirees, and retrainees (Cross, 1978; Lenning & Hanson, 1977); and physically handicapped students (Coffing, Hodson & Hutchinson, 1973).

In order to effectively improve student affairs programs, it is also important to identify and assess the needs of particular non-student groups such as: the families of students, prospective students, high school counselors, dropouts, alumni, and the local community members. Student affairs staff are often involved in developing informational materials and providing institutional and program information and advice to prospective students, parents, and high school counselors. They are also responsible for programs and activities such as college-high school relations, student-parent relations, parent visitation days, orientation programs for prospective students and parents, student exit interviews, former student relations, college-community relations, job placement programs, community work-study programs, etc.

Which groups should be of concern in assessing needs depends on where the institutional context in the student affairs program is found. For example, the institution's size, purpose and mission, goals, and constituencies all are directly related to the kind of groups likely to be the foci of needs assessment. A comprehensive taxonomy of broad groups in postsecondary education that might be the target audiences for needs assessments is presented in Appendix A, and each of these groups (e.g., students) could be separated into a number of overlapping subgroups. This taxonomy constitutes one dimension of the NCHEMS Outcomes Structure (Lenning, Lee, Micek & Service, 1977).

The importance of specifying whose needs are of concern cannot be over-emphasized. For example, too many assessments of students' needs have focused on "students in general" as the target group with little or no subgrouping. It should also be emphasized that target groups can be too specific in nature. Focusing separately on groups that are not particularly unique makes the needs assessment unduly cumbersome and may decrease the usefulness of the assessment data for planning purposes.

The taxonomy in Appendix A suggests important target groups that might otherwise be overlooked. To illustrate, the category titled "association communities" emphasizes that consideration should be given to the needs of the student affairs profession; e.g., the need for sharing innovations, experiences, and research with colleagues throughout the country.

CLARIFYING THE CONCEPT OF NEED

In most cases, needs assessment studies have been based on the discrepancy definition of need: i.e., a need exists if there is a discrepancy between "what should be" and "what is currently the case." During the 1960's, process and procedural discrepancies between the actual and the ideal were generally included. However, since Kaufman, Corrigan, and Johnson (1969), the focus in the needs assessment literature has tended to be entirely on discrepancies in outcomes or results.

More recently, some discussion has centered on whether a discrepancy concept of need is adequate or necessary for an effective and productive needs study. For example, Scriven (1977) refers to this definition as the primary reason that needs assessment models employed in the past by evaluators "are farcical and decisions based on them are built on soluable sand" (p. 25). One problem with the discrepancy concept of need is that it has led many needs assessors to equate "wants" or demands with needs. "Wants" may very well be indicators of the presence of need, particularly if "wants" develop into demands or expressions of anguish. Nevertheless, an authentic need may not exist. For example, some students may want or demand something merely because other students have it, because it will attract attention, or to keep other students from getting it. In other words, the real need may not be the expressed need. Conversely, students may have needs and not realize them, or they may recognize the need but not be willing to act upon what the need implies. For example, a student may recognize the need for counseling but not want to request it, or be unwilling to take the necessary steps to implement the counselor's suggestions.

It is important to identify and analyze wants and demands in an assessment of need. However, most program needs assessments have not gone beyond this point but merely have equated "wants" and "demands" with needs. Needs assessors should use any additional evidence that they can find or gather to assist in determining whether "wants" and "demands" indicate "real needs" and whether other needs are also present.

Another problem with the discrepancy or deficiency definition occurs when the need has been fulfilled. In discrepancy-based needs assessment, "met needs" are not considered to be needs, even if the deficiency would reoccur were the support withdrawn that has satisfied or met the need. Assessments of need by student affairs staff should identify and assess the satisfied needs of the target groups so that staff are prepared to act should conditions change and deficiencies appear. In other words, staff should be sensitive to maintenance needs (need for "lots") as well as incremental needs (need for more) (Scriven, 1977).

Also related to the consideration of what is a need is the fact that because someone can benefit from something does not satisfy the criterion of need (Scriven, 1977). For example, a gift of one million dollars would benefit most people; but having less than a million dollars would not put most people into an "unsatisfactory condition." According to this view, a need is present only when an unsatisfactory condition exists or would exist if the need were not being met. But who decides what is an unsatisfactory condition, and what criteria should be used in making that judgment?

For the purpose of this chapter, a "need" is considered to be a combination of discrepancy and level of necessity. The degree to which elements of both components exist should be judged by a relevant person or group using objective criteria and methodologies that have been mutually agreed upon by the assessor(s) and the target group. The relevant person or group to determine when the combination of necessity and discrepancy constitute need, and the point at which needs are partially or fully met, depend on the situation and context. However, it is important to remember that the amount of need varies directly with both the level of necessity and the amount of discrepancy — the same amount of necessity with increased discrepancy means greater unmet and overall need and vice versa. Furthermore, as Burton and Merrill (1977) have suggested, unmet needs can be met by lowering the threshold of necessity, closing up the discrepancy (overcoming the deficiency), or a combination of both. For example, a student affairs professional's need to publish a study can be reduced by lowering the expectations of the profession or institution concerning publication or by the staff member closing the discrepancy through completing a study and publishing it.

WHAT NEED? WITH WHAT TYPES OF NEEDS SHOULD WE BE CONCERNED?

For any individual or group, there are many different needs that could be of concern. How then do student affairs staff determine which types of needs are most important to identify and assess for a particular person or group, and program?

In a comprehensive review of the literature on needs and needs assessment, Lenning, Beal, Cooper, and Passmore (submitted for publication) have identified a number of need schemas. Many of these categorizations are pertinent to the concerns of student affairs staff and can stimulate thinking about the process of determining which needs should be assessed for various target groups.

An early classification of needs was developed by Murray *et al.* (1938) based on interviews with college students at Harvard and resulted in the development of a variety of *need for achievement* and *need for affiliation* scales. Some of these scales were objective and some projective in nature. Murray postulated 20 manifest (leading to overt action) and eight latent (not leading to overt action but to active imagination and fantasies) needs.

Maslow's (1954) hierarchy of needs is another schema that has greatly influenced student affairs professionals. According to Maslow, needs at a particular level cannot be met until those at lower levels in the hierarchy have been satisfied. There have been a number of protentially useful attempts to operationalize Maslow's formulation (e.g., Groves, Kahalis & Erickson, 1975).

Developmental tasks related to maturity and chronological age in which earlier tasks must be mastered or accomplished before individuals can move on to further tasks suggest a different set of needs. For example, Cronbach (1963) has referred to several basic needs including: affection, adult approval, peer approval, independence, competence, and self respect. In an earlier and more extensive formulation, Havighurst (1952) identified ten primary ordered developmental tasks for adolescents, eight for early adulthood, seven for middle age, and six for later maturity.

It is also possible to classify needs in terms of goals. For example, Beatty (1976) has related needs to goal-state continua. Her prescriptive needs for individuals are determined by societal norms and standards, while motivational needs are thought to be determined by the individual's goals. Lenning (1977a) has compiled numerous classifications of educational goals found in the literature for individuals, society, and individuals plus society. In some instances the categories are very detailed and narrow in focus, while in others the categories are broad.

Closely related to goals are outcomes. As mentioned earlier, needs assessment studies have generally focused on needs in terms of outcomes or results. For example, Chickering (1969) identified seven developmental vectors for college students each of which had two or more subcategories of outcomes. Bowen's (1977) identification of numerous types of long-term impacts on graduates and society is another example. Appendix B shows a comprehensive generic taxonomy of possible outcomes that could be used with any of the target group categories in Appendix A. Many of these outcomes could constitute important student affairs program needs.

Environmental needs and the processes needed to bring about the desired outcomes also deserve consideration. Chickering (1969, 1974), Aulepp and Delworth (1976), and Baird (1976) have discussed educational environmental factors and processes that can facilitate particular types of student outcomes. In addition, Lenning *et al.* (1974a, 1974b) compiled a comprehensive review of nonintellective factors found to be related to various types of educational outcomes such as GPA, persistence, motivation, attitudes and values, social skills, confidence, and self-concept.

Needs can also be related to problems. For example, each of the 11 problem areas considered by the college student form of the *Mooney Problem Check List* (Mooney & Gordon, 1950) can imply particular needs: (1) health and physical development, (2) finances-living condition-employment, (3) social and recreational activities, (4) social-physical relations, (5) personal-psychological relations, (6) courtship-sex-marriage, (7) home and family, (8) morals and religion, (9) adjustment of school work, (10) the future vocational and educational, and (11) curriculum and teaching procedures. There is also an "adult" form of this checklist that may be more appropriate for certain student groups. A converse strategy to the above has been promoted by Campbell and Markle (1967), who have developed techniques for transforming educational needs into well-defined problems. They contend that educators need carefully designed problem-formulation training in order to translate needs to problems effectively.

Bradshaw (1972) and Burton and Merrill (1977) have proposed an additional typology of needs that could be useful in student affairs programming. The categories in this typology are: (1) normative needs, (2) felt needs, (3) expressed needs, (4) comparative needs, and (5) anticipated or projected needs. Still another potentially useful classification of needs for student services consists of basic (primary, root, or underlying) human needs versus secondary (derived, learned, or deduced) needs. Monette (1977) has labeled these two categories "innate needs" and "acquired needs."

WHAT APPROACHES AND PROCEDURES SHOULD BE USED FOR CONDUCTING STUDENT AFFAIRS NEEDS ASSESSMENTS?

Conducting needs assessment is an important activity related to student affairs program evaluation. Few suggestions have been put forward as to how such assessments can systematically and effectively be carried out within student affairs, however. This section will discuss how to conduct assessments of individual and group needs.

ASSESSING INDIVIDUAL NEEDS

Any program designed to identify the needs of individual students is of central importance to student affairs. Assessment procedures utilized in this context can assist a student in identifying current needs and clarifying strategies for future change. Data relating to individual personality characteristics, perceptions, values, goals, and interests can provide a framework within which a student can move towards continual growth and development.

An example of a needs clarification model was initiated at Azusa Pacific College as a means of enhancing planned growth among individual students. The strategy was formulated as part of a project conducted by graduate students in 1977-1978. In the first step, a conceptual framework for the project was created by examining various developmental and learning theories. The six-stage model that was adopted was largely based on Chickering's (1969) seven vectors. The areas chosen for examination of personal needs among college students included: Personal/Emotional, Social/Interpersonal, Intellectual/Cognitive, Values/Religious Orientation, Career/Life Planning, and Physical Fitness.

The next step involved the selection of appropriate assessment tools for each of the six areas. The following criteria for selecting the best available assessment tools were used:
1. Instruments should assess each area of need using a clearly defined conceptualization of that need.
2. A comparative analysis of the alternative assessment tools should be conducted taking into consideration the:
    a. Degree of congruence between stated purpose of instrument and the needs assessment/clarification purpose;

    b. Availability of appropriate instruments;
    c. Data regarding the instrument's validity, reliability, and standardization;
    d. Costs involved — funds available.

The instruments chosen for the six areas were: Personal/Emotional (*California Psychological Inventory*), Social/Interpersonal (*Fundamental Interpersonal Relations Inventory*), Values-Religious Orientation (The University of Wisconsin Survey Instrument and University and Society: Student Perspectives) and selected values clarification exercises — *(Yourself Halfway and Values Clarification)*, Cognitive/Intellectual *(Omnibus Personality Inventory* and *Learning Styles Questionnaires)*, Career/Life Planning *(Hall Occupational Orientation Inventory)*, and physical fitness tests. Instrument selection should be made according to individual variables appropriate to the institution, students, or staff being considered.

A five-part sequential plan was formulated to facilitate the process of clarifying student needs (see Figure 1). Pertinent bibliographic materials were also included to provide students with background information as well as material for future references.

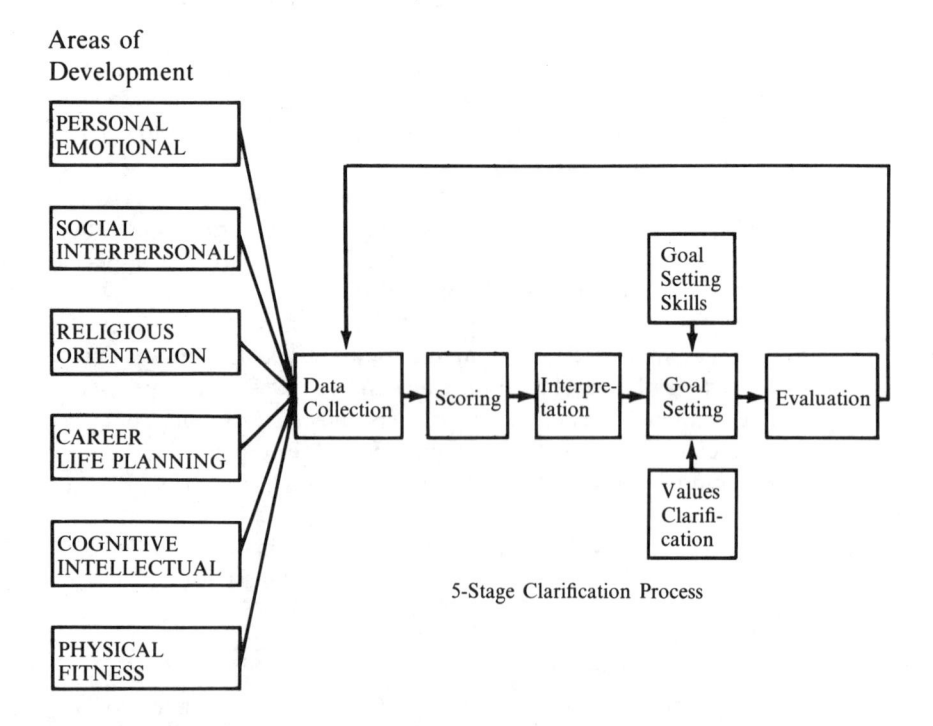

Figure 1. A procedural model for student need clarification
a Reprinted from McAleenan and Deddo (submitted for publication)

15
A STUDENT AFFAIRS APPLICATION OF THE CIPP EVALUATION MODEL

Robert F. Rodgers

This case study describes an application of the CIPP Evaluation model (Stufflebeam, Foley, Gephart, Guba, Hammond, Merriman & Provus, 1971) to the development of a new student affairs program at The Ohio State University. Stufflebeam's model is designed to provide decision makers with systematic information at each phase of program development. Although program development may not appear to be an important topic in times of austerity in higher education, there are several reasons to support both program development or redevelopment and systematic evaluation.

First, program development and evaluation lead to higher quality programs at more efficient cost/benefit ratios. Too often in student affairs, new programs are designed, implemented, and institutionalized in less than one term without having been systematically evaluated. It usually is not clear whether the program responds to or anticipates a demonstrated need; the intended audience may be only vaguely defined; and goals may not be explicit. Further, the procedures of a given design may be "lost" due to staff turn-over or the fact that programmatic designs often are not explicitly detailed in writing. Finally, *ad hoc* program development probably is more expensive in the long run than systematically developed and evaluated programs. This is due to the fact that systematic evaluations gather data relevant to the problems mentioned above and provide built-in "go" versus "no-go" decision making points throughout the program development process.

Second, contraction in higher education will require most institutions to develop programs to attract non-traditional students. Although this application of Stufflebeam's model was not directed at a new clientele, it does demonstrate its applicability in student affairs and provides rationale for its general use.

THE CIPP EVALUATION MODEL

Stufflebeam's approach to evaluation is called the CIPP (Context, Input, Process, Product) evaluation model. In order to understand the CIPP model, the definition of decision types and their relationship to evaluation and program development will be described.

According to Stufflebeam (1973) decisions can be classified as a function of whether they relate to *ends* or *means* and *intentions* or *actualities*. Figure 1 represents the alternatives: (1) intended ends are *goals* for a program. *Planning decisions* will determine goals and objectives for a program. (2) Intended means are the *design* of a program. *Procedural and structural decisions* are made as alternative designs are created and considered. (3) Actual means are the procedures and structure *actually implemented or used. Implementation decisions* are made to use or refine the design of the program. (4) Actual ends are made to use or refine the design of the program (4) Actual ends are the outcomes or attainments of the program as implemented. Recycling decisions judge attainments and accept, amend, or terminate the program.

	INTENDED	ACTUAL
ENDS	GOALS Planning Decisions to determine goals and objectives	ATTAINMENTS Outcome Recycling Decisions to judge & react to attainments
MEANS	DESIGNS Procedural or Structuring Decisions to design programs	DESIGNS IN USE Implementation Decision to use & refine procedures or structure in a program design

Figure 1. Types of decisions

There are four types of evaluation associated with the four decision types: context, input, process, and product. Context evaluation provides information for planning decisions in order to determine objectives. Input evaluation provides information for procedural and structural decisions in order to select a program design. Process evaluation provides information for implementation decisions in order to accept, refine, or correct the design as actually implemented. Product evaluation provides information for recycling decisions in order to accept, amend, or terminate the program.

The decision types and evaluation types can now be related to program planning. There are many ways to conceptualize program planning processes (e.g. Parker, 1972; Micek &Arney, 1973). The following program planning steps represent a synethesis of several approaches and illustrate the relationship between program planning and the CIPP model:

1. Assessment
2. Develop Goals and Objectives
3. Design a Program
4. Design an Implementation Plan for the Program
5. Plot Run of the Program
6. Evaluate the Pilot Run
7. Adopt, Amend, or Drop the Program
8. Institutionalize the Program
9. Evaluate the Institutionalized Program

In Figure 2 program planning steps, evaluation types, and decision types are related.

CONTEXT EVALUATION

Context evaluation serves both the assessment and development of goals and objectives steps in program development. Its *purposes* are to : (1) define the characteristics and parameters of the environment to be served; (2) determine general goals and specific objectives; (3) identify and diagnose the problems or barriers which might inhibit attainment of goals and objectives. Its *tasks* are to: (1) define the environment, both *actual* and *desired;* (2) define *unmet needs* and *unused opportunities;* and (3) *diagnose problems or barriers.* Finally, its *methods* are: (1) conceptual analysis to define the limits of the setting to be served; (2) empirical studies to define unmet needs and unused opportunities; (3) judgment of experts and clients on barriers and problems; and (4) judgment of experts and clients on desired goals and objectives.

INPUT EVALUATION

Input evaluation serves the two design steps (program design and implementation design) of program development. Its *purposes* are to: (1) design a program (intervention) to meet the objectives; (2) determine the resources needed to deliver the program; and (3) determine whether staff and available resources are adequate to implement the program. Its *tasks* are to: (1) develop a *plan* for a program through examinations of various intervention *strategies;* and (2) develop a *program implementation plan* which considers time, resources, and barriers to be overcome. The first task requires identification and assessment of the following:
   (a) strategies for achieving objectives
      — time requirements,
      — funding and physical requirements,
      — acceptability to client group,
      — potential to meet objectives,
      — potential barriers;

(b) capabilities and resources of the staff in the setting
— expertise to do various strategies (interventions),
— funding and physical resources,
— potential barriers.

The second task can be developed only after the essential dimensions of the first task have been defined. The second task is essentially an organizational intervention problem — how to gain entry, acceptance, and institutionalization of the program. *Methods* for conducting input evaluation are lacking according to Stufflebeam. Student affairs staff must accept this challenge and begin to design and disseminate creative methodologies.

PROCESS EVALUATION

Process evaluation serves the pilot run and/or institutionalization steps of program development. Its *purpose* is to provide decision makers with information necessary to determine whether the *implemented version* of the design should be accepted and standardized, amended, or discontinued. Its *tasks* are to: (1) identify discrepancies between actual implementation and intended design; and (2) identify defects in the design or implementation plan. The *methods* for process evaluation include the following characteristics:

(a) A person is assigned exclusively to the role of evaluator;

(b) This person monitors and keeps a record of setting conditions, program elements as they actually occured, barriers, and unanticipated factors;

(c) This person gives feedback on discrepancies and defects to decision makers.

PRODUCT EVALUATION

Product evaluation is the kind of study which usually is associated with evaluation. It serves program development steps of *outcome evaluation* for pilot projects and institutionalized programs. The *purpose* of product evaluation is to provide information to decision makers related to the outcomes or attainments of a program in order for them to decide whether to continue, modify, refocus, or terminate the program. Its *task* is to develop an experimental, quasi-experimental, case-study or descriptive research design for the program. Stufflebeam recommends that relevant data be collected at time intervals during and after the program. The *methods* of product evaluation included traditional research techniques, operational definitions, multiple measures of objectives, and monitoring for unanticipated results. Output results should be compared to predetermined standards or comparative bases when they are communicated to decision makers.

Program Planning Stage	Supported by Evaluation Type	to make Decision Type
1. Assessment	Context Evaluation	Planning Decision
2. Develop goals and objectives	Context Evaluation	Planning Decision
3. Design a program	Input Evaluation	Procedural & Structural Decisions
4. Design an implementation plan	Input Evaluation	Procedural & Structural Decisions
5. Pilot run the program	Process Evaluation	Implementation Decisions
6. Evaluate outcome of pilot run	Product Evaluation	Recycling Decisions
7. Adopt, amend, drop the program	Product Evaluation	Recycling Decisions
8. Institutionalize the program	Process Evaluation	Implementation Decisions
9. Evaluate Institutionalized program	Product Evaluation	Recycling Decisions

Figure 2. Relations among program planning evaluation, and decision making.

SUMMARY

CIPP evaluation encompasses the entire scope of a program development or redevelopment process. It functions in the planning stages and in evaluation of delivery. At each step, CIPP provides information to decision makers in order to help them decide whether to proceed, recycle, or drop the process and/or program. Appendix A summarizes these features.

THE CASE STUDY

The CIPP model was used to develop and evaluate new programs for Greek social organizations at the Ohio State University (OSU). The staff involved in the project were the Coordinator of Greek Affairs, two graduate student interns, and a faculty member from Student Personnel Work. Many members and alumni of the Greek community ultimately were involved in the process over a two and a half year period.

CONTEXT EVALUATION: OSU PROJECT

In order to define the contextual factors in the OSU Greek environment and to determine if there were unmet needs worthy of further development, four kinds of assessment were conducted: (1) a descriptive profile; (2) conceptual and rational analyses by experts; (3) structured interviews with pledges, officers, and alumni advisors; and (4) behavorial observations.

DESCRIPTIVE DATA

The descriptive profile was collated from data in the files of the Greek Affairs Office. It included the number of chapters, chapter sizes, average length of membership, class rank of officers, pledge class sizes, length of pledgeship, age and class rank of pledges, and percentage of initiations. Briefly, there were 66 Greek groups on the OSU campus. Chapter size varied from 12 to over 100 members. The mean active membership for sororities was 2.2 years, and for fraternities it was 3.2 years. The majority of the officers were juniors with, seniors being the second largest group of officers. Pledge classes ranged in number from 1 to 35 persons. The majority of the pledges were 18 or 19 year old freshmen. Pledgeship lasted a minimum of 10 weeks or one quarter. An average of 60% of the initial pledges were initiated.

CONCEPTUAL AND RATIONAL ANALYSIS BY EXPERTS

The Coordinator of Greek Affairs, the graduate student interns, and the faculty member met regularly to analyze the OSU Greek system.

All sessions were tape recorded and written notes were kept by one of the staff members. The initial sessions focused upon the chapters. Basically, the evaluators examined the following:

(a) What are members' behaviors and values?
- in meetings and committees
- in programs and projects
- at social occasions
- in rushing activities
- as friends living together

(b) Are there discrepancies between what "is" and what "ought to be"?

The meetings also focused on pledges and pledge education programs. Again, what were their behaviors and values? What were the discrepancies between "is" and "ought"? These questions were discussed in reference to the following:
- their meetings,
- their programs and projects,
- their interpersonal relationships
- the content of pledge education programs, i.e., what values and behaviors are modeled and reinforced?

The results of these sessions were summarized in writing and used to develop structured interview formats for the next assessment.

INTERVIEWS WITH PLEDGES, OFFICERS, ALUMNI ADVISORS

Structured interviews on the content listed above were conducted with pledges, officers, and alumni advisors. Chapters were selected by using three chapter characteristics: (1) size; (2) mutuality of persons rushed; (3) and the Greek advisor's subjective ratings of prestige. From each of these three categories, two fraternities and two sororities were randomly selected. As a result, 12 chapters (6 fraternities and 6 sororities) were invited to participate in the project. Requests to interview 4 pledges (randomly selected by the staff), 4 officers, and 2 alumni advisors per chapter resulted in over 100 interviews over a time period of one quarter. All interviews were taped and the data were summarized.

BEHAVIORAL OBSERVATIONS

The same fraternities and sororities also were systematically observed by two graduate interns on a planned schedule. Behaviors at social events, projects and programs, pledge education sessions, initiation week, and informal house interactions were observed, categorized, and summarized. The results confirmed staff predictions that espoused and observed behaviors would be somewhat different.

Some Conclusions From the Context Evaluation

All four types of assessment were useful. If time and resources permit, all four are recommended. In this project one academic year was invested in conducting, analyzing, and summarizing the data. Certainly less rigorous versions of each of four types of assessment are possible and are recommended over doing only one type more rigorously.

Briefly, Greek groups were found to hold similar ideals and general goals. These may be summarized as follows:

(1) forming a brotherhood or sisterhood of close, personal friends who like to socialize, study and participate in athletics and service projects in sharing and caring ways;
(2) providing organizational experiences in leadership, team work, and collaboration;
(3) fostering the development of individual members and pledges;
(4) developing relationships for a lifetime, not only for the duration of college.

Reality often falls short of espoused ideals. For many the ideals are only partially achieved. There were problems in the following areas:

(1) Cliques tend to form and fractionalize the total group. Limited friendships, suspicion, and internal distrust often result.
(2) Internal competition among cliques is a common problem. Competitive behaviors are used in collaborative situations.
(3) There is a tendency to involve only elite members in activities in order to "win" and thus supposedly to accrue prestige. This is contrasted to the involvement of as many members as possible in activities in order to "develop" the members, and then to win if you can under those conditions.
(4) Individual and group financial problems and financial mismanagement are common problems.
(5) Behaviors of student leaders often reveal an absence of skills in leadership, group processing, decision making, etc.
(6) Pledge education programs tend to emphasize and reinforce the problem behaviors outlined above for the chapters. In other words, the socialization process of pledgeship tends to guarantee the problems will persist.

In short, to the extent the groups were less collaborative, less team oriented, less friendship oriented, and less developmental in operations, then stated goals were not being achieved.

In order to determine general goals and specific objectives and identify possible barriers, a committee comprised of the four staff members, three pledges, three officers, and two alumni advisors served as decision makers. The data from all four assessments were presented to the group. They made judgments about whether there were needs worthy of further development, prioritized the needs, and identified and diagnosed barriers. It is strongly recommended that both staff and students be involved in the process of negotiating entry into the organization (Hornstein, Bunker, Burke, Gindes & Lewicki, 1971) and attempting to improve the quality of the subsequent judgments. It is also important to note a distinction between a *need* and a *desired objective*. A need implies the client's willingness to provide support (financial and otherwise) for a program. A desired objective is espoused but is not supported with dollars and other resources.

In the OSU project the group decided remedial interventions were *needed* in the short run, and proactive/developmental interventions were *needed* in order to change the socialization process of pledge training for the long term. The students and alumni tested the *need* versus *desired objective* distinction with their constituencies. The barriers identified were:

(1) Some Greeks believe universities really are not supportive of Greek organizations, and therefore, the project could be viewed with suspicion.
(2) There were 66 groups to be served.
(3) Alumni support would be critical, especially for sororities.

In short, entry could be a problem. An implementation plan would need to take into account these potential barriers.

INPUT EVALUATION: OSU PROJECT

There were two areas of need in which programs were designed in the OSU project: (1) chapter intervention; and (2) pledge education intervention. The design of a new pledge education program will be reviewed. As mentioned earlier, creative methods for conducting input evaluations are lacking. Hence, in order to conduct an input evaluation in the OSU project, methods had to be developed. The tasks of an input evaluation, the processes or activities used as methods, and the persons involved in the activities are summarized in Table 1.

Formulate Specific Objectives

The staff-student-alumni committee used consensus methodologies (Pfeiffer & Jones, 1973) to arrive at general goals for the program. The staff then used Mager's (1962) recommendations for formulating specific learning objectives. Learning objectives should (1) clearly state what pledges are expected to be able *to do, to know,* and *to feel* as an outcome of their learning experiences; (2) how well they are to do, know, or feel them; and (3) under what (physical and psychological) conditions they are to do, know, or feel them.

The staff found Mager's criteria to be rigorous, difficult to fulfill, and in some cases, inappropriate for use outside the classroom. Nevertheless, they found his categories and standards very useful in

Table 1
Input Evaluation:
Ohio State Methodology

GOALS	PROCESS OR ACTIVITY	WHO
1. Formulate Specific Objectives	1. Group Consensus Session	1. Staff/Student Committee
2. Generate various strategies	2. Brain Storming Session	2. Staff
3. Evaluate strategies and select one for design purposes	3. Evaluation Session (1 week later) – Individual Assessment and Ranking – Group Consensus on Assessment and Ranking	3. Staff
4. Develop a specific design and implementation plan for the design	4. Individual Creativity and Knowledge of Interventions	4. One person from staff
5. Critique, Revise, Accept a specific design and implementation plan	5. Evaluation Session. Check for Internal Consistency	5. Staff

formulating objectives. Detailed doing, knowing, and feeling objectives were developed for outcomes of the intervention and each part of the design.

GENERATE VARIOUS STRATEGIES

The staff held a brainstorming session to identify strategies which might be used to fulfill the goals and objectives of a new pledge education program. This session required, and was limited by, the professional knowledge of the staff. In Table 2 illustrations from the OSU session are summarized.

Table 2
Input Evaluation: Summary
OSU Brainstorming Session

STRATEGY TYPE	SPECIFIC INTERVENTION TYPE
1. Laboratory Education	- leadership labs - personal growth labs - communication labs - interpersonal communications labs - values clarification labs - weekend labs tended labs - total group labs - officers only labs
2. T-oriented Groups	- Tape led groups - weekend groups - time extended groups
3. Process Consultation	- processing meetings
4. Data-Based Interventions	- Survey feedback - Problem solving retreats

EVALUATE STRATEGIES AND SELECT ONE FOR DESIGN PURPOSES

As individuals working alone, each staff member assessed and prioritized the strategies from the brainstorm session. Each person was asked to use the following questions in developing two priority listings:
  (1) Which strategy can best fulfill the objectives? Why? Defend yourself with research and/or a rationale.
  (2) Which strategy is most compatible with context evaluation data and items such as time requirements, potential barriers, staff competencies, and number of client groups?
  Responses to the first questions require professional knowledge

of interventions, research findings and their respective applications. If staff members lack this expertise, experts should be invited to participate in this activity.

As a group, the staff then met to compare assessments and rankings and to work for consensus on a strategy to use for a specific design. A laboratory education strategy using structured group experiences was selected emphasizing themes of leadership, communications, team building, and personal growth.

DEVELOP A SPECIFIC DESIGN

"Designs by committees look like camels." That is, structured group laboratories designed by committees often lack logical sequencing and pacing, and sometimes reflect questionable content (Jones & Pfeiffer, 1973). These designs may look like camels when race horses are needed. Hence, it is recommended that one person have responsibility for initial design(s). This is a professional task. Professional expertise in design considerations and knowledge of various structured group experiences were required in the OSU case.

CRITIQUE, REVISE, ACCEPT A SPECIFIC DESIGN

A formal evaluation session was used to critique, revise and accept a specific design and implementation plan. A checklist for internal consistency was used as a final evaluation. The checklist is reproduced in Figure 3. A specific design, antecedent conditions, and implementation plan resulted from the meeting.

PROCESS EVALUATION: OSU PROJECT

Rather than institutionalize the new pledge education program with the Greek system, a pilot project involving the pledge classes of two sororities was initiated. In these pilot projects, the new pledge education program initially was added to the regular weekly meetings of the pledge classes. During the first hour, traditional pledge activities were conducted. During the next two hours, one or two structured group experiences were conducted with the group. The experiences were sequenced to achieve the objectives over the 10 weeks of pledgeship. The location of the meeting was the sorority house. A staff person, the pledge trainer, and an alumni advisor (if available) participated in this process.

In order to identify discrepancies between actual implementation and intended design and to identify defects in the design, antecedent conditions, or the implementation plan, a different staff person assumed the role of evaluator. The evaluator studied the design, antecedent conditions, and implementation plan. The evaluator ob-

	Yes	No
1. Staff qualifications are sufficient for performing the design?	___	___
2. Program clearly related to staff's mission?	___	___
3. Design can be performed by trained paraprofessional?	___	___
4. Administrative support is sufficient for program development and planning?	___	___
5. Facility descriptions are adequate for program operation?	___	___
6. Time allocated for program is sufficient to accomplish program goals?	___	___
7. Activities in the design are related to goals?	___	___
8. Alternative activities defined in order to respond to unique demands?	___	___
9. Design can deliver on output objectives?	___	___
10. Design can be done within the budget?	___	___
11. Design will be acceptable to clients (Students and alumni)?	___	___

Figure 3. Checklist for internal consistency of designs.

served and made a record of the conditions under which the meetings were held, program elements as they actually occurred, and unanticipated factors. This information was summarized and discrepancies and defects were identified. Then the information was presented to a decision making group comprised of the staff, pledge trainer and alumni advisor.

After the second week, a decision was made to recycle the design. Changes in the setting, the specific structured experiences used to implement some of the objectives, and the implementation plan were judged to be needed.

The program was redesigned and then used with two sororities in a second pilot test. In the new design, the format involved two weekend retreats away from the sorority houses. The first retreat was held the first weekend after pledging. General themes were: acquaintanceship, purposes of Greek life, team building, communications, collaboration, and personal feedback. The second retreat was held on a weekend prior to initiation. Leadership styles, decision making, principles of planning and execution, power and influence, and commitment to action in the chapter were its themes. In between retreats, the pledge trainer consulted with one staff person so that her weekly activities would reinforce the objectives of the retreats. The staff remained the same, as did the role of the evaluator. This design was completed by both sorority pledge classes.

SOME CONCLUSIONS FROM THE PROCESS EVALUATION

Pilot testing the designs was very beneficial. Although the initial design was believed to be adequate, unanticipated events and defects in the implementation plan made redesign essential. If the initial design had been institutionalized without the pilot test, it is possible the clients would have been alienated to the point that a revised intervention could not have been attempted until several years later; i.e., after many members had graduated. The pilot projects took one year to accomplish; however, they probably saved time in the long run and certainly improved the quality of the design.

Only a staff person familiar with the theoretical nature of the intervention could have served in the role of evaluator. Discrepancies in the setting conditions, implementation plan, and appropriateness of the structured experiences required technical knowledge of the intervention strategy.

PRODUCT EVALUATION: OSU PROJECT

In order to provide decision makers with information on the *outcomes or attainments* of the pledge education program, a comparison group pre-test, post-test research design was used.

The comparison group for each sorority was the sorority which had the largest number of mutual persons on previous bid lists and who were subjectively rated as approximately equal by the Coordinator of Greek Affairs. The comparison group sororities were asked to conduct their usual pledge education programs. The testing sessions were the only unusual events in their education programs. An additional comparison group of randomly selected, non-Greek freshmen women also agreed to participate in the study. Both experimental and comparison groups took the *Personal Orientation Inventory (POI), Fundamental Interpersonal Relationship Orientation-Behavior (FIRO-B), Leadership Styles Inventory (LSI),* and *Cognitive Concepts Scale (CCS)* before and after their pledge education programs. The *Group Functioning Inventory (GFI)* was administered to the pledge classes after the programs. The participants both in experimental and sorority comparison groups are being followed throughout their undergraduate careers. Data will be collected on number of dropouts during pledgeship, chapter offices sought, when the women run for these offices, whether they are elected, and their length of active membership.

The experimental sorority pledge classes scored significantly higher than both comparison groups on the *GFI* and *CCS*. There were no significant differences on the *FIRO-B* scales. On the *POI*, the experimental and comparison pledge classes were not significantly different on pre-test. In contrast, the non-Greek women scored lower than the pledges on every scale at pre-test and significantly lower on self-actualizing values (SAV), self-acceptance (Sa), and synergy (sy). Post-test *POI* results indicated the experimental pledges and non-Greek women moved in positive directions on all scales. The comparison pledges exhibited slight negative movement on 10 of the 13 POI scales. The experimental and comparison pledge groups evidenced the most post test difference on the scales of self-actualization (SA) and of time competence. (Tc). Hence, women who began their respective pledge programs at almost identical levels moved in opposite directions and were significantly different on two scales at the end of the pledge period.

The preliminary results were presented and discussed at a meeting of the staff, students, and alumni who participated in the context evaluation. A judgment was made to institutionalize the program.

SUMMARY AND CONCLUSIONS

The CIPP evaluation model proved to be a useful approach to program planning in this application. Context evaluation was especially important. If the assessment step in program development is taken seriously and is done well, then the chances of avoiding many of the problems cited earlier (*ad hoc* programs based upon unclear needs, vague definitions of persons to be served, unclear goals, etc.) are increased. Stufflebeam et al., (1971) defines the goals and tasks of a context evaluation and suggests several appropriate methodologies. In the OSU project CIPP goals and tasks were accepted; however, mothodological adaptations using four data collecting techniques were tested. The picture of the context as seen by the four kinds of data seemed to be more useful than that of any single part.

The OSU project also experimented with consensus and brainstorming methodologies for input evaluation. Concepts from the Delphi technique (Brown & Helner, 1964; Lipsetz, 1972) were used to design the steps for selecting an intervention strategy after the brainstorming session. The nature of these steps included elements of the following:

(a) Independent judgment of experts on priorities, with written rationales required;
(b) two priorities were solicited: one relative to the objectives, and one relative to the limitations of the context;
(c) the synthesis of two sets of priorities and their rationales in a verbal consensus session.

Finally, the combination of a pilot test and process evaluation probably saved the program. Without the pilot effort, the entire system might have been alienated by the faulty design. Without the process evaluation, concrete information upon which to redesign the program would not have been available.

The CIPP model can be implemented in systematic and formal ways which require lengthy time spans and some expense, or in quicker and less expensive ways. Some programs cannot justify elaborate and expensive implementations; others need to be systematically developed. In either case, CIPP concepts provide guidance for the task.

It has been alleged that the use of systematic processes stifle creativity and lead to mediocre results. In the OSU experience, this was not the case. The systematic processes of the CIPP model were compatible with flights of fantasy, and they provided the discipline needed to help creative efforts meet the demands and limitations of reality.

The CIPP model has all the limitations of any other model. It provides processes and not content. Implementation requires professional expertise in evaluation methodologies and the content area under consideration. The model cannot carry out professional tasks for a student affairs evaluator. It can define the steps of program design and evaluation and their order. The quality of a program, however, is a function both of the steps and the quality of the content which is processed through them. There is no substitute for professional expertise in evaluation methodologies and program content.

REFERENCES

Brown, B., & Helner, O. *Improving the reliability of estimates obtained from a consensus of experts.* Rand Corporation, Technical Report P-2986, September, 1964.

Hornstein, H.A. et al. *Social intervention.* New York: Free Press, 1971.

Jones, J.E., & Pfeiffer, J.W. *The 1973 annual handbook for group facilitators.* La Jolla, California: University Associates, 1973.

Lipsetz, A. *Delphi as an intervention technique in developing a plan of change for student affairs.* Unpublished doctoral dissertation, The Ohio State University, 1972.

Mager, R.R. *Preparing instructional objectives.* BXELMONT, Calif: Fearon, 1962.

Micek, S.S., & Arney, W.R. *Outcome-oriented planning in higher education: An approach or an unpossibility?* Boulder, Colorado: Western Interstate Commission for Higher Education, 1973.

Parker, C.A. *Student development — The new look.* Paper presented at the state convention of Ohio Student Personnel Association, 1972.

Pfeiffer, J.W., & Jones, J.E. *A handbook of structures experiences for human relations training, Vol. IV.* La Jolla, Calif: University Associates, 1973.

Stufflebeam, D.L. Foley, W.J., Gephart, W.J., Guba, E.G., Hammond, R.L., Merriman, H.O., & Provus, M.M. *Educational evaluation and decision making.* Itasca, Illinois: Peacock, 1971.

Appendix A:
Flow Chart for Program Development and CIPP Evaluation

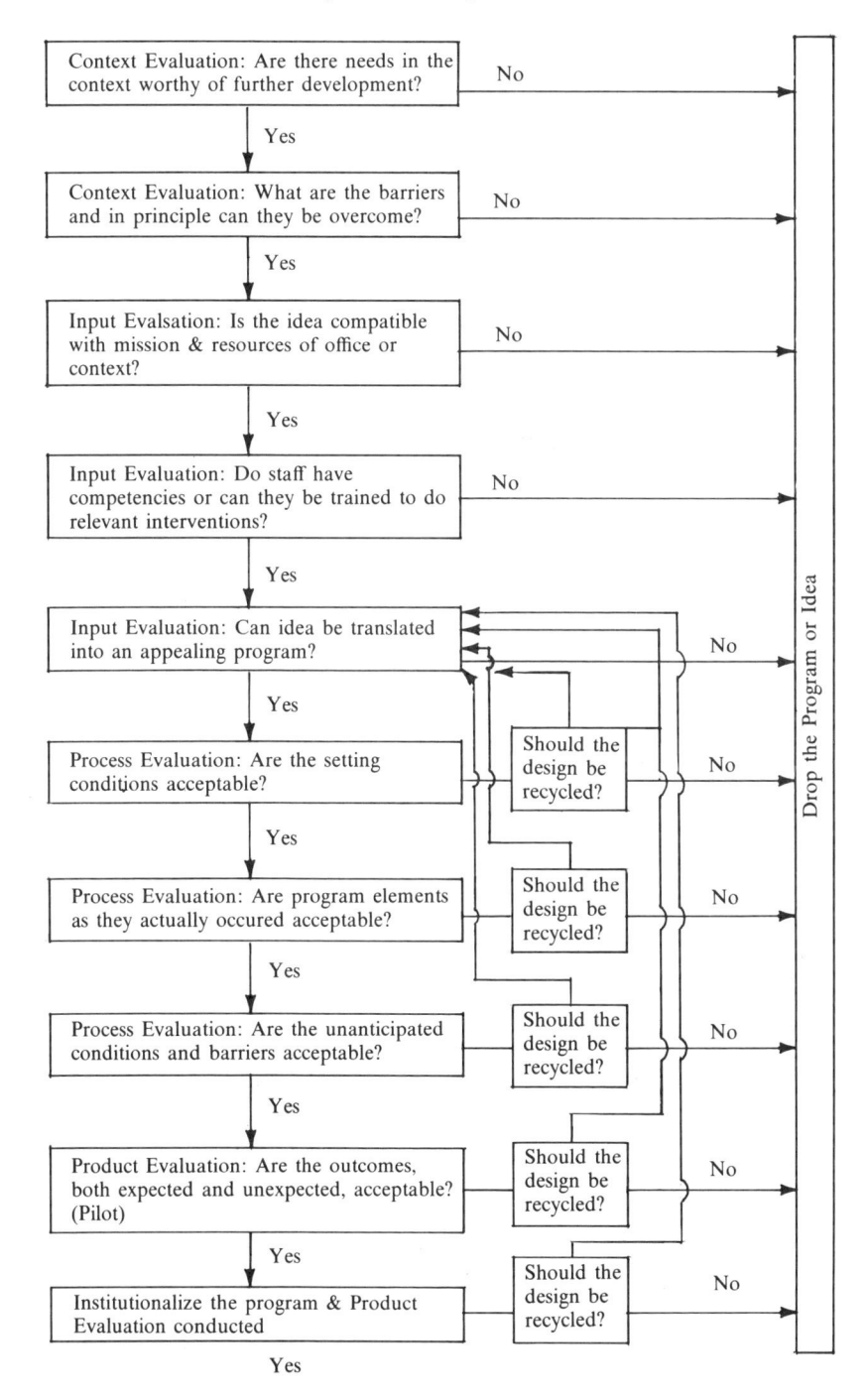

- Context Evaluation: Are there needs in the context worthy of further development? — No → Drop the Program or Idea
- Yes ↓
- Context Evaluation: What are the barriers and in principle can they be overcome? — No → Drop the Program or Idea
- Yes ↓
- Input Evalsation: Is the idea compatible with mission & resources of office or context? — No → Drop the Program or Idea
- Yes ↓
- Input Evaluation: Do staff have competencies or can they be trained to do relevant interventions? — No → Drop the Program or Idea
- Yes ↓
- Input Evaluation: Can idea be translated into an appealing program? — No → Drop the Program or Idea
- Yes ↓
- Process Evaluation: Are the setting conditions acceptable? — Should the design be recycled? — No → Drop the Program or Idea
- Yes ↓
- Process Evaluation: Are program elements as they actually occured acceptable? — Should the design be recycled? — No → Drop the Program or Idea
- Yes ↓
- Process Evaluation: Are the unanticipated conditions and barriers acceptable? — Should the design be recycled? — No → Drop the Program or Idea
- Yes ↓
- Product Evaluation: Are the outcomes, both expected and unexpected, acceptable? (Pilot) — Should the design be recycled? — No → Drop the Program or Idea
- Yes ↓
- Institutionalize the program & Product Evaluation conducted — Should the design be recycled? — No → Drop the Program or Idea
- Yes

16
COMPARING APPLES AND ORANGES: COORDINATING EVALUATION AND DECISION MAKING
Jack McKillip

There are three sides to program evaluation in student affairs. On one is the *evaluator* who may feel the need to be independent or even ignorant (Scriven, 1973) of the organizational contingencies for the program, to have a bias toward outcome measures and to be steeped in the single program-independent variable analogy. On the second side is the student affairs *administrator* or *decision maker* who has the ultimate responsibility for judging the overall worth of the programs being studied. This perspective will usually include multiple programs, an action orientation, and concern with political and logistic aspects of program operation. The third side is the *question:* How is (are) the program(s) doing? The meaning of this question depends upon the context in which it is asked and varies along a dimension anchored at one end by concern for social policy formation and at the other by normal management functions related to student affairs activities, e.g., bugetary allocations and personnel decisions. Much has been written about how to pose evaluation questions when the concern is social policy formation (e.g., Riecken & Boruch, 1974) but little about evaluation questions which arise as part of the normal decision making processes of administrators in student affairs.

THE CENTRAL PROBLEM: COMPARING APPLES AND ORANGES

The chief characteristic of the typical management perspective is that it usually necessitates inter-program comparisons. When merit raises or budget reductions are necessitated, individuals or programs involved in quite different activities often will be compared. Figure 1 presents a short description of the services provided by the Division of the Student Health Service at a major university. While the range of activities is quite large, it is not unlike (in breadth) that offered by many university-based student affairs units. For purposes of evaluation, each of these programs may be approached on at least two levels.

On one level the evaluator asks how well the program has been meeting its goals and objectives. What impact is it having on the problem it was designed to address? An evaluator with a research perspective may well stop at this level, evaluating each program on its own terms. For example, it has been demonstrated that the Lifestyling program can effect changes in diet, exercise and stress (McKillip & Kamens, 1977) and that the Sex Education Workshops can increase growth in sexuality (Voss & McKillip, 1979) and can increase the use of contraceptives (McKillip, Workman, & Dickson, 1978). When presented with this information, the administrator of a Student Health Service might be pleased but also confounded. How can these data be used to make decisions? How can a 5% decrease in smoking associated with the Lifestyling program be compared with a 10% increase in the use of contraceptives associated with the Sex Education Workshops? Thus, while the respective evaluations were rigorously designed to measure program impact, the evaluation questions were not framed in a way that the answers would provide information useful to the decision maker.

The administrator's task is even more complicated than that of comparing various program impacts, since other criteria of worth such as political support and administrative complexity must also be considered. The decision maker's task might include comparison of a program showing 5% impact, 80% student support, and requiring 5 hours per week direct supervision with another program showing 10% impact, 60% student support and requiring 10 hours of weekly supervision. Not only must the decision maker compare apples and oranges (inter-program) but, to do so, must also integrate taste, shape and color (intra-program)!

---

1. Lifestyling: education and support for students to modify behaviors in the areas of diet, smoking, exercise, stress and environmental awareness.
2. Sexuality Counseling: sexual dysfunction counseling and growth groups.
3. Sex Education: workshops and lectures on contraception, venereal disease, sex roles and sexual values clarification.
4. Synergy: crisis oriented mental health service providing emergency counseling, housing and food.
5. Medical Self-Care: education concerning proper use of medical facilities and appropriate situations for self-treatment of symptoms.
6. Alcohol program: education and support for responsible alcohol use.

Figure 1. Service programs provided by prevention program division of student health services, Southern Illinois University at Carbondale.

Part of the difficulty in generating useful information is related to defining the evaluation question on the individual program level and not at the level of the sponsoring unit or organization. The most obvious benefit of asking the question within the context of the organization's strengths and weaknesses is the potential for input to the decision maker. However, to say that an evaluation must be multi-faceted or must include measures of both process and outcome, is not to give the evaluator much insight into the concerns which the administrator must consider.

One common and apparently rigorous solution is to reduce all evaluation questions to some variation on cost, e.g., cost-benefit or cost-effectiveness ratios. Aside from the many problems which are inherent in the use of these techniques, they tend to overemphasize the importance of the criterion of cost for the program. In the context of ongoing student affairs programs, cost should be only one of the criteria which is considered. Other criteria are related to goals and the nature and capabilities of the sponsoring organization or unit. Another common response is to ignore or neglect the problem. This occurs when the decision maker leaves decision criteria unexplicated and the evaluator must divine measures from a list of somewhat pious and vaguely stated organizational goals and objectives. Even where the administrator and evaluator attempt to address the various facets of the evaluation question straight on, the lack of structure in the process makes it more difficult and less fruitful than it can be. Other unsatisfactory solutions can be thought of, such as ignoring evaluative information and making awards or cutbacks across the board. However, these generally leave the evaluator out of the process.

SMART: SIMPLE MULTI-ATTRIBUTE RATING TECHNIQUE

When inter-program comparisons seem desirable, evaluation questions should be defined in a manner that will enable the evaluator to collect the type of information that will be useful to the decision maker. One of the simplest and most flexible of proposed solutions is the Simple Multi-Attribute Rating Technique (SMART) (Edwards, 1971; Edwards, Guttentag & Snapper, 1975). This technique has been used for such diverse decisions as the choice of experiments to be included in NASA's Skylab satellite and of desegregation plans to be implemented by the Los Angeles Public School Board. Most importantly, SMART provides guidance to the evaluator confronted with the task of evaluating a diverse set of programs in a manner to be used in organizational decision making.

In the present context, SMART offers three important advantages. First, it provides a common measure of the worth of completely different programs. The output of the technique is a quantified measure of the worth (called Utility) of a program which is comparable to the measured worth of other programs. Second, the technique focuses on the goals and constraints of the organization which sponsors the various programs. In this sense SMART provides subjective, i.e., internally generated, rather than objective, i.e., externally generated, criteria of worth. Third, the technique provides an explicit decision process which can be used both for evaluation and for planning. Not only does SMART result in an overall judgment of worth, it also identifies areas of strength and weakness for each program. SMART consists of ten steps. These will be detailed below with examples taken from its application to the Prevention Programs Division, Student Health Service described in Figure 1.

Step 1: Identify the persons, organizations, or units which have a stake in the decision(s) to be made. This may involve only the chief administrator for a unit or might also include senior staff in the unit, representatives from parallel units and/or supervising bodies, and student representatives.

Constraints as to whom to include in the process depend on the normal decision processes of the unit. In independent or hierarchically organized units, few participants need be included. Where the evaluation may have important implications for other units or a consensus decision model is used, broad participation is indicated. At Prevention Programs, it was decided to include heads of the individual programs described in Figure 1 and the administrator of the unit. Student representatives would have been included if an appropriate campus group could have been identified. Generally SMART seems robust in the face of differing value orientations (see comments on this topic under Step 7).

Step 2: Identify the program evaluation question. As described above, this question will usually be "How are our programs doing?" However, the technique is flexible enough to consider a whole range of questions, for example, "Where should we expand?" or "How should we spend our limited, new equipment funds?" The decision criteria which are relevant for one question may not be important for another. For example, the ability of a program to attract grant money was not of great importance for evaluating the worth of ongoing programs at Prevention Programs but is a topic of constant discussion when the question of adding new services is raised. The point here is that the result of the evaluation process will depend on the question as posed at this step.

Step 3: Identify the programs and activities to be evaluated. Program designations may be made on the basis of function rather than formal organizational demarcation. At Prevention Programs this task was fairly simple because service functions tended to follow organizational lines. However, it was necessary to divide the sexuality services program into counseling and education components. It should be noted that the level of application of SMART within the organization is quite arbitrary, depending upon where evaluation questions are raised. When single programs involve diverse activities (for example the Synergy program described in Figure 1 which includes a crisis telephone line, drug education and peer counseling), SMART can also be applied.

Step 4: Identify the decision criteria or dimensions of value which are important for answering the evaluation question (from Step 2). Often these criteria are implicit rather than explicit and considerable time is required to identify them. Participants must describe the characteristics which they think made a program valuable to their unit and the criteria they use in determining how well programs are doing. As a stimulus to this step, participants at Prevention Programs were asked to respond to the following questions:
1. If another staff member were to suggest a new program, what questions would you be likely to raise?
2. Consider _____ (a program you value highly). If it were run by some organization other than Prevention Programs, how would it be different?
3. Consider the last time you were really proud to be attached to Prevention Programs. Why did you feel this way?
4. Consider _____ (a program in which you are not involved). Why does Prevention have such a program?
5. Consider the last time you were particularly upset about how a program was being run at Prevention Programs. What was it about the program that upset you and what corrective measures did you suggest?

Decision criteria are then elicited in a group session which includes a period of non-evaluative brainstorming. Any and all suggestions are accepted, without regard to overlap or consensus. Often goals and criteria are thought of in hierarchies. However, at this stage it is useful to ignore hierarchies and simple specify the criteria which are relevant to the question posed.

After the brainstorming session, considerable paring of the list of criteria is necessary. Overlap can be eliminated by attempting to identify hierarchies among criteria by redefining criteria on a slightly more general level, by consolidation, and by reversing the preferred level of the criterion, i.e., whether it should be maximized or minimized. Three principles should guide the process of winnowing the list of criteria: (1) a final list of 15 is a practical maximum and 8 is a good target; (2) criteria should be defined so they are at least monotonic, i.e., the more (or the less) the better; (3) participants' evaluation of performance on any one dimension (as good or bad) should be independent of their evaluations of performance on any other dimension. This last principle would be violated if high performance on one dimension – e.g., generating student support – were only valued if performance on another dimension were high (or low) – e.g., demonstrating impact.

1. Demonstrated Impact (27)
    Concerns addressed by this criterion include:
    a. Is there agreement on the goals and objectives of the program/activity?
    b. Can and does the program show that it is effective in meeting its goals and objectives?
    c. Does the program reduce medical costs for crisis care delivery?
2. Student Need and Participation (19)
    Concerns addressed by this criterion include:
    a. Does the program meet an expressed need of the students?
    b. Does the program meet an assessed need (by prevention staff) of the students?
    c. Do students participate in the program/activity to a degree indicating to staff that the program is filling a fairly widespread student need?
3. Philosophic Congruence (10)
    Concerns addressed by this criterion are:
    a. Is the program preventive rather than curative?
    b. Is the program holistic?
    c. Is the program innovative?
4. Student Support (9)
    Concerns addressed by this criterion include:
    a. To what extent are students aware of the program?
    b. Does the program/activity promote acceptance of Prevention and its function among students?
    c. To what extent are students willing to fund Prevention programs (via Health Service fees) regardless of whether they use this particular program?
5. Administrative Support (7)
    Concerns addressed by this criterion include:
    a. To what extent does the program/activity have the support of administrators in the Health Service hierarchy?
    b. To what extent does the program have the support of administrators of other programs (e.g., Counseling Center, Rehabilitation, Psychology) and to what extent are they willing to publicize this prevention program?
    c. To what extent does the program/activity have the support of administrators and board members of SIU?
6. Resource Utilization (7)
    Concerns addressed by this criterion include:
    a. Does the program fit the present staff capabilities?
    b. What is the cost of the program in terms of use of physical space, percentage of budget, and staff time?
    c. Can Prevention accommodate the program within existing resources?

d. How efficiently does the program use resources (e.g., number of client contacts per hour of staff time)?
7. Staff Satisfaction (7)
   Concerns addressed by this criterion include:
   a. Does the program contribute to staff commitment to Prevention?
   b. Does the program enhance staff interpersonal interactions?
   c. Does the program improve/maintain staff morale at desired levels?
8. Attracts Interns (7)
   Concerns addressed by this criterion include:
   a. Does the program attract volunteer (e.g., practicum/intern students) staff to help maintain it?
   b. Does the program contribute to the overall attractiveness of Prevention such that volunteers are willing to commit themselves to working for any programs needing staff time?
9. Duplication (4)
   Concerns addressed by this criterion include:
   a. Does the program duplicate services offered by other organizations?
10. Generating Grant Money (3)
    Concerns addressed by this criterion include:
    a. Does the program generate its own funding via grants?
    b. How much of the costs of the program does its grant funding cover?
    c. Are there other resources the program can attract besides money (e.g., space)?
    d. Does the program generate publicity both for the particular program and for Prevention?

Figure 2. Decision criteria and importance weights for evaluation of prevention program activities.

Figure 2 presents the decision criteria developed for evaluation of Prevention Programs Services. These final definitions were concretized after much discussion. Under each of the 10 decision criteria, Figure 2 presents subcriteria or indicators, many of which were generated during the brainstorming session. This hierarchical arrangement is extremely useful in guiding the selection of measures actually used in the evaluation.

The criterion of Resource Utilization (#6) provides an example of the redefinition at a more general level allowing incorporation of related concepts. Originally this criterion was labelled "cost", as indicated by sub-criterion 6b. This concept was broadened to include the demands made by a program on staff capabilities (6a) and efficiency with which a program delivers services (6d). An example of combining criteria is provided by Student Need and Participation (criterion #2). This criterion resulted from concern based on need assesments and utilization patterns. Note that all of the decision criteria are monotonic. Either more is always preferred to less or the opposite. While disagreements are probable at this stage, the usual experience is surprise at the degree of consensus on identifying the important criteria.

Step 5: Rank the criteria in order of importance. This step is usually accomplished as a continuation of the group process initiated in Step 4. As a starting point, each individual is asked to rank the final set of criteria agreed upon at Step 4. Then the rank orders are pooled. Discussions about disagreements with the aggregate ordering are useful for understanding what is meant by each of the criterion and for achieving consensus about their relative importance. Disagreements at this stage can usually be resolved by a process of negotiation.

In discussions during this and the following step, attention should be given to the levels of performance considered to be minimal and maximal. For example, it was decided that the minimal level for Student Support (criterion #4) and Administrative Support (criterion #5) was somewhat more positive than indifference — not active hostility! The ordering of the criteria presented in Figure 2 represents the ordering generated by this step at Prevention Programs with some minor reversals.

Step 6: Rate the decision criteria on importance. This is done by assigning the least important criterion a value of 10 and then deciding how much more important (if at all) is the next least important criterion. Assign this second criterion a number which indicates this ratio. For example, if the second criterion were twice as important as the first it should be assigned a 20; if it were three times as important, a 30. In the Prevention Programs example, the least important criterion (Generating Grant Money) was assigned a 10 and the next least important criterion (Duplication) a 12. This indicated that Duplication was 20% more important than Generating Grant Money.

This process of assigning numbers to reflect ratios of importance is continued with an additional criterion (the next least important) added each time. During the next repetition, Attracting Interns was assigned a 20 indicating that it was twice as important as Generating Grant Money and about two-thirds more important than Duplication. During each repetition each criterion is compared with every other one being considered, so that by the time the most important criteria are added to the process, there will be many comparisons to perform. At any time, participants may want to change the ratings of some criteria and perhaps even ordinal positions of others.

Individual differences which develop at this stage are important to consider as they probably reflect differences in approach and perspective. If a compromise solution cannot be agreed upon, it should be left to the administrator or decision maker to make a final assignment (the buck must stop somewhere!).

Step 7: Transform these ratings so that they sum to 100 (purely an arbitrary choice). This is done by summing over all ratings, dividing each by this sum and multiplying by 100. The resulting importance weights represent the percentage of the evaluation which depends on each criterion. In the Prevention Programs example (these weights are shown in parentheses in Figure 2), the highest weight was assigned to Demonstrated Effectiveness (27). This indicated that 27% of the evaluation of each program or activity depends on this criterion. Similarly, 19% of each evaluation depends on Student Need and Participation. Assuming the weights yield a ratio scale of the importance of the criteria, a comparison of the importance weights indicates that Demonstrated Impact is judged to be three times more important than Student Support and almost four times more important than Administrative Support.

A number of characteristics of the decision criteria described in Figure 2 are important. First, the criteria are *evaluative.* They represent a judgment about what is valuable to Prevention Programs. Generally, more is better, although for the cost dimension of Resource Utilization and for Duplication, "less" is better. The importance weights indicate that it is not so much the data but Prevention Program's evaluation of the data that is relevant. Second, these criterion define worth *subjectively;* i.e., from the perspective of the Prevention Program Division. Another group or organization, e.g., a student advisory committee, may have a much different definition of what makes a worthwhile Prevention Program activity. If differences at Steps 4 – 6 cannot be reconciled and the arbitrating choice of a single decision maker is unacceptable, separate identification, ranking and ratings should be done. It may be appropriate in some situations for advisory groups or minority factions to generate their own scaled set of decision criteria. Finally, note that while Prevention Programs attaches much importance to impact of its programs (criterion #1), most of the evaluation depends on other factors, i.e., 73%.

Step 8: The program evaluation can now begin. The evaluator has the dependent measures (from Figure 2) which are needed by the decision maker. Each program and activity needs to be "measured" on each of the decision criterion. A number of approaches to this measurement are possible, ranging from subjective, global estimates by experts to objective, experimentally derived scores. For the former, an appropriate expert should be identified for each criterion and given the task of assigning each progam a value representing the extent to which the program maximizes (or minimizes, as the case may be) the particular criterion. Judgments should be made on a scale from 0 to 100 where 0 is defined as the minimal plausible (not possible) level and 100 is the maximal plausible level as described in Step 5. The location of the 0 and 100 points for the experts needs to be the same as for those who generated the decision criteria if the importance weights are to be valid. For example, the criterion of Administrative Support would be of much greater importance if it were thought to include active hostility instead of only variations in support.

Other criteria can and should be measured in objective or comparative units. For example, "effectiveness in meeting program goals" and "degree of reduction of medical cost" are two of the indicators of demonstrated impact. Both measurements necessitate assessment of a comparison group of non-program participants to determine impact (McKillip, 1979; McKillip & Voss, 1978). These objective measurements can then be transformed to the 0 – 100 scale used for expert judgments or aggregated according to some weighted formula. Following the general principles outlined in SMART, it may be decided for the criterion of Demonstrated Impact that "consensus on goals" has an importance weight of 20, "effectiveness in meeting goals" 50 and "reduction of medical costs" 30.

Step 9: Calculate Utilities values for each program. The formula for this calculation is: $U_i = {}_j w_j u_{ij}$. Where U_i is the aggregated Utility value or SMART generated measure of worth of a specific program; w_j is the importance weight assigned to a particular decision criterion; and u_{ij} is the value assigned to the program on the particular decision criterion. The product $w_j u_{ij}$ is summed (j) over all decision criteria to generate the Utility value for the program. Utility values can range from 0 to a maximum of 10000. Figure 3 presents fictional utility value for the service programs listed in Figure 1 (the higher the value the better).

	U_i
Lifestyling	5000
Sexuality Counseling	3500
Sex Education	6000
Synergy	8000
Medical Self-Care	2000
Alcohol Program	4000

Figure 3. Fictional utility values for service programs of prevention programs.

Step 10: The evaluation question can now be answered. The evaluator has provided the decision maker with a global rating (Utility) on how well each of the programs and activities of the organization are performing. These ratings can be used as input to evaluate decisions of management. For example, on the basis of Figure 3, the Synergy Program is an extremely worthwhile activity of Prevention Programs. Organization rewards should be forthcoming. On the other hand, the Medical Self-Care Program is of only marginal worth, barely one quarter that of Synergy. Remedial action is indicated. As a guide to planning, administrators and staff should attend to the values assigned to each program on the decision criteria (u_{ij}s). Low values point to areas for future activities and high values point to strengths.

In some situations a criterion of cost will have an importance far above that assigned to any of the other criteria. In this case, SMART can be applied ignoring criterion of cost and the resultant Utility values used to compute a Utility/Cost ratio.

SUMMARY

SMART can be used as a tool for defining program evaluation questions. These procedures can be a tremendous aid to an evaluator. A major reason that results of program evaluations are often ignored is because they address only the official goals of a program and neglect the actual decision criteria used by the sponsoring organization. The utility of SMART is enhanced in most typical student affairs management situations by the administrator's need not only to integrate a number of diverse value dimensions but also to make comparisons between programs in quite different activities and objectives.

The components of SMART need not remain fixed, however. Since organizations and goals change, evaluation and planning can be aided by a periodic redefinition and weighting of decision criteria. Furthermore, alternatives exist for almost all of the steps described above. Three are worthy of note. First is the question of weighting. A number of authors (e.g., Einhorn & McCoach, 1977) advocate equal weighting of criteria rather than the unequal weighting suggested here. Practically, the use of equal weights would greatly simplify the technique by eliminating Steps 5 and 6. Unequal weighting fits better intuitively but the evaluator or student affairs staff member may want to make comparisons over a range of situations before choosing one over the other. Second, there is the general question of whether the assumption of a monotonic relationship between decision criteria and worth is valid. It is argued that in some situations a median, rather than maximum or minimum, value on a decision criterion has the highest utility. In practice, however, the monotonicity assumption has always seemed defensible. In situations where the assumption is clearly violated, decision criterion values (u_{ij}s) can be assigned on the basis of deviations from the optimal level. Finally, there is concern about corruption of decision criteria. There are two versions here. One is that alert service providers will direct all of their efforts toward the decision criterion with the highest importance weight, ignoring the others. If this tendency occurs, decision criterion values (u_{ij}s) could be assigned on a logarithmic scale so that after attaining relatively high levels of value on the most important criterion, alert service providers would focus attention on other criteria (the general principle is to find a scoring rule such that payoff [U_{is}] is maximum if it leads staff to distribute efforts proportionately with importance weights). A second version is that the specification of decision criteria will lead to the neglect of activities not covered by these criteria. The solution is to include these unspecified dimensions, with appropriate weights, in the process.

A number of writers have suggested (e.g., Cronbach, 1977; Deutscher, 1976) that the major criterion of success for program evaluation is the degree to which results are utilized. If this is true, SMART will aid the evaluator and the student affairs administrator.

REFERENCES

Cronbach, L.J. Remarks to the new society. *Evaluation Research Society Newsletter,* 1977, *1,* 1-3.

Deutscher, I. Toward avoiding the goal-trap in evaluation research. In C.C. Abt (Ed.), *The evaluation of social programs.* Beverly Hills, Calif.: Sage Publications, 1976.

Edwards, W. Social utilities *The Engineering Economist,* Summer Symposium Series, 1971, *6,* 119-129.

Edwards, W., Guttentag, M., & Snapper, K. A decision-theoretic approach to evaluation research. In E.L. Struening & M. Guttentag, (Eds.), *Handbook of evaluation research.* Beverly Hills, Calif.: Sage Publications, 1975.

Einhorn, J.J., & McCoach, W. A simple multiattribute utility procedure for evaluation. *Behavioral Science,* 1977, *22,* 270-282.

McKillip, J. Impact evaluation of service programs, three flexible designs. *Evaluation Quarterly,* 1979, *3,* 97-104.

McKillip, J., & Kamens, L. Evaluation of a positive health care program. In R.V. Robertson (Ed.), *Health care research in Illinois.* Springfield, Ill.: Southern Illinois Univeristy, 1977.

McKillip, J., Workman, K., & Dickson, S. *Evaluation of the Human Sexuality Services birth control rap workshops.* Evaluation report, Student Health Services, Southern Illinois Univeristy at Carbondale, 1978.

McKillip, J., & Voss, J.R. *Why do we need a control group? Why should we randomize? Some answers for evaluative researchers.* Presented at the meeting of the American Personnel Guidance Association, Washington, April, 1978.

Riecken, H.W., & Boruch, R.F. *Social experimentation.* New York: Academic Press, 1974.

Scriven, M. Goal-free evaluation. In E.R. House (Ed.), *School evaluation: The politics and process.* Berkeley, Calif.: McCutchan, 1973.

Voss, J.R., & McKillip, J. Program evaluation in sex education: The effectiveness of sexual awareness weekend workshops. *Archives of Sexual Behavior,* 1979, in press.

17
EVALUATING A LIVING-LEARNING PROGRAM
Philip C. Chamberlain

Academic and student affairs administrators have indicated an interest in integrating academic programs with the living environment of the residence hall (Buckner, 1977; Magnarella, 1975). The residential college concept with living and learning intimately related is a tradition on many campuses. But in many large institutions living and learning have become educationally and administratively separated due to growth in size and program diversity. In an effort to encourage out of class interest in academic activities, a good deal of experimentation with different kinds of living-learning arrangements has been attempted. One such experiment is the subject of this evaluation case study.

BACKGROUND TO THE CASE

Indiana University-Bloomington is typical of many large state university campuses located in small urban communities. It is characterized by a large sprawling campus on which the living needs of the majority of students are met through residence hall complexes or through fraternities and sororities for those who prefer an alternative living style. Still other students choose to live off campus, and though their number is large, they represent a minority of all students enrolled. The campus is overwhelmingly residential and dominated by residence halls and classroom buildings where the quality of both the living and learning environments is of major importance to campus administrators.

There is diversity in the age, types and size of residence halls available to students on the Indiana campus. They range from older, smaller units characterized by collegiate-gothic architecture built prior to World War II to large, multi-storied, modern designed structures built during the growth years of the 1950s and 1960s. Differences in institutional priorities between the two eras can be discerned in the differences between the halls. In the newer residence centers the preordinate need is to house large numbers of students easily and efficiently, while the older halls seem to foster a more intimate educational environment where academic traditions and collegialism are implicit. Not surprisingly, the older residence halls are located in close proximity to the present geographic center of the campus, while the modern units are found on the outer fringes. Accessibility to the center of the campus where most academic activity occurs is one criterion which is commonly used by students today in choosing a residence hall.

The post-war period also witnessed a large increase on the campus in the diversity of academic programs and in the numbers of faculty and administrators. This in turn created a need in the late 1960's for increased space for academic and administrative offices. It was not surprising, therefore, that the older residence centers located near the center of academic activity were considered for possible conversion into needed office space. It was thought that the large newer halls would be able to absorb the students who would be displaced as the older halls were converted. The proposal to transform the older halls into administrative quarters met with considerable opposition from the Division of Student Life, and from many faculty members, particularly many senior professors. Despite the opposition, one of two eligible halls was converted. The second hall continued to serve as a residence center, with the understanding that it would become an innovative living-learning center. Furthermore, an important factor in assuring its continuance as a residence center would be the extent to which its innovative program was diffused into the mainstream of campus academic and residential life. Thus the Living-Learning Center (LLC) was created in 1970 as an alternative living style where regular classroom instruction and an enriched academic climate was to be infused into the residence center. An advisory board comprised of faculty, administrators and students was authorized to define and implement the mission of the LLC. The board subsequently considered program evaluation as a method to substantiate the allocation of special academic resources. Interest in evaluating the LLC's worth increased steadily over time as the amount of financial resources available for the campus generally became less plentiful due to changes in state legislative funding practices for the University. It was in this situation that an evaluation of the LLC was conducted by an evaluation team in the spring of 1978 at the request of the Advisory Board's Evaluation Steering Committee. The essential element of the case as described herein was to determine *the degree to which the LLC had developed a program which not only could be distinguished from other residential settings on the campus, but was also sufficiently viable to attract support and resources based on its intrinsic worth.*

THE EVALUATION PROBLEM

Evaluation strategies usually are designed to measure the input, process or output of an organization. These strategies work well in student affairs work when the effectiveness of an admissions program or a financial aids system is of interest or when there is a question as to whether a particular educational program is related to some aspect of student achievement. These evaluation strategies do not serve well other kinds of student affairs activities, especially if the activities are largely value-based and exist to meet a qualitative need for a particular constituent group. Union boards and student foundations are two examples of such activities. Their continued existence may rest with the intrinsic worth they possess and the value satisfaction they provide for individuals who identify with them. Their effectiveness, therefore, should be measured by the intensity of sentiment or value placed on them using an evaluation strategy that is sensitive to the peculiar elements these activities possess. This can pose a problem, however, as many strategies do not seek these data.

The reason for the problem stems from the characteristics of these value-based programs. They often do not evidence the variables for measurement required by most evaluation strategies; e.g., formal administrative structures, precise role descriptions for participants, and observable program outcomes. Instead, these programs and activities tend to derive decisions by group consensus, rely upon implicit rather than explicit values as standards, follow normative behavior patterns, and hold the constituent membership together by equal parts of trust and reciprocity. In short, these activities and programs have many of the properties of institutions and institutionalized programs. The LLC was such a program.

SELECTING THE STRATEGY

Few evaluation strategies have been developed to respond to the unique properties of institutionalized organizations and programs. One such strategy has been developed by Esman and Blaise for the Inter-University Research Program in Institution Building (Mann, 1975). The framework of the strategy is based on the premise that an institution is more than an organization; it is a collection of values and behaviors having unique importance for one or more constituent groups. The framework is composed of nine variables, each containing sets of questions that suggest the kinds of data that must be collected and from which subjective judgments of the strength of the institution can be made. While the strategy was developed initially for use in developing new institutions in emerging countries, a modified version (Academic Institution Building Model) has been used to evaluate existing collegiate institutions (Chamberlain, 1975). Its major feature is that it is a process model which can be used either by internal or external evaluators.

The AIB Model assumes that institutions and institutionalized programs exist to serve the unique needs of constituent groups, and that there is a relationship between the level of constituent need the institution or program attempts to satisfy and the level of resources the constituents will provide. This balance reflects the degree of success the institution or program has achieved in establishing its worth. The criteria for measuring this balance are: (1) the survival of the institution's unique elements over time, (2) the level of administrative autonomy the institution or program exhibits, and (3) the influence or spread-effect the institution or program can exert in its operational environment. The Academic Institution Building Model, therefore, attempts to evaluate the way an institution or program is linked with its environment. This relationship can be depicted schematically with the nine model variables.

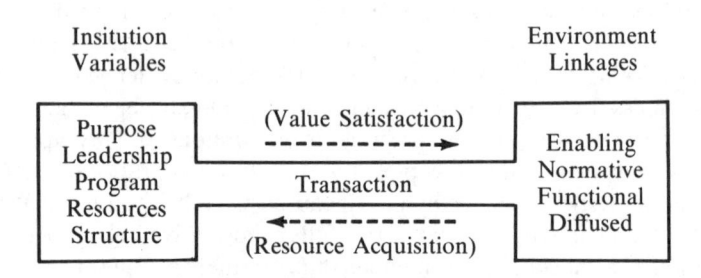

Insitution Variables		Environment Linkages
Purpose Leadership Program Resources Structure	(Value Satisfaction) ------------> Transaction <------------ (Resource Acquisition)	Enabling Normative Functional Diffused

The five institution variables and the four environment variables each have a precise working definition which is provided later under case study findings. The kinds of data the model requires is determined by the particular institution or program being analyzed, and are usually different across evaluation settings (institutional properties do not tend to generalize). Furthermore, the conclusions drawn from these data tend to be subjective. It is important, therefore, that the data are analyzed by a team of knowledgeable evaluators. The validity of the conclusions derived through consensus in this way rests not with the model solely, but also with the quality of the data collected and the general knowledge of the institution or program held by the evaluation team. It is this feature that makes the model particularly suitable for use with institutions and institutionalized programs. In general, the larger the number of knowledgeable evaluators, the greater the validity of the conclusions. This case study was conducted by a team of six evaluators, all of whom had first hand experience with the LLC.

DATA COLLECTION AND ANALYSIS

The AIB Model suggests a team evaluation approach. As the validity of the conclusions are influenced by the degree of consensus drawn, it is important that data requirements be determined mutually by team members. The data defined for the LLC evaluation were: (1) demographic data such as grade point averages and academic majors of approximately one hundred LLC students and a matched group of approximately one hundred other students residing in other residence halls; (2) descriptive data such as program objectives and offerings drawn from the dozen or more LLC publications produced in the seven years of its existence; and (3) qualitative data defined as the expressed opinions obtained through approximately one hundred interviews with individuals having knowledge of the Center. Each evaluation team member was responsible for reviewing all the data prior to a series of team discussions from which answers were derived for the evaluation questions posed by each variable of the model. Definitions for the variables and the team's findings for each are presented below.

FINDINGS

This section reports the major findings from the evaluation. They are organized to follow a detailed description of the model variables to which they relate.

PURPOSE

Purpose is defined as the specification of values, objectives and operational methods underlying social action. The purpose is viewed as the stable reference point of the organization and of its interaction with the environment to which all other variables are related. The questions of the purpose variable are:
1. *Specificity.* To what extent do the elements of the purpose supply the necessary foundation for social action in a given situation?
2. *Relationship to existing norms.* Do the elements of the purpose conform to socially expected and sanctioned behavior?
3. *Relationship to the preferences and priorities of the society.* Do the elements specify the relationship of the purpose to the intermediate goals and targets of the campus?

Findings: From its inception in 1970, the LLC was to provide an academically enriched residential environment. This has been clearly stated in publications of the LLC and is presently articulated as "an environment in which student creativity, intellectual growth and self-direction can be maximized." All who are associated with the LLC were found to subscribe to this creed. These statements have been judged as providing a clear set of values and objectives which has guided the LLC in its overall development. It is also evident these values and objectives are consistent with the educational norms of higher education generally and with the preferences and priorities of the campus specifically.

The purpose of the LLC as generally stated and understood was found to have a serious limitation, however. It was found to lack the specificity necessary to differentiate between types of academic experiences most suitable for the Center and for providing criteria by which students could be selected who could profit most from this unique educational environment. While some argued that the lack of specificity enhanced the diversity and variety of experiences available at the Center, the data also indicated that confusion existed concerning how the LLC differed from other residential settings. While this problem of purpose specificity was not found to be of concern within the LLC, it was found to be troublesome to some individuals and groups on campus such as directors of other residence halls. Moreover, lack of specificity in the LLC's purpose statements did not provide explicit criteria against which program success could be measured.

LEADERSHIP

Leadership is defined here as the group of persons who are actively engaged in the formulation of the purpose and program of the organization and who direct its operation and relationships with the environment. On the basis of this definition, the leadership group is not restricted to those who are formally charged with the direction of the organization. Leadership is viewed as a unit, with the variables or determinants of leadership being significant for the group, rather than in terms of each individual. The questions related to the leadership variable are:
1. *Political viability.* Do the members of the leadership group have political acceptability and survival power?
2. *Professional status.* Do the members of the leadership group have status or rank in the professional group and field of activity within which the program is found?
3. *Technical competence.* Do the members of the leadership group possess the technical competence in regard to the functional area and technologies needed by the program?
4. *Continuity.* Is there continuous association of members of the leadership group with the program?

Findings: The major leadership group for the LLC was the Advisory Board which had responsibility for the Center's overall development. Though the number on the Board fluctuated occasionally, there existed a continuing majority which remained relatively unchanged in its make-up. In this group was found a former campus vice-chancellor who, while in that position, was instrumental in implementing the concept of LLC and who served as chairman of the Board from its beginning. In this group also was the Dean of Students, the campus Director of Residence Life and Halls of Residence, the campus Business Manager and several faculty members committed to the LLC concept. The rest of the Board was comprised of students and administrative staff from the LLC. These individuals were responsible for operationalizing LLC's purposes and programs and for coordinating LLC activities with the campus environment. These individuals provide adequate administrative competence required to protect and nurture the LLC.

In addition to the Advisory Board, the leadership function of the LLC was accommodated by a student government which had considerable authority for determining student life policy. Policy concerns of the body ranged from academic offerings to cafeteria regulations.

INTERNAL STRUCTURE

This model variable is defined as the structure and processes established for the operation of the institution and for its maintenance. The distribution of functions and authority, the processes of communication and decision-making, and other relationship and action patterns, are essential for the analysis of institution building and maintenance. Internal structure and processes determine the efficiency and effectiveness of program performance as well as the identification of participants with the organization's purposes and programs. The questions in this variable are:
1. *Identification.* What are the mechanisms and processes which enhance identification of participants with the program?
2. *Consistency.* Does the internal structure conform to the rules and specifications of the institution's purpose and program?
3. *Adaptability.* Does the internal structure have the capacity to change over time to accommodate shifts in program emphasis and other changing conditions?

Findings: The operational structure of the LLC reflected the attempt to infuse academic programs into the residence hall. There were two administrative units: one responsible for overseeing the residence hall program of the Division of Student Life, with the other having the special function of carrying out the programs of the LLC.

The residence life unit was headed by a hall coordinator who also supervised a group of approximately 10 residence hall assistants. This kind of administrative unit (and its trained personnel) was common to every residence hall on the campus. Among other things, it provided disciplinary supervision in the halls and leadership for planning extracurricular and curricular programs for students.

The second administrative unit in the LLC was the Office of the LLC Director. The Director was responsible for administering the academic programs within the LLC and providing the administrative linkage with the academic departments on the campus which offered course sections in the LLC or provided faculty for student-designed seminars. There had been three LLC directors since its beginning. The two most recent were both faculty members from the College of Arts and Sciences who were given released time from their regular teaching assignments. The source of these directors reflected a formal shift in sponsorship of the LLC to the College of Arts and Sciences in 1972 from the University Division (an administrative undergraduate advising unit). The shift was made to better provide the academic resources required by the Center. In addition to the LLC Director, a faculty member from the College of Arts and Sciences lived in the hall and assisted with academic advising.

For the most part, the internal structure of the hall was found to be consistent with the specifications of the LLC program. There appeared to be an adequate structure to administer the various programs unique to the LLC. Furthermore, the shift to external unit sponsorship in 1972 suggested that the LLC had the capacity to adapt to change.

Some confusion about the operational structure was thought to exist, however, apparently due to ambigious role definitions of the LLC Director and the Residence Life Coordinator. LLC student members were frequently unaware of who had administrative responsibility for which program.

PROGRAM

Program is defined as those actions which are related to the performance of functions and services constituting the output of the institution. The questions of the program variables are:
1. *Consistency.* Are the programs consistent with the rules and specifications contained in the purpose of the institution?
2. *Stability.* Are the outcomes of the program reliable in terms of quality, quantity, and in time perspective?
3. *Feasibility.* Are the programs feasible with regard to physical and human resources?
4. *Contribution to needs.* Does the program contribute to satisfying the specified needs of the campus?

Findings: The LLC's formal program was comprised of special sections of regular campus course offerings, special student-designed seminars taught by regular faculty and a variety of non-credit courses to meet students' special interests. The non-credit courses were frequently taught by the students themselves. In a typical year a dozen or more credit courses and approximately 20 non-credit courses were offered by the LLC. The Center's informal program ranged from student theatrical productions to receptions for noted speakers visiting the campus.

The various programs were rated as being highly consistent with the LLC's purpose, feasible with regard to available resources, and contributing to the academic and social needs of the campus. Without a needed level of specificity in the LLC's stated purpose, however, it was difficult to determine the degree to which the program was consistent or stable over time. It was not easy to determine whether the overall program had developed cohesive elements or stability to distinguish it from similar programs elsewhere on the campus. The character of the program seemed to be determined largely by the preferences of each class of LLC students.

When comparing the academic records of LLC students with other students living elsewhere on the campus, achievement as measured by grade point average was not significantly different, nor was the pattern of academic majors. The major difference between the groups was found from the results of standardized tests *(Omnibus Personality Inventory* and the *College Student Questionnaire)* administered to both student groups which indicated LLC students tended to be more psychologically independent, creative and liberal in their outlook.

RESOURCES

Resources are defined as the physical, financial, human and technological inputs of the institution. Program decisions, and even decisions concerning purposes and leadership, may be influenced by the capacity to mobilize resources, and the sources from which they can be obtained. The sources will also affect the interdependencies of the institution with other institutions. The questions of the resource variable are:

1. *Availability.* Are the physical, human and technological requirements available for the functioning of the institution and the performance of the program?
2. *Sources.* Are the sources from which the resources have been obtained stable, and alternative sources to which the institution has access been identified?

Findings: The major resources of the LLC came from two sources. Academic resources, both human and financial, came largely from the College of Arts and Science. Although other academic divisions from time to time offered courses in the LLC, it was Arts and Sciences that provided the full time director and special funds for enriching the Center's program. These resources had been both stable and adequate across time.

The other resource (and for many the most important) was the physical structure in which the LLC was located. As previously alluded to, it is an older hall, built in the 1930s, and located close to the academic center of the campus. More significant is its size. It is a relatively small unit housing several hundred students. It was constructed so as to provide for an intimate collegiate atmosphere by housing students in still smaller groups in different building units. Prior to the establishment of the LLC, it had for many years been known as the Men's Residence Center (MRC) and membership eligibility was based on the variable of sex. Over the years an image of selectivity had developed about the MRC along with its own set of traditions (the University swimming team, for example, had traditionally lived in the Center due to its proximity to the University pool). There had always been a distinguishing character to the Center with which many identified, and it was this identification that helped prevent it from being converted into administrative office space in the late 1960s. For the LLC, therefore, the MRC with its continuing image was its major resource for program development, even though the LLC was coeducational and used the whole facility. This reliance was clearly indicated in the fact that the LLC frequently referred to itself as the LLC-MRC.

ENABLING LINKAGES

Enabling linkages are the relationships with organizations and social groups which control the allocation of authority and resources needed by the institution to function. This category is comprised of the specific organizations and groups with which enabling linkages exist. The questions of the enabling linkage variable are:
1. *Specifications.* Are relationship definitions with external groups clear?
2. *Importance.* Is the relative importance of these relationships understood?
3. *Influence.* Does the institution possess ability to influence these relationships?

Findings: The primary enabling linkages of the LLC were the College of Arts and Sciences and the Division of Student Life. The significance and importance of the relationships were clearly reflected in the composition of the LLC Advisory Board on which several of the chief administrators from these units served. It is through the Advisory Board that the LLC had the potential to significantly influence these relationships. The LLC's enabling linkages were found to be one of its strongest assets.

FUNCTIONAL LINKAGES

The entities in this category are the organizations with which complementary or competitive relationships exist. Included are linkages with organizations which constitute the real or potential competition or which perform similar functions and services to those of the institution. In its relationship with these organizations an institution will strive for complementarity with them. The questions of the functional linkage variable are:
1. *Specifications.* Are relationship definitions with external groups clear?

2. *Importance.* Is the relative importance of these relationships understood?
3. *Influence.* Does the institution prossess ability to influence these relationships.

Findings: The groups which constituted the potential for functional linkages for the LLC were the other residence centers on the campus. Though no other center had the formalized purpose and resources of the LLC, most did maintain programs which were intended to academically enrich their programs. These academic programs were defined by each residence center and tended to be informal. They ranged from hall-sponsored movies to non-credit courses and faculty lectures. The quality of these programs tended to be a function of the interest of the residence life staff in each residence unit. There was no formal linkage between the LLC and these other programs due, in large part, to the fact that the LLC derived its sponsorship directly from the College of Arts and Sciences. No significant cooperative or competitive relationships were identified during the evaluation.

NORMATIVE LINKAGES

Normative linkages describe the institutional norms and values which are relevant to the purpose and programs of the institution. This includes both the socio-cultural norms and the operating rules and regulations. As an example, an institution may be influenced by the rules and regulations of a professional association or organization even though no enabling or functional linkage exists with that body. The significant entities in this category are those norm and value protecting institutions which enhance or hinder changes introduced by the institution. The questions of the normative linkage variable are:

1. *Specifications.* Are relationship definitions with external groups clear?
2. *Importance.* Is the relative importance of these relationships understood?
3. *Influence.* Does the institution possess ability to influence these relationships?

Findings: The LLC had salient normative linkages with the academic units from which it derived its purpose. It was from such units as the College of Arts and Sciences that the LLC took its special meaning as an alternative style for the University to fulfill its educational mission. Moreover, it was the residential college model of Oxford and Cambridge that established the norms and values for the university generally and for the LLC specifically. Although the importance of the norms and values espoused by the LLC were acknowledged, they had not been clearly operationalized.

DIFFUSED LINKAGES

Not all the relationships between an institution and its environment are with specific social organizations. The establishment and operation of an institution is also affected by the more diffused support or resistance in its immediate enviroment and in the larger society. Thus, diffused linkages refer to public opinion and relations with the public such as those expressed in the news media. The questions of the diffused linkage variable are:
 1. *Specifications.* Are relationship definitions with external groups clear?
 2. *Importance.* Is the relative importance of these relationships understood?
 3. *Influence.* Does the institution possess ability to influence these relationships?

Findings: The LLC projected a limited image on the campus largely due to its relatively small size as a residence center (numbers of residents and physical structure). Its primary linkage with the College of Arts and Sciences tended to delimit outside interest. Within the Division of Student Life the LLC was considered to be a privileged activity, but the size of the program, compared to the overall residence program on the campus, was not viewed as large enough to create a serious equity concern for other residence centers.

CONCLUSIONS

The evaluation question posed for this study was whether the LLC since its inception had developed a program which not only could be distinguished from other living styles on the Indiana University – Bloomington campus, but also was sufficiently viable to attract support and resources based on its developed intrinsic worth. The conclusions are discussed below according to the criteria of the AIB Model for judging the quality of the relationship of the institution with its environment.

1. *Did the LLC have unique elements and did they survive over time?*

The intent in structuring the LLC was to provide students an alternative living style characterized by an enriched academic environment in a residential setting. In this regard the intent had been fulfilled. No other residence hall had the range and quality of academic programs as did the LLC. It was clear that the element of academic enrichment was a success.

Whether academic enrichment as an element by itself, however, is sufficient for measuring the success of the LLC is not clear. If this was the only necessary variable, then a question may be raised of the standard to be used for determining whether the environment has been *adequately* enriched. Without such a standard, the claim could be made that all residence halls are living-learning centers; some are just poorer than others. While this is probably true, it does not answer the most important question: Did the LLC achieve a uniqueness solely its own that could be used as a reason for its continued existence the level of enrichment notwithstanding? Were there elements unique to the LLC that had become highly valued, which in their aggregate were sufficient to attract resources and support? The conclusion is that in the main it did not.

The basis for the conclusion is that the specificity of the LLC's purpose was insufficient to discriminate between types of programs and activities appropriate to its mission. The result was a program determined annually by what the LLC members themselves desired with no assurance of program continuity. This might have been judged satisfactory, however, if the criteria existed to provide for LLC membership which was differentiated from the rest of the student body.

2. *Did the LLC establish administrative autonomy?*

The LLC was set up initially with an Advisory Board with representation from the major administrative units with which it had to relate. Moreover, this representation consisted of the chief administrators of these units. Through the Advisory Board the LLC had from its inception a high level of autonomy.

The most important question, however, is whether the LLC as an innovative program was able to derive a level of autonomy based on the success or worth of the program irrespective of the quality of the Advisory Board. It is difficult to answer this question completely because of the difficulty of differentiating leadership from program. Nevertheless, a qualified "no" was offered based on the general perception of the LLC by those in cognate units on the campus. It was difficult for them to distinguish a substantive difference in the LLC program from what was considered appropriate in other halls.

It appeared that the level of operational autonomy which the LLC did enjoy was due mainly to the composition of its Advisory Board, not the character of the LLC itself.

3. *Did the LLC exert influence or have a spread effect it its operational environment due to the success of its innovative elements?*

The concept of learning being combined with living on a campus is an important and cherished value in American higher education. It is an element generic to the system. However, the LLC did not define this element in such a fashion so as to be a distinctive educational model for operationalizing this value. This is not to say that the LLC did not have many supporters on the campus who were interested in its growth and development. As an operational entity, however, its perceived success was not sufficient to be replicated elsewhere.

It was concluded that the LLC was an administrative entity integrated with a unique residence hall, and as such, enriched the hall. But it was the character of the hall itself that gave reason for the LLC to exist, not the converse as was originally intended. The apparent reason for this relationship was the failure of the LLC to develop one of the basic prerequisites of an institutionalized program — specificity of purpose sufficient to develop a program with a uniqueness greater than that of the residence hall facility in which it was placed. This is not to imply that the LLC has not developed a level of worth to an identified constituency. Indeed, it has survived! It does suggest, however, that without the physical facility, the LLC would probably be without a significant part of its *raison d'etre*.

REFERENCES

Buckner, R. Restructuring residence hall programming: Residence hall educators with a curriculum, *Journal of College Student Personnel*, 1977, *18*, 389-392.

Chamberlain, P.C. The new management tools: Problems and potential, *NASPA Journal*, 1975, *12, 8*, 171-178.

Magnarella, J. The University of Vermont's living-learning center: A first year appraisal, *Journal of College Student Personnel*, 1975, *16*, 30-35.

Mann, A.G. (Ed.) *Institution-building: A reader*. PASITAM, Bloomington, Indiana; 1975.

18
BUILDING A WOLF-PROOF HOUSE: INTEGRATING EVALUATION IN STUDENT AFFAIRS

George D. Kuh

Once upon a time there were three pigs (Otl, Ood, and Pro by name) who were faced with the problem of coping with the big bad wolf.

The first pig (Otl) was simply "out to lunch." "What is a big bad wolf?" he said as he built his straw house.

The second pig (Ood) was an old-timer in this wolf-fending business, and he saw the problem right away. What he needed to do was build a house strong enough to resist the huffing and puffing he had experienced before. After all, he had received his Ph.D in wolf-fending 20 years ago, and the old reliable brick and plaster house repelled the big bad wolf every time.

The third pig (Pro) was a little green at this wolf business for she had just received her Ph.D. She decided the wolf problem required careful consideration. As a part of the process, she interviewed experienced wolf-fenders and reviewed the literature related to recent wolf behaviors. She listed the design objectives of a wolf-proof house, determined the functions that the house should serve, and analyzed wolf-coping strategies. After considering all this information, she designed, built, and tested the house (obviously she was an empiricist and still a green professional for she had not yet been huffed and puffed at).

All this time, the second pig laughed at the third pig and vehemently declined to enter into this kind of folly. He had build wolf-proof houses before, and clearly he was alive and prospering, wasn't he? He said to the third pig, "if you know what you are doing, you don't have to go through all of that jazz." And with this, he joined the first pig (who of course, had finished his straw house well ahead of the second pig) and went fishing, or rooting, or whatever it is that pigs do during their normal work hours. The third pig adhered to her systematic approach, and designed, pilot-tested, and evaluated her work against all possible contingencies.

One day the mean old wolf passed by the three houses. From the wolf's perspective, one house looked peculiar, but the others looked the same (after all, a brick house is just a brick house!). The wolf thought that a pig dinner was just what he wanted.

The story of the first litle pig is well known. As the big bad wolf walked up to the second pig's house, he uttered a warning to the old-timer which was roundly rejected by Ood as usual. With this

253

rebuff, the wolf, instead of huffing and puffing, pulled out a sledge hammer, knocked the door down, and ate the "out of date" oldtimer for dessert. Still not satiated, the wolf walked to the third pig's house and repeated his act. Suddenly, a trap door in front of the house opened and the wolf dropped neatly into a deep, dark pit and was never heard from again.

MORALS:

1. They're not making wolves like they used to.
2. It's hard to teach old pigs new tricks.
3. If you want to keep the wolf away from your door, you'd better plan ahead and evaluate systematically (Rodgers, 1978).

The preceding chapters have largely espoused the merits of systematic evaluation without fully confronting the issues related to the second moral. The contributors to this book seem to agree that the student affairs profession can benefit from more colleagues like "Pro" and fewer who resemble "Otl" and "Ood." In order for student affairs to include more Pros among its ranks, two major issues must be addressed:
1. How can more student affairs staff members acquire the skills necessary to adequately design and conduct evaluations?
2. What must be done to more adequately integrate the evaluation function into divisions of students affairs?

PREPARING STUDENT AFFAIRS STAFF FOR EVALUATION

At least three additional questions must be raised when considering the preparation of student personnel staff for evaluation activities:
1. What are the necessary skills?
2. Who is to be trained?
3. Who should do the training?

REQUISITE SKILLS FOR EVALUATORS

A number of researchers have attempted to determine the skills or competencies characteristic of well-prepared evaluators. For the most part, these inquiries have dealt with evaluation as a generic discipline rather than with activities germane to particular professions (e.g., education) or settings (e.g., higher education). Anderson and Ball (1978) have synthesized the various evaluator competencies that have been suggested in the literature. This section relates their conclusions to student affairs.

Some of the basic requirements of many student affairs preparation programs such as statistics and research design/methodology involve content areas with which student affairs evaluators should be familiar. This is true even for those who are more comfortable with qualitative approaches which rely less on "hard" data such as the Issue Resolver (Responsive and Transactional), Reporter, or Unbiased Judge (Goalfree or Adversary) strategies discussed in Chapter 3. This suggestion (qualitative evaluators having minimal quantitative skills) is somewhat analogous to the abstract painter who is also expected to know how to draw (Anderson & Ball, 1978).

Student affairs evaluators should have a working knowledge of the various existent evaluation models. Brown (Chapter 3) has succinctly summarized the major perspectives from which evaluation can be approached. Additional sources to which the conscientious student affairs staff member can refer are included in the references at the end of each chapter. It is not unusual, however, for evaluators to become enamored with or exhibit preference for one or two of the approaches. It is also probable that an individual's preferred model will not always be the most appropriate approach to the variety of evaluation questions inherent in student affairs. While the abstract painter may some day need to produce a drawing, the student affairs evaluator should be prepared to apply principles of a less preferred model. In other words, the unique configuration of variables in the setting to be evaluated (see Chapter 2) should influence the choice or synthesis of strategies employed.

Other technical competencies also may be required to answer some evaluation questions. Application of psychometrics, unobtrusive techniques, and case study methodologies may be most appropriate for some evaluation plans. Academic departments such as psychology, educational inquiry and business often can provide technical assistance in these areas. The office of institutional research may also prove to be an invaluable liason and collaborative unit. In many institutions, this office is responsible for collating evaluation and accountability data to be used by top level decision-makers. By establishing working relationships with the institutional research office, divisions of student affairs may be able to influence how evaluative questions for student affairs are framed and the kind of data used to answer these questions. In this way, student affairs may have a greater influence over its own destiny as well as be able to more clearly communicate the importance of its institutional role.

Another area which is of inestimable importance encompasses knowledge about the practical application of consultation theory including change strategies. In addition to the contributors to this monograph, Brown (1978), Kurpius (1978), Keating and Hurst (1978), and Hamilton and Meade (1979) have emphasized the importance of effective interpersonal relations and the application of individual and organizational change strategies to the evaluation process. Many of the interpersonal skills required for effective change agent behavior are typically exhibited to acceptable degrees by the types of individuals who choose student affairs as a profession, particularly by those who work from the perspective and use the skills of a counseling psychologist.

A high level of proficiency in expositional skills (written communication particularly) is also critical to the success of a student affairs evaluator. The clarity with which the evaluation plan is designed and communicated is second in importance *only* to the form in which the results of the project are communicated to the respective relevant constituencies (see Chapters 2 and 7; Brown, 1978).

WHO IS TO BE TRAINED?

At first blush, this question seems fairly straightforward and simple. "Every student affairs staff member should be prepared to conduct evaluations!" It is probably unrealistic, however, to assume all student affairs staff will exhibit the requisite skills discussed above for at least two reasons. The first reason is related to the second moral of the fable which introduced this chapter. At present, the majority of student affairs staff have been trained prior to any systematic emphasis on program evaluation in graduate-level preparation programs. Given the demands of daily responsibilities, it is unlikely (and unfortunate) that many practitioners will be able to acquire the necessary skills. Second, all student affairs staff do not have (nor should have) an interest in evaluation and related activities. In fact a relatively small proportion of student affairs staff seem to seek out quantitative coursework or experiences. This is not surprising given the fact that only about 10% have undergraduate majors in traditionally quantitative areas such as business, mathematics, and the natural sciences (Kuh, Greenlee & Lardy, 1978). Of course, a fairly substantial number of aspiring student affairs workers come from the social sciences including psychology and education, and many have had an introduction to measurement techniques as undergraduates. Because evaluation coursework *per se* is not usually offered at the undergraduate level, few students have any academic experience in this area prior to the student affairs preparation program.

While it is impractical to train everyone in the profession to become evaluators, it may not be unrealistic to assume that most student affairs staff should be familiar with evaluation as a form of inquiry distinct from research and development activities. Graduate students should be encouraged to take a course in evaluation. In a study of currently enrolled graduate students preparing for student affairs work, only about a quarter indicated that they would complete an evaluation course as a part of their academic program (Kuh, Greenlee & Lardy, 1979). It is likely that in a majority of cases this type of course probably introduces basic measurement principles necessary but not sufficient to understanding the unique purposes and strategies of program evaluation. Perhaps the most realistic suggestion for sensitizing students to the need for evaluation is that a brief introduction to the principles of program evaluation be incorporated in a required course such as "Introduction to College Student Personnel" or a "Practicum Seminar" (the problems associated with this suggestion will be discussed in the next section).

Who shall be trained? Perhaps the best answer is any student affairs professional who exhibits a desire to learn how to conduct evaluations in post-secondary education. The profession is not likely to be overrun with such persons, however. In fact, the dearth of trained evaluators with student affairs expertise is likely to continue for some time. But when students or colleagues indicate an interest in acquiring these skills, they should be encouraged and professionally rewarded.

WHO SHOULD DO THE TRAINING?

The traditional academic response to this type of question is, "the faculty." In many settings the response may be quite appropriate. Some preparation programs, however, do not have faculty who have the requisite skills described in the preceding sections and, therefore, are not in a position to teach them to students or practitioners. In fact, this lack of expertise is a major obstacle to retooling the profession. If the definition of "faculty" is expanded to include staff from other university departments, the probability that evaluation skills can be acquired by students will increase. In many institutions with graduate programs, departments of educational psychology or educational inquiry offer coursework in evaluation (as distinct from research design, statistics or tests and measurements). Depending on the institution and/or instructor, the course emphases tend to fluctuate between evaluating public school programs (preschool, elementary, secondard) and federally-funded social programs such as Head Start. Rarely examined are evaluation programs germane to higher education and student affairs in particular.

Some would agree as to whether offering evaluation coursework with such a narrow focus (i.e., evaluation in student affairs) is pedagogically efficacious. Legitimate arguments can be made to support either side of the issue (see Schulberg & Perloff, 1979). What is most important, however, is whether persons are, in fact, acquiring the skills necessary to conduct evaluations in student affairs.

A variety of self-instructional workbooks are available which purport to assist novices in the systematic planning and implementation of the evaluation (e.g., Fink & Kosecoff). All too often, however, these materials assume a rather sophisticated level of expertise in research design and/or statistics and, like professors of educational evaluation, typically make use of illustrations from public schools or social service agencies. These texts may be of some help to student affairs staff, but an individual staff member will probably need additional assistance in designing and conducting evaluations.

At present, it seems the most likely option available to student affairs graduate students may be the service course(s) in evaluation methodology offered by educational psychology or inquiry faculty. Of course, a seminar or component of a course specifically devoted to evaluation methods and concerns related to student affairs work would be preferable. Those who plan to seek positions in Research and Evaluation (R & E) units in divisions of student affairs should also plan to take additional available coursework in educational inquiry as well as gain practical experience by assisting with evaluations of student affairs programs on their campus. Administrators are usually receptive to the offer of free "help" in conducting evaluations *provided* that the students are reasonably well prepared for the technical challenges inherent in the evaluation and exhibit a high degree of professionalism (maintaining confidentiality, exercising mature judgment, etc.)

Somewhat different obstacles confront practitioners who wish to acquire evaluation skills. Traditional professional development activities such as attending programs at national and regional meetings are possible formats through which evaluation principles can be introduced. In general, however, participants do not report an appreciable amount of skill acquisition as a result of these types of sessions (Miller, 1975; Rhatigan & Crawford, 1978).

Special institutes or workshops focusing specifically on evaluation in student affairs is an alternative which deserves careful consideration. Workshops for career planning, attrition, and residence life have been fairly numerous but evaluation workshops have rarely been offered (participation in such a workshop has been associated with more favorable attitudes toward evaluation activities – see Coan, 1976). The advantage of a 3-5 day workshop format are that participants: (1) can be exposed to a variety of evaluation models and methods; and (2) are immersed for an intensive time period in a different environment which emphasizes, supports, and rewards evaluation as a priority activity. However, workshops tend to be relatively expensive per individual staff person attending. Also, because the "back home" setting is often far less supportive of evaluation (Coan, 1976), newly acquired skills and attitudes often atrophy shortly after the workshop experiences.

Another viable option for practitioners is inservice sessions devoted to teaching evaluation skills to student affairs division staff (Miller, 1975). If an R & E unit or staff expertise in evaluation does not exist within the division, faculty from psychology or educational inquiry departments are often more than adequate resources. They do, however, tend to be somewhat less "applied" in their presentations.

In addition, there are a number of well-qualified student affairs professionals who are available to consult in the area of evaluation. When using either an internal or external consultant, the expectations of the consultant and staff participants should be clearly articulated and negotiated prior to the inservice.

The advantages of an inservice staff development session in evaluation are threefold: (1) a relatively large number of staff can participate at a fraction of the per person cost of attending a workshop; (2) the sessions can be structured to emphasize evaluation questions presently confronting the division; (3) staff can subsequently support one another in evaluation efforts as they have shared a common experience. The major disadvantage is that the consultant or inservice presenter(s) will probably emphasize a particular "favored" strategy, thereby excluding other approaches with potentially equal utility for the division and staff. Careful selection of the consultant can, of course, ameliorate the potential negative consequences of an inservice session.

INTEGRATING EVALUATION INTO STUDENT AFFAIRS

The issues related to the preparation of evaluators in student affairs seem to be manageable. Whether divisions of student affairs are willing or able to support (financially and psychologically) an R & E unit or a trained student affairs evaluator is another matter. To better understand how evaluation activities might be integrated into divisions of student affairs, three categories of obstacles must be considered: (1) attitudes of student affairs staff members; (2) financial constraints; and (3) administrative structures.

ATTITUDES TOWARD EVALUATION

It is not unusual for student affairs staff to avoid public discussions of professional competence and colleague performance (Stamatakos, 1978). In fact, in many preparation programs affiliated with counselor education departments, non-evaluative behavior exhibited by counselors-in-training is expected as it is considered a necessary therapeutic condition (Rogers, 1961). In addition, the student affairs staff member's relative unfamiliarity with evaluation activities is probably related to this attitude. In order for systematic evaluation in student affairs to be institutionalized, the negative or ambivalent attitudes toward evaluation as a professional responsibility must be modified. For this reason, the contributors to this monograph have attempted to underscore the value of evaluation to student affairs.

It is not enough, however, for an occasional publication to extoll the virtues of program evaluation. The attitudes and behaviors of practitioners can only be modified by campus-specific interventions explicitly designed to *change* the status quo.

The work of Lewin (1951) has indicated that to bring about attitude (and eventually behavior) change, the environment or peer group which has supported the undesirable attitude must be impacted. The homeostasis of the system or environment must be disrupted so that previously held attitudes are no longer functional. During this fluid period characterized by ambiguity and a search for stability, new ways of thinking can be introduced and, if consistently supported over time by persons in authority and peers, will take the place of previously held opinions and beliefs. To be sure, this is an oversimplified description of the change process. The point, however, is that in order for evaluation to become a valued activity, all student affairs staff — from the chief student affairs officer to para-professionals — must understand and appreciate evaluation.

Most successful changes or innovations in educational practice have been of the incrementalism genre (Stufflebeam, Foley, Gepbart, Guba, Hammond, Merriman & Provus, 1971); i.e., a developmental research-based process designed to improve educational practice through a series of small changes to a system. For evaluation to be perceived as a viable activity, a student affairs division should probably "start small" (see Chapter 8). After an evaluation of a limited scope activity (short term program involving few staff and participants) has been completed, the report written, and the decisions made, similar small scale efforts should be conducted in other units within the division. Within 18 months or so (depending on the size of the institution), it is possible that most units will have experienced an evaluation.

There are data which indicate that the more experience students in student affairs preparation programs have had with research and evaluation activities, the more they are likely to see merit and be comfortable conducting similar activities (Kuh, Lardy & Greenlee, 1979). So in one sense, this suggestion is analogous to the parent-child dinnertime conversation, "try it, you'll like it." In another sense, however, it is a risky proposition. While evaluations illuminate strengths, they can also identify weaknesses in programming and staff. The former should be emphasized, particularly in the early stages of integrating an evaluation component into a division of student affairs.

If evaluation is to be considered a valued activity, the reward system must also reflect and operate with this value in mind. Evaluation should be an activity which is conducted as part of a typical work assignment, not a task to be completed evenings and weekends. Evaluation must be defined as an objective inquiry into the merit of a given endeavor. As such, areas in need of improvement may be identified. These findings should not be suppressed nor should extra-ordinary efforts be put forth by the staff to present the "best possible picture" of the respective program or service. In this regard,

Penn's comments (Chapter 12) concerning salary negotiations and program or staff evaluation mut be reemphasized. Every effort should be made to separate the two activities, i.e., the evaluation of an individual's performance in order to design appropriate staff development activities should be discussed apart from the determination of salary adjustment.

Successful integration of an evaluation component in student affairs requires that staff share a perspective which nurtures and *values* evaluation as an activity important to maintaining to organization's vitality. Student affairs preparation programs can do much to inculcate this perspective in young professionals. But chief student affairs administrators and middle managers must also exhibit favorable attitudes toward evaluation before it can become an effective tool in practice.

During this period of contraction in postsecondary education it is unlikely that student affairs divisions will be able to create a full-time position for a person trained in evaluation. Yet, there is a need for someone to gather and analyze the data required to generate support for student affairs programs among institutional budget officers and the various publics involved (students, faculty, community, etc.). These responsibilities will likely be added to the work scope of an existing staff position, but they might also be covered by creation of a part-time doctoral internship in student affairs. If a particular type of expertise required for an evaluation is not available within the division, it may still be found elsewhere on campus. Inter-departmental consultation and services are often available through the Office of Institutional Research or from a faculty member from an appropriate department. As staff vacancies occur, successful candidates may very well have to exhibit competency and interest in evaluation. As the staff is exposed to and acquires evaluation skills, the process of evaluation will become more natural and ongoing, and will become a valued activity.

The evaluation process can be expensive. While the evaluator's time is probably the largest single expenditure, the participation of others related to the program or unit being evaluated and that of the decision maker and support personnel (data processing, secretarial pool, etc.) must be considered also. The costs can be minimized, however, if small scale evaluations are well conceived. For example, some of the information required to evaluate a student activities program may already exist in some form in the student activities office or elsewhere on campus. After consideration of the evaluation questions and the existing data, an experienced evaluator may be able to suggest modifications in regularly scheduled office procedures which will result in the required information.

Larger scale evaluations such as those reported in Chapters 15-17 are somewhat more expensive to conduct. Once again, by making use of expertise on campus and student assistance, it is possible to conduct a reasonable scale evaluation for about $200 excluding supplies and clerical support. A particularly intriguing possibility is "evaluator reciprocity" whereby staff from a nearby institution serve as evaluators for another institution's programs and vice-versa (Kuh, 1977). If logistical problems can be minimized, the likelihood of objective, low cost evaluations would be increased by such an arrangement.

Reporting the findings from an evaluation can be a time consuming and therefore an expensive task, particularly when a written report is expected and persons from off the campus serve on the evaluation team. One recent approach, the Evaluation By Discussion Model (Kuh & Ransdell, in press), was designed to reduce the time required for preparing a report as well as to minimize the costs associated with off campus consultants. This model was conceptualized specifically for use in postsecondary institutions and is particularly suited for Issue Resolver or Unbiased Judge evaluations in student affairs.

It is possible for a Research and Evaluation unit to pay for itself in several years. For example, if the unit identified various factors in the college environment related to attrition and suggested specific interventions which resulted in a drop in the attrition rate, the initial R & E unit start-up costs could be considered a wise investment (see Chapter 7, also Noel, 1978). In the final analysis, how a student affairs division invests its resources is a manifestation of values. Administrators who believe evaluative data are important for decision making will find a way to support systematic evaluation activities.

ADMINISTRATIVE STRUCTURE

Where does an evaluator or an R & E unit belong in the student affairs administrative hierarchy? In order to maintain as much objectivity and autonomy as possible, the evaluator should be in a staff relationship with the chief student affairs officer and not have line responsibilities for staff other than those assigned to the R & E unit (Harpel, 1976). It is important that those for whom the evaluation data can be most helpful are intimately acquainted with the procedures and results. For example, when conducting an evaluation of a particular unit (e.g., orientation), the evaluator should determine the data needs with the staff members responsible for the programs (e.g., orientation staff). Formative feedback should be provided to the staff as the relevant data become available. Staff reactions to the feedback should be solicited so that modifications or additions to the data collection procedures may be made to better meet staff needs. Final reports or summative discussions should be shared with the respective units as well as the chief student affairs officer. The content and/or style of these reports should vary depending on the audience (see

Chapter 2).

If the evaluation is authorized for a specific purpose by the chief student affairs officer, the evaluator will probably communicate directly with that person. Needless to say, evaluations commissioned in this manner are likely to arouse suspicion and anxiety on the part of staff. Therefore, a unilateral approach to commissioning an evaluation should be avoided if at all possible. As a general rule, evaluation efforts will have greater utility and be better received if they are coordinated through the unit or program being evaluated.

Most smaller institutions and many community colleges may not have the necessary resources to adequately staff an R & E unit. However, an individual or a group of staff members could form a special task force which would assume responsibility for coordinating or consulting about evaluation activities. Again, line relationships between evaluators and the program to the evaluated should be avoided. In many institutions, this will be impossible. Biases can be identified, however. Because the intent of an evaluation in student affairs is to improve services and practices, most biases can be dealt with in as straightforward a manner as is possible without comprising the integrity of the results. In those instances where conflicts cannot be ameliorated to an acceptable extent, an outside evaluator is recommended.

For most institutions, integrating evaluation in student affairs must be considered an innovation or a change in standard procedures or practices that is designed to improve services for students. The various ways in which an organization could institutionalize an innovation (planned change) have been discussed by a number of observers (e.g, Chin & Benne; Havelock, 1969; Seiber, 1976). In general, the process usually includes five steps: (1) a "model" (exemplary student affairs evaluation program or R & E unit) must exist; (2) the potential adopter (a division of student affairs interested in integrating evaluation as a part of its activity) must become aware of the "model"; (3) the potential adopter examines the "model" and *decides* to adopt or adapt the exemplar for use in the organization; (4) the organization implements the "model"; (5) support for the "model" is provided over an extended period of time. Evaluative studies of planned change have concluded that the failure of many educational innovations can be attributed to the insufficient support for the new practice *after* the decision has been made to implement the innovation.

The implications for integrating evaluation in student affairs are clear. While there may be support and enthusiasm for systematically conducting evaluations in student affairs, these efforts must be nurtured and supported by the division over a considerable number of months if this innovative practice can favorably influence the quality of services for students.

CONCLUSION

Evaluation activities as they have been presented in the preceding chapters have emphasized improvement of services for students. However, as institutions of higher education grapple with the realities of decreasing enrollments, reversion quotas, and budget constraints, evaluation and accountability practices may be necessary for the *survival* of divisions of student affairs as they presently exist.

The preceding chapters have outlined a number of procedures which are relatively easy to implement *provided* a commitment to integrating evaluation within student affairs is supported by favorable attitudes, resources, and appropriately prepared staff. In almost every chapter a number of salient issues have been raised about which student affairs staff must be cognizant — whether evaluating or being evaluated.

This book only begins to speak to the myriad of evaluation needs in students affairs. It would be a mistake, however, for student affairs staff to wait until more elaborate conceptual papers are disseminated or more elegant evaluation models are designed specifically for student affairs. In the past, the profession has relied on allied disciplines to provide the required expertise and direction. As far as evaluation in student affairs is concerned, the time to experiment is now. In fact, the future is now. As we move into the 1980's, we would do well to systematically plan and evaluate our programs and products.

Keeping the wolf away from our door is *not* the major objective of evaluation in student affairs. Integrating evaluation with program development will result in improved services for students and living and learning environments more consistent with the purposes of higher education.

REFERENCES

Anderson, S.B., & Ball, S. *The profession and practice of program evaluation.* San Francisco: Jossey-Bass, 1978.

Brown, R.D. How evaluation can make a difference. In G.R. Hanson (Ed.), *Evaluating program effectiveness.* San Francisco: Jossey-Bass, 1978.

Chin, R., & Benne, K. General strategies for effecting changes in human systems. In W. Bennis, K. Benne & R. Chin (Eds.), *The planning of change.* New York: Holt, Rinehart & Winston, 1969.

Coan, D. Effects of a workshop on perceptions about evaluation. *Journal of College Student Personnel,* 1976, *17,* 186-189.

Fink, A., & Kosecoff, J. *An evaluation primer.* Washington, D.C.: Capitol, 1978.

Hamilton, M.K., & Meade, C.J. (Eds.) *Consulting on campus.* San Francisco: Jossey-Bass, 1979.

Harpel, C.L. Planning, budgeting and evaluation in student affairs programs: A manual for administrators. *NASPA Journal,* 1976, *14,* i-xx.

Havelock, R.G. *Planning for innovation through the dissemination and utilization of knowledge.* Ann Arbor, Michigan: Institute for Research, Center on Research on Utilization of Scientific Knowledge, 1969.

Keating, L.A., & Hurst, J.C. The evaluator as consultant. In G.R. Hanson (Ed.), *Evaluating program effectiveness.* San Francisco: Jossey-Bass, 1978.

Kuh, G.D. *Evaluation of the College Student Personnel Administration Preparation Program at Indiana University.* Unpublished manuscript, Indiana University, 1977.

Kuh, G.D., Greenlee, F.A. & Lardy, B.A. Professionals in the making: A profile of graduate students in college student personnel. *Journal of College Student Personnel,* 1978, *19,* 531-536.

Kuh, G.D., Lardy, B.A., & Greenlee, F.A. Research orientation of graduate students in college student personnel. *Journal of College Student Personnel,* 1979, *20,* 99-104.

Kuh, G.D., & Ransdell, G.A. Evaluation by discussion: An evaluation design for post-secondary programs. *Journal of Higher Education,* in press.

Kurpius, D. Consultation theory and process. An integrated model. *Personnel and Guidance Journal,* 1978, *56,* 335-338.

Lewin, K. Principles of re-education. In K.D. Benne (Ed.), *Human relations in curriculum change.* New York: Dryden, 1951.

Miller, T.K. Staff development activities in student affairs programs. *Journal of College Student Personnel,* 1975, *16,* 258-264.

Noel, L. (Ed.) *Reducing the dropout rate.* San Francisco: Jossey-Bass, 1978.

Rhatigan, J.J., & Crawford, A.E. Professional development preferences of student affairs administrators. *NASPA Journal,* 1978, *15* (3), 45-52.

Rodgers, R.F. Personal communication. August 17, 1978 (Original source unknown).

Rogers, C.R. *On becoming a person: A therapist's view of psychotherapy.* Boston: Houghton-Mifflin, 1961.

Schulberg, H.C., & Perloff, R. Academia and the framing of human service delivery program evaluators. *American Psychologist,* 1979, *34,* 247-254.

Seiber, S. Change agents in education. In *Handbook of contemporary education.* New York: Bowker, 1976.

Stamatakos, L.C. Unsolicited advice to new professionals. *Journal of College Student Personnel,* 1978, *19,* 325-329.

Stufflebeam, D.L., Foley, W.J., Gephart, W.J., Guba, E.G., Hammond, R., Merriman, H.O., & Provus, M.M. *Educational evaluation and decision making.* Itasca, Illinois: Peacock, 1971.

SUBJECT INDEX

A
Accountability 1, 2, 7, 13, 55, 78, 86, 91, 96, 104, 107, 166
Admissions 53-60
Adversary model 48
Assertiveness training 44

B
Bias: and evaluator values 48, 153
    observer 46, 47
Budget 13, 53, 86, 90

C
Career planning 15, 104
Change 91, 173-175, 259, 260, 263
Chief student affairs officer: 121-131
C.I.P.P. model 34, 98, 207-223
Cost-effectiveness 98, 207, 227
Counseling center 21, 86-93

D
Decision-making 15-16, 22, 29, 39, 87, 88, 140, 225, 227, 235
Delphi technique 221
Discrepancy model 34-37

E
Environment 87, 88, 137, 142, 143, 212, 239
Evaluation: as a management tool 150-152
    attitudes toward 117, 259
    communication in 44
    context 137, 142, 164-166, 209, 212-214
    criteria 16, 124, 125, 128, 153, 229, 234
    definitions of 2, 3, 13-14, 133
    formal 14-17, 121, 122, 155, 156
    informal 14-17, 38, 39, 79, 96, 97, 121
    integration into student affairs 253-265
    interpretation of results 39, 175, 198
    instrumentation 69, 70, 100-102, 108, 109-112, 157, 158, 172, 197, 220
    key questions and issues 15-30, 64, 81-83
    preparing reports 39, 43, 261
    purposes of 3, 8, 13-14
    standards 156, 157, 249
    team approach to 67, 68
    use of testimony in 48, 59
    utilization of results from 59, 71, 72

Evaluator: as change agent 40-41, 91
    external 24-25, 46, 67
    internal 24-25, 67
    roles of 23-25, 33-49
    skills 25, 35, 41, 88-91, 254-256
    training 83, 102, 256-259
Evidence 48, 134, 135
Experimental researcher model 44-46, 49
External audiences 1, 96, 104

F
Formative evaluation 21, 22, 35, 36

G
Generalizability of evaluation results 22-23
Goals: adequacy of 166
    formulation of 7, 34, 63, 64, 105, 106, 160, 193
    measurement of 28, 34, 55, 107, 124
Goal-free model 46-47, 98
Greek affairs 212-211

H
"Hawthorne effect" 45

I
Inputs 108, 109, 137, 143, 209, 210, 215-218
Interviews 70, 213
Issue resolver model 37-42, 49

L
Living-learning center 80, 239-250

M
Management By Objectives (MBO): 3, 4, 83, 84

N
Naturalistic inquiry 29, 42-44
Needs assessment: definitions of 25-26, 185, 187-191
    group 82, 86, 87, 105, 113, 185, 193-198
    individual 185, 191-193
    taxonomy of target audiences for 202, 203

O
Obstacles to evaluation 8-9, 99
Obtrusive measures 70
Organizational development (OD) 4, 42, 95

Organizational effectiveness 149
Orientation 63-74
Outcomes 109, 139, 140, 142, 145, 210

P

Paraprofessionals 65, 68
Participant-observer 42-43
Placement (see Career Planning)
Politics 19, 26, 27, 37, 244
Process evaluation 28, 35, 210, 218-220
Product evaluation 28, 35, 210, 220, 221
Program: continuation 27, 146
        development 88, 138, 207
        impact 46, 47, 66, 146, 172, 177-179, 225, 230
        modification 72, 117
        monitoring 35, 36
        objectives 33, 34, 138
        planning 27, 53, 108
Programming 95, 107

R

Randomization 23, 44, 173, 175, 176
Reliability 71, 171, 172, 197
Reporter model 42-44, 49
Research: contrasted with evaluation 2, 3, 17-18, 89
        definition of 2
Research and evaluation unit in student affairs 67, 68, 258, 260-262
Residence life 15, 22, 26, 27, 35, 36, 45, 77-85, 144, 171, 239-250
Responsive evaluation 37-40

S

Side effects 46, 47, 135, 136
Simple Multi-Attribute Rating Technique 227-236
Staff: development 73, 78, 79, 125, 126, 129, 151, 194, 258, 259
    effectiveness 149
    evaluation 108, 149-160
Students: assertiveness 44
        autonomy 3
        independence 17
        non-traditional 63, 65, 86
        recruitment 53, 54, 56, 57
Student activities 95-103
Student development 163-182
Summative evaluation 21, 22, 36
Systematic planner model 33-37, 49
Systems model 136-140

T
Transactional model 40-42

U
Unbiased judge model 46-48, 49
Unintended effects (see Side effects)
Unobtrusive measures 69, 70, 213

V
Validity 71, 153, 171, 172, 197, 242
Values: comparative 19, 20
      decision 19
      explication of 134
      idealization 19, 20
      imbued in program evaluation 241
      instrumental 19
      intrinsic 18, 19
      personal 18, 37
      professional 18, 37

Y
Yield analysis 57-59

NAME INDEX

Abernathy, L. 53, 54, 60
Aiken, J. 65, 74
Anderson, S. B. 254, 255, 265
Appleton, J. R. 128, 131
Arney, W. R. 208, 222
Aulepp, L. 87, 93, 190, 195, 199
Ayres, J. 66, 74
Baird, L. L. 190, 199
Ball, S. 254, 255, 265
Barr, M. J. 30, 31, 63, 65, 74
Bates, M. 194, 200
Beach, D. 153-155, 160
Beal, P. E. 189, 195, 200
Beatty, P. T. 189, 199
Beeler, K. 159, 160
Benne, K. 263, 265
Bergin, A. E. 89, 93
Birch, E. E. 128, 131
Bishop, J. B. 7, 10
Blaesser, W. W. 41, 50
Blaska, B. 106, 119
Bloland, P. A. 96, 103
Bonner, D. 66, 74
Boruch, R. F. 225, 237
Bowen, H. R. 190, 199
Boyer, J. 1, 10
Bradshaw, J. 190, 199
Brickell, H. M. 46, 50
Broskowski, A. 92, 93
Brown, B. 221, 222
Brown, R. D. 8, 9, 10, 13, 33, 47, 50, 72, 74, 92, 98, 103, 164, 180, 255, 256, 265
Buckner, R. 239, 252
Bunda, M. A. 185, 199
Bunker 215
Burck, H. D. 2, 8, 10, 186, 199
Buros, O. K. 172, 180
Burton, J. K. 189, 190, 199
Butts, T. 63, 74
Campbell, D. T. 44, 50, 176, 177, 180
Campbell, V. N. 190, 199
Carnegie Commission 180
Casse, R. M., Jr. 7, 10
Celio, D. L. 71, 74
Chamberlain, P. C. 239, 241, 252
Chambers, G. 101, 103
Chickering, A. W. 146, 167, 169, 180, 186, 190, 191, 199
Chin, R. 263, 265
Coan, D. 258, 265
Coffing, R. T. 186, 196, 199
Coffman, D. 90, 93
Cohen, M. D. 125, 131
Cole, C. W. 175-177, 181
Conrad, R. W. 68, 74
Cooper, E. M. 189, 195, 200
Corazzini, J. 86, 87, 93
Corrigan, R. E. 187, 200
Crawford, A. E. 258, 265
Cronbach, L. J. 2, 10, 172-175, 180, 189, 199, 236, 237
Cross, K. P. 8, 10, 19, 31, 170, 180, 186, 199
Curry, M. K. 53, 60
Damarin, S. 174, 182
Dannells, M. 63, 65, 74, 167, 181
DeCoster, D. A. 82, 85
Deddo, G. 192, 193, 199
Delworth, U. 87, 88, 93, 190, 195, 199
Deutscher, I. 236, 237
Dickson, S. 226, 237
Doherty, P. 167, 181
Dressel, P. L. 2, 4, 10, 84, 85, 165, 180
Dutton, T. 128, 131
Dyle, R. B. 182
Ebel, R. L. 163, 180
Edwards, R. M. 106, 119
Edwards, W. 227, 237
Einhorn, J. J. 235, 237
Eisner, E. W. 48, 50
English, F. W. 195, 199
Erickson, D. L. 189, 200
Erikson, E. 167, 169, 180
Escott, S. 1, 10
Feldman, K. A. 173, 80

271

Fenske, R. H. 164, 180
Fink, A. 257, 265
Fischer, G., Jr. 110, 119
Fisher, C. F. 124, 131
Fisher, M. B. 8, 10
Flentje, H. E. 1, 10
Flores, T. R. 186, 200
Foley, W. J. 2, 11, 137, 147, 207, 222, 260, 265
Freeman, J. 7, 10
Furby, L. 172-175, 180
Ganshaw, T. F. 167, 181
Garnder, D. E. 98, 103
Gephart, W. J. 2, 11, 137, 147, 207, 222, 260, 265
Gillis, A. L. 7, 10
Gindes 215
Glass, G. A. 16, 31
Gleazer, E. J. 53, 60
Goodenough, D. R. 182
Goodman, J. 80
Gordon, L. V. 190, 201
Gowin, D. B. 18, 31
Greenlee, F. A. 256, 262
Gross, R. F. 126, 131
Groves, D. L. 189, 200
Guba, E. G. 2, 10, 29, 31, 43, 50, 137, 147, 207, 222, 260, 265
Gulick, L. 127, 131
Guttentag, M. 227, 237
Hamilton, M. K. 225, 265
Hammond, R. L. 2, 11, 137, 147, 207, 222, 260, 265
Hanniford, G. W. 100, 103
Hanson, G. R. 4, 10, 163, 186, 200
Harpel, R. L. 2, 7, 10, 151, 160, 262, 265
Harris, C. W. 172, 173, 180
Harshman, C. L. 7, 10, 80, 85
Harshman, E. F. 7, 10, 80, 85
Hartanov, T. F. 80, 85
Harvey, J. 98, 103
Harvey, O. J. 169, 180
Havelock, R. G. 263, 265

Havighurst, R. J. 189, 200
Hawkes, F. 2, 11, 92, 93
Hays, D. G. 195, 200
Heath, D. 167, 169, 180, 181
Heath, R. 167, 170, 181
Helner, O. 221, 222
Henderson, C. 1, 10
Hodkinson, H. L. 1, 10
Hodson, W. A. 186
Holland, J. L. 167, 181
Hornstein, H. A. 215, 222
House, E. R. 33, 50
Howell, H. A. 8, 10
Huebner, L. 93
Hull, S. B. 104, 114-117, 119
Hunt, D. E. 167, 169, 180, 181
Hurst, J. C. 67, 71, 74, 90, 93, 255, 265
Hutchinson, T. E. 186, 196, 199
Iscoe, I. 90, 93
Johnson, D. W. 187, 200
Jones, J. E. 215, 218, 222
Justice, S. H. 30, 31, 63
Kahalas, H. 189, 200
Kamens, L. 226, 237
Kapel, D. E. 186, 200
Karp, S. A. 182
Katz, J. 169
Kaufman, R. A. 187, 195, 199, 200
Keating, L. A. 67, 74, 255, 265
Keniston, K. 167, 169, 181
Kerlinger, F. N. 2, 10
Kiersy, D. 194, 200
Killen, K. 157, 160
Kiresuck, J. 90, 93
Knefelkamp, L. 167, 168, 181
Kohlberg, L. 167, 169, 181
Kosecoff, J. 257, 265
Kozall, C. E. 7, 10
Krumboltz, J. D. 2, 11
Kuder, J. M. 80, 85
Kuh, G. D. 53, 54, 58, 60, 63, 65, 74, 80, 104, 167, 171, 181, 253, 256, 260-262, 265
Kunkel, R. 135, 146

Kurpius, D. 255, 265
Lardy, B. A. 102, 103, 256, 262
Leach, E. R. 54, 60
Lee, Y. S. 146, 147, 187, 200, 203, 205
Lenning, O. T. 146, 147, 163, 165, 166, 172, 173, 181, 185-187, 189, 190, 195-197, 200, 203, 205
Levine, M. 48, 50
Levinson, D. 167, 181
Levy, S. R. 7, 11
Lewicki 215
Lewin, K. 259, 265
Lewis, L. 153, 156, 157, 160
Liebeler, L. 193, 199
Linn, J. K. 195, 200
Lipsetz, A. 221, 222
Loevinger, J. 169, 181
Lopez, H. 65, 74
Lord, 174
Mable, P. 82, 85
Madson, D. L. 80, 85
Mager, R. R. 195, 200, 215, 222
Magnarella, P. J. 80, 85, 239, 252
Mann, A. G. 241, 252
March, J. G. 125, 131
Marcia, J. 169, 181
Markle, D. G. 190, 199
Marsee, S. E. 54, 60
Maslow, A. H. 189, 200
Maxey, E. J. 165, 181
Mayhew, L. B. 165, 180
McAleenan, A. 185, 192, 193, 200
McCannen, R. 66, 74
McCoach, W. 235, 237
McKaig, R. N. 95
McKelfresh, D. A. 80, 85
McKillip, J. 225, 226, 234, 237
Meade, C. J. 255, 265
Merrill, P. F. 189, 190, 199
Merriman, H. O. 2, 11, 137, 147, 207, 222, 260, 265
Messick, S. 174, 182

Micek, S. S. 146, 147, 187, 200, 203, 205, 208, 222
Miller, T. K. 2, 7, 8, 11, 77, 85, 164, 181, 185, 201, 258, 265
Millman, J. 18, 31
Mitchell, M. A. 66, 74
Monette, J. L. 191, 201
Mooney, R. L. 190, 201
Moore, M. 88, 93
Moore, P. 102, 103
Moore, W. Jr., 186, 201
Mullen, J. 7, 10
Munday, L. A. 165, 181
Murray, H. A. 189, 201
Nash, R. J. 83, 85
Nevin, J. R. 100, 103
Noel, L. 262, 265
Nudd, T. R. 10
Nunnally, J. C. 172-176, 181
O'Donnell, T. 10
Oetting, E. R. 2, 3, 7, 11, 17, 31, 89, 92, 93, 175-177, 181
Oliaro, P. M. 126, 131
Parker, C. A. 167, 168, 181, 208, 222
Parker, G. G. 56, 60
Passmore, J. R. 189, 195, 200
Paterson, J. F. 182
Penn, J. R. 149, 159, 160, 260
Perloff, E. 2, 8, 11
Perloff, R. 2, 8, 11, 257, 265
Perry, W. G., Jr. 164, 169, 182
Peterson, D. W. 54, 60
Peterson, G. W. 2, 8, 10, 186, 199
Pfeiffer, J. W. 215, 218, 222
Phillips, B. A. 77
Piaget, J. 169, 182
Pipe, P. 195
Polscello, S. M. 95
Prince, J. S. 2, 7, 8, 11, 77, 85, 164, 181, 185, 201
Provus, M. M. 2, 10, 34, 35, 50, 137, 147, 207, 222, 260, 265
Ransdell, G. A. 262
Rhatigan, J. J. 258, 265

273

Rickard, S. T. 124, 131
Riecken, H. W. 225, 237
Riker, H. C. 77, 79, 85
Rippey, R. M. 40, 41, 50
Robinson, D. 150, 160
Rock, M. 153, 156, 157, 160
Rodgers, R. F. 80, 85, 207, 254, 265
Rogers, C. R. 259, 265
Rogers, D. G. 84, 85
Rosnow, R. L. 45, 50
Rowland, L. 154, 160
Sample, S. B. 1, 10
Sanders, J. R. 2, 3, 11, 14, 17, 31, 33, 50, 97, 103
Sanford, N. 164, 169, 182
Saurman, K. B. 83, 85
Schmidt, M. R. 106, 119
Schreck, T. C. 7, 11
Schroder, H. M. 169, 180
Schuh, J. H. 77
Schulberg, H. C. 92, 93, 257, 265
Scott, S. H. 79, 85
Scriven, M. 21, 29, 31, 46, 47, 50, 166, 182, 187, 188, 201, 225, 237
Seiber, S. 263, 265
Service, A. L. 146, 147, 187, 200, 203, 205
Shaffer, R. H. 4, 11, 121, 126, 131
Sharf, R. S. 78, 85
Sherman, R. 90, 93
Simon, L. A. 78, 85
Sims, O. S., Jr. 7, 10
Slaikey, K. 90, 93
Smith, T. T. 71, 74
Snapper, K. 227, 237
Sovilla, E. S. 104, 119
Stake, R. E. 21, 31, 33, 37-39, 50
Stamatakos, L. C. 8, 11, 126, 131, 259, 265
Stanley, J. C. 44, 50, 176, 177, 180

Stear, C. 55, 60
Stern, G. G. 167, 182
Stevens, N. D. 113, 119
Stimpson, R. 78, 85
Stone, J. C. 43, 50
Strupp, H. H. 89, 93
Stufflebeam, D. L. 2, 6, 8, 9, 10, 34, 50, 98, 137, 147, 207, 210, 221, 222, 260, 265
Styles, M. A. 104
Taft, R. 159, 160
Terranova, C. 66, 74
Thomas, W. G. 106
Thuveson, G. 193, 199
Tilley, D. C. 54, 60
Travis, C. 44, 50
Trembley, E. L. 78, 85
Truitt, J. W. 126, 131
Tucker, L. R. 174, 182
Tucker, S. 135, 146
Tyler, R. W. 2, 11, 34, 50
Urwick, L. 127, 131
Utz, P. A. 101, 103
Vaillant, G. 167, 182
Van Eaton, E. N. 63, 74
Voss, J. R. 234, 237
Walberg, H. 50
Warsaw, P. 90, 93
Watson, J. F. 100, 103
Weigel, R. 90, 93
Weiss, C. H. 26, 31, 89, 93
Wergin, J. F. 31
Whittington, T. B. 80, 85
Widick, C. 167, 168, 181
Wilson, S. 93
Witkin, B. R. 185, 197, 201
Witkins, H. A. 170, 182
Witmire, D. E. 53, 60
Wolf, R. L. 48, 50
Wood, P. 66, 74
Workman, K. 226, 237
Worley, C. W. 102, 103
Worthen, B. R. 2, 3, 11, 13, 17, 31, 33, 50, 97, 103
Yancey, B. D. 30, 31, 63